The Declaration's Forgotten Liberties

Charles A. Castleberry

The Declaration's Forgotten Liberties (Forgotten Liberties, Book 1)

Copyright © 2025 by Charles A. Castleberry

All rights reserved. No part of this publication may be reproduced, distributed, or transmitted in any form or by any means, including photocopying, recording, or other electronic or mechanical methods, without the prior written permission of the author, except in the case of brief quotations embodied in critical reviews and certain other noncommercial uses permitted by copyright law. Please do not participate in or encourage piracy of copyrighted materials in violation of the author's rights.

No part of this book may be used for the training of artificial systems, including systems based on artificial intelligence (AI), without the copyright owner's prior permission. This prohibition shall be in force even on platforms and systems that claim to have such rights based on an implied contract for hosting the book.

Cover Image Citation:
Ferris, Jean Leon Gerome, Artist. *Writing the Declaration of Independence, / J.L.G. Ferris.* ca. 1932. Cleveland, Ohio: The Foundation Press, Inc., July 28. Photograph.

Library of Congress Control Number: 2024924413

Paperback ISBN: 978-1-965092-50-7
Hardcover ISBN: 978-1-966283-40-9

1. Main category— History › United States › Colonial Period
2. Other category— History › United States › Revolution & Founding
3. Other category— History › United States › General

Published by American Real Publishing
Binghamton, NY
americanrealpublishing.com

Introduction

The Declaration of Independence: More Than Just Words

The Declaration of Independence is one of the most important documents in history—but how well do we really understand it? Over time, myths, misunderstandings, and even deliberate distortions have clouded the true story of America's founding. This book sets the record straight.

Have you ever wondered:

- What were the real reasons the colonies broke away from Great Britain?
- Why was Thomas Jefferson chosen to write the Declaration?
- What had Jefferson written about independence before 1776?
- What did John Adams write in April and May of 1776 that preceded the Declaration?
- Why were the May 15 Virginia Resolution and the June 7 Lee Resolution so important?
- If the Declaration says, "all men are created equal," why did Jefferson own slaves?
- What happened to the original passage condemning slavery—and why was it removed?
- Did Jefferson and Adams really spend two weeks in a Philadelphia tavern writing the Declaration?
- Is it true that Jefferson drew from George Mason when writing the Preamble?

The answers to these questions are important. They help us understand the America we inherited.

A Bold New Idea

The Declaration wasn't just a rebellion against Britain—it was the birth of a radical idea. Jefferson and the Founders weren't just fighting for independence; they were asserting that governments should exist to serve the people—not the other way around.

But declaring independence didn't secure liberty overnight. It took a bloody war, a Constitution, and generations of struggle to turn those words into reality. Even today, the fight for freedom continues, both in America and around the world.

This book goes beyond the famous phrases and explores the forgotten stories that shaped our nation. You'll discover:

- How Jefferson replaced the word subjects with citizens—a moment that changed history.
- Why British trade laws hurt everyday colonists far more than just a tax on tea.
- The truth behind the Three-Fifths Clause—and why it wasn't what most people think.
- How early abolitionists, as well as slave owners like Jefferson and Mason, tried (and failed) to stop the importation of slaves—even proposing laws to end slavery.

Why the Grievances Still Matter

Many people think of *The Declaration of Independence* as just a historical document, but its grievances weren't just complaints—they were lessons. The Founders knew that if future generations didn't understand these injustices, they could happen again. That's why these grievances are more than words on a page—they shaped the Constitution, guided America's laws, and continue to influence our rights today. Each Grievance tells a story, and some are truly eye-opening!

A Call to Think for Yourself

History isn't just about what we're told—it's about what we discover for ourselves. This book invites you to go beyond the textbooks, ask questions, and explore the ideas that shaped America. The Founders believed in thinking critically, debating ideas, and standing up for what is right.

As you read, ask yourself:

> Would I have had the courage to sign my name to the Declaration, knowing it could cost me everything?

The Power of Words

One of the most remarkable things about *The Declaration of Independence* is that it wasn't a clash of mighty armies on a battlefield—it was the voice of a revolution, a declaration of bold ideals and enlightened principles, crafted by a master wordsmith. Words that changed the world.

Jefferson's words galvanized the colonies, leading to the creation of a new nation. His words continue to ignite movements for freedom worldwide. Never underestimate the power of words—or the courage to speak them and stand firmly for the cause of liberty and justice.

The Story of Slavery in America

Many people learn about slavery in America, but few understand how it fit into the larger global picture. The horrors of slavery are often the "elephant in the room"—a painful truth that shaped nearly every aspect of our nation's history.

This book includes compelling charts and graphs that compare the role of different nations in the Trans-Atlantic Slave Trade—a brutal system that spanned more than three centuries and involved far more countries than just Great Britain and the American colonies. In it, you'll also find clear explanations of the Three-Fifths Clause and the 20-Year Clause in the U.S. Constitution—two often-misunderstood issues. These charts will help you see how decisions made during the nation's founding affected both the fight against slavery and the long road toward liberty and equality.

Why This Story Still Matters

The Declaration of Independence was the first step toward securing the rights and freedoms we enjoy today. But the fight for liberty didn't end in 1776. Even after independence, slavery continued in America, leading to a long struggle for abolition, civil rights, and justice.

Sadly, slavery still exists in the world today. Millions of people—men, women, and children—are trapped in forced labor, human trafficking, and other forms of modern slavery. While this may seem like a problem from the past, it remains a global crisis that needs awareness and action.

That's why this book also explores slavery today. By understanding how past generations fought against oppression, we can recognize our responsibility to raise our voice for freedom in our own time. The principles in *The Declaration of Independence*—that all people are created equal and deserve life, liberty, and the pursuit of happiness—are still relevant.

What Inspired This Book
Key moments that inspired this book

The first was reading a book published by Barnes & Noble containing our founding documents and the writings of many Founders. One entry caught my attention—**Thomas Jefferson's *Summary View of the Rights of British America*,** written in the summer of 1774. Jefferson wrote it for Virginia's delegates, who were soon to attend the First Continental Congress, but they considered it too radical.

As I read it, I began to recognize ideas that would later appear in *The Declaration of Independence*. My research revealed that nearly every principle and Grievance in the Declaration had its roots in this earlier work. Further investigation showed that every principle and Grievance in the Declaration is now protected by law in the U.S. Constitution.

The second event was my introduction to the Rough Draft of *The Declaration of Independence*. Glenn Beck, who owns a rare copy of this draft, brought it to St. George, Utah, as part of a large historical exhibit at the St. George Tabernacle. For three days, I presented this document to thousands and witnessed their amazement as they listened to its powerful words.

What touched most people was learning of the Slavery Clause in the Rough Draft. Most had never heard of it, and were disheartened to learn why it was removed from the official Declaration. The trajectory of our nation may have been so different had it remained.

As I give presentations in many cities, I am often requested to put these findings into a book. Three years later, here we are—**ready to celebrate 250 years of Independence!**

More Secrets Await in the Afterword

By the time you finish this book, you'll have explored the Declaration's hidden truths and forgotten stories. But there's more. In the Afterword, you'll meet forgotten heroes—men and women who sacrificed for liberty, beginning a century before 1776.

In *The Declaration's Forgotten Liberties* you'll read of:

- **The 1688 Germantown Petition Against Slavery,** America's first written protest against the practice.
- **The boy who fell off the Mayflower**—but survived to help shape the New World.
- **The "Quaker Comet,"** a dwarf abolitionist as mighty as a lion.
- **A Black man who plotted the stars and our nation's capital**—and challenged Jefferson.
- **The fearless Daughter of Liberty** known as the Mother of the Boston Tea Party.
- **Black and Native American heroes** whose stories lift and inspire.

From Subjects to Citizens

History does not fade because it is old. It fades when it is simplified, softened, and turned into *fables* that ask nothing of us.

Over time, America's founding has been wrapped in comforting legends—neat, heroic, and incomplete. Hard questions were smoothed away. Contradictions were ignored. Complexity was traded for slogans. What remains in many tellings is not history, but a set of familiar *MythTakes*—repeated so often that they are mistaken for truth.

The Declaration of Independence is not a fairy tale. It is a legal indictment, written with precision, urgency, and consequence. It was composed by one man, but it spoke for many. Thomas Jefferson knew exactly what he was doing—and what it would cost. He was not a perfect man. But he was a serious one, wrestling openly with liberty, power, human dignity, and responsibility—giving voice to convictions already shared by his countrymen.

With the ear of a musician, Jefferson did not merely write an indictment against King George III; he composed it. Like a symphony, the Declaration builds in movements—introducing principle, establishing grievance, and resolving in action—calling a people to cast off the status of subjects and assume the responsibilities of citizens.

In its wake, men pledged their lives, their fortunes, and their sacred honor—not as a flourish of words, but as a binding commitment. What followed was not inevitable. It was chosen—and purchased with the blood of a generation.

He'd Already Written It

When it came to articulating the principles and grievances in the *Declaration of Independence*, Jefferson was no novice. He did not begin the Declaration in June 1776—he had been developing those ideas for years, testing and refining them in earlier writings before bringing them together in a final expression of independence. What appears in the Declaration is not the beginning of those ideas—it is their synthesis.

Independence Already Underway

By the summer of 1776, independence was not merely being debated and its success was far from assured—but it was already in motion. Congress had begun transferring authority to the people, colonies were forming new governments, and the structure of a new nation was taking shape. *The Declaration of Independence* did not initiate this transformation; it explained it, justified it, and presented it to the world.

To understand the Declaration rightly, we must see not only what it says—but why it was written, what had already been written, and what had already been done. The Declaration was not the starting point of independence—it was its explanation.

Not Relics, But Responsibilities

Whether the Declaration continues to live up to its promises depends on us. Are we willing to act as responsible and engaged citizens? Will we seek out and support trustworthy representatives? The *Declaration*, the *Revolution*, and the *Constitution* made a *new nation* of *citizens*—no longer *subjects* to a distant king. That implies *responsibility*.

The Declaration's forgotten liberties are not relics of the past—they are responsibilities of the present.

Table of Contents

- INTRODUCTION 4
- TABLE OF CONTENTS 8
- PROLOGUE: THE JOURNEY BEGINS 10
- AMERICA'S CHARTERS OF FREEDOM 18
- THE GOLDEN APPLE IN A SILVER FRAME 22
- OPENING LINE OF THE DECLARATION OF INDEPENDENCE 24
- WHEN, IN THE COURSE OF HUMAN EVENTS 26
- WE HOLD THESE TRUTHS 28
- DID GEORGE MASON INSPIRE JEFFERSON'S PREAMBLE? 30
- WHEN A LONG TRAIN OF ABUSES 34
- LET FACTS BE SUBMITTED TO A CANDID WORLD 42
- PRESENTING THE GRIEVANCES 44
    1. He Refuses to Assent to Necessary Laws 46
    2. He Forbids Passing Laws of Pressing Importance 48
    3. He Suppresses Representation 50
    4. He Burdens Legislatures with Fatiguing Measures 52
    5. He Dissolves Parliaments & Opposes Rights 54
    6. He Endangers Us by Neglecting Elections 56
    7. He Controls the Settlement of Lands & Naturalization 58
    8. He Blocks Local Administration of Justice 62
    9. He Has Made Our Judges Dependent on His Will 64
    10. He Erected New Offices & Sent Swarms of Officers 66
    11. He Keeps Armies Among Us in Times of Peace 68
    12. His Military is Superior to Our Civil Authority 70
    13. He Subjects Us to Foreign Jurisdiction 72
    14. For Quartering Large Bodies of Troops 74
    15. He Protects Foreign Soldiers by Mock Trials 76
    16. For Cutting Off Global Trade 78
    17. Taxation Without Representation 82
    18. Deprived of Trial by Juries 84
    19. Transporting Us Beyond Seas for Trial 86
    20. Enlarging the Borders of a Neighboring Province 88
    21. Taking Away Charters and Valuable Laws 92
    22. Suspends Legislatures & Assumes Power 96
    23. Abdicating Governance and Protection 98
    24. He Plundered, Ravaged, Burnt & Destroyed 100
    25. Foreign Mercenaries Terrorize Our People 102
    26. Taken Captive to Bear Arms Against Fellow Citizens 104
    27. Inciting Insurrections & Unleashing Merciless Forces 106
- THE SLAVERY CLAUSE 108
- THE KING IS DISQUALIFIED BY HIS TYRANNY 114

ENEMIES IN WAR, IN PEACE FRIENDS	116
THEY PLEDGED THEIR LIVES	118
SIGNING THE DECLARATION	120
THE PRICE THEY PAID	122
COMPARING THE GRIEVANCES	123
WORKING COMPOSITION DRAFT	130
JEFFERSON'S EPIPHANY	131
BEFORE THE DECLARATION	132
JOURNEY TO PHILADELPHIA	134
REFINING THE LANGUAGE OF LIBERTY	135
CLASSICAL EAR AND ARCHITECTURAL PROSE	139
NOTES ON THE STATE OF VIRGINIA	140
A WOLF BY THE EARS	142
AFTERWORD	**144**
THE "DUTY BOYS" OF 1619	145
THE ORIGINS OF SLAVERY IN AMERICA	146
SLAVE SHIP BROOKES	147
TRANSATLANTIC SLAVE TRADE	150
HORRORS OF SLAVERY IN AFRICA	151
THE THREE-FIFTHS COMPROMISE	156
THE THREE-FIFTHS AND 20-YEAR COMPROMISES	158
AMERICAN SLAVE MERCHANTS	162
THE DISTORTED LEGACY OF JEREMIAH DIXON	163
THE FIRST SLAVERY PROTEST	164
A HOUSE DIVIDED AGAINST ITSELF CANNOT STAND	166
BLOOD AND TREASURE: THE CIVIL WAR	168
FORGOTTEN HEROES	170
COLONEL GEORGE MIDDLETON	172
JOHN HOWLAND	174
BENJAMIN LAY	176
SARAH BRADLEE FULTON	178
MERCY OTIS WARREN	180
BENJAMIN BANNEKER	182
FRANCES ELLEN WATKINS HARPER	186
POLLY COOPER, ONEIDA ANGEL OF VALLEY FORGE	189
THE FIGHT GOES ON	190
A FINAL REFLECTION	192
BIBLIOGRAPHY	194
END NOTES	196

Prologue: The Journey Begins

A Journey Into Forgotten Liberties
Welcome to an incredible journey into history.

The Declaration's Forgotten Liberties is more than a story about the past—it helps us understand how America was built and why freedom, justice, and unity still matter today. The Declaration of Independence is 250 years old, yet its words still shape our nation. What did it really mean? How did it change the world? And what can we still learn from it today?

A Surprising Family Discovery
I grew up on the West Coast, far from where the Revolution took place. Years later, I found myself in Pennsylvania, learning about relatives who lived there long before America became a country.

One of my ancestors was Heinrich Kesselberg, later known as Henry Castleberry. He and his future wife, Catherine, immigrated separately from Germany to Pennsylvania in the 1680s. Their story connects to one of the first written protests against slavery in America. Family tradition holds that Catherine was present at that early protest.

The 1688 Germantown Protest Against Slavery
In 1688, four men in Germantown, Pennsylvania, wrote the first official protest against slavery in the American colonies.

One of them was Abraham op den Graeff, a weaver and farmer whose family later married into mine. He lived near Evansburg, Pennsylvania, and is buried nearby in the Skippack Mennonite Cemetery.

Over time, four Castleberry stone homes were built on that land. Two remain today. One—the Derrick Castleberry House—served as General George Washington's headquarters on September 20, 1777. My wife and I restored the home next door.

Abraham and many early German immigrants were Quakers and Mennonites—people who believed in peace and equality. At a time when slavery was common, even among some Quakers, they chose to speak out. Their words became the 1688 Germantown Petition Against Slavery.

Escaping Wars and Religious Persecution in Europe
While these ideas were taking root in Pennsylvania, conditions in Europe told a very different story.

As Africans were being taken from their homelands and enslaved, millions in Europe suffered under war and religious persecution. Armies moved across the land, seizing food, livestock, and supplies, leaving civilians to face famine, displacement, and death. In many regions, more civilians died than soldiers.

Families faced difficult choices. Some stayed and hid. Others crossed borders. Many left everything behind.

They were escaping not only war, but also tyranny and punishment for their beliefs. *Martyrs Mirror*, first published in 1660, records the suffering of over 4,000 people who were tortured or executed for their faith. These accounts help explain why so many risked everything in search of a new beginning.

Finding Home

The people who left Europe had faced terrible hardships—wars, religious persecution, and constant danger. They were desperate to find a place where they could live in freedom and safety.

That place was Pennsylvania. William Penn, the colony's founder, invited German Quakers and Mennonites to settle in his land, promising them religious freedom and a fresh start. In 1683, a group of them left their homes in the Rhine and Rühr River Valleys and boarded a ship called the *Concord*, bound for America.

One of the largest family groups on the ship was the Op den Graeff brothers, cousins of William Penn. They traveled with their families, including their elderly mother, hoping to build a better life. The Concord became known as the *"German Mayflower"* because of its important role in bringing German refugees to America.

For these early immigrants, America was a place of hope—a chance to live in peace without fear. But when they arrived in Pennsylvania, they found something quite shocking: Slavery was everywhere.

Restoring the Old Home

The photos on the next pages show a special place—the Casselberry farm in Evansburg, Pennsylvania, first purchased in 1722. Over 200 years ago, four Castleberry (Casselberry) homes were built on this land.

In 2016, my wife, Vanet, and I purchased one of them—the abandoned Anne E. Casselberry House. We spent the next five years restoring it to its former beauty. This home is part of the Evansburg National Historic District, which helps preserve the history of William Penn's vision for Pennsylvania. Here's what the photos show:

1. **Anne E. Casselberry House:** The original section was built in the mid-1700s, with an addition in 1798. The sturdy stone walls are nearly two-feet thick. We remained true to colonial colors and schemes as we restore this home.
2. **1820s Addition:** This is the "new" addition. This part of the house has a modern kitchen, a "winder staircase," and a bedroom and bath upstairs. A fun feature of this kitchen is the Dutch door.
3. **Colonial Kitchen:** This home has two kitchens! We kept the colonial kitchen just as it was in the 1700s. Visitors love it!
4. **Updated Second Kitchen:** This kitchen is in the 1820s addition. It has a Dutch door that leads to a porch which was added some time later.
5. **Dining Room:** This room, plus the entry hall, staircase, and an upstairs bedroom, were built between 1795 and 1800. The fireplace woodwork and cabinets are original.
6. **The Casselberry Barn:** A German stone bank barn built in 1831. The name John Casselberry and the date August 1831 are carved into the stone.
7. **Derrick Casselberry House:** Washington's Headquarters! On September 20, 1777, George Washington stayed here during the Revolutionary War. The first section was built in 1734. This photo is from a century ago. Today, most of the white stucco has been removed and it is in need of restoration.
8. **President Washington's Visit:** Washington honored fallen soldiers at St. James Episcopal Church. This reenactment includes historical actors and Father Mike Sowards, who shared historical documents with me. Local stories say Washington spent the night at Anne E. Casselberry House.
9. **Tomb of Unknown Soldiers (Revolutionary War):** This burial mound holds over 150 unknown soldiers. The Daughters of the American Revolution placed a plaque to honor them. The first church on this site was built in 1700, replaced by a stone church in 1721. Today's "new chapel" was built in 1845.[1]

1. Anne E. Casselberry House with two front doors—mid 1700s phase on the left, 1790s addition on the right

2. 1820s addition on back left before restoration

3. Mid 1700s colonial kitchen in the front left of the house

4. Updated 2nd kitchen in the 1820s addition

5. Dining room and fireplace, circa 1795 with original woodwork

6. Casselberry German Bank Barn, circa 1831

7. Adjacent Derrick Casselberry House, first phase circa 1734

8. Re-enactment of President Washington visiting fallen comrades

9. Tomb of Unknown Soldiers, Revolutionary War, placed by the Daughters of the American Revolution

A Visit from President Washington

On **September 20, 1777**, during the Revolutionary War, **George Washington** stayed at the **Derrick Casselberry House**, which sits near the home we restored.

He was there to honor **fallen soldiers**, including those buried in the nearby **Tomb of Unknown Soldiers**. More than 150 Revolutionary War soldiers are buried in that sacred place.

Local stories say that **after visiting the cemetery, Washington may have spent the night at the Anne E. Casselberry House.**

A Web of Family History

The more I researched my family history, the more surprises I found!

One of my ancestors, **John Howland**, was a passenger on the **Mayflower**. He signed the **Mayflower Compact**, which helped shape the government of Plymouth Colony. He even worked as a clerk for the governor—so it's very possible he **wrote the Mayflower Compact himself!**

Another ancestor, **John Rolfe**, played a major role in Jamestown's history. In **1609**, he was shipwrecked on the island of Bermuda before finally arriving in **Jamestown**. He later introduced **sweet tobacco seeds** to the colony—creating the American **tobacco industry**.

John Rolfe married **Pocahontas**, and together they had a son. They traveled to England, but tragically, Pocahontas died just before their planned return to Jamestown.

These discoveries weren't always easy to process. The **tobacco industry** later became tied to **slavery**, something I struggled with as I learned more. But history is full of **both triumphs and tragedies**—and we must study both to understand our past.

Jefferson's Vision and The Declaration of Independence

As I continued my research, I found more and more connections between early American documents. One of the biggest discoveries was how Thomas Jefferson prepared for writing the Declaration long before 1776.

Two years earlier, in 1774, he wrote *A Summary View of the Rights of British America*, outlining ideas that would later appear in the Declaration. He wrote that for the Virginia delegates to the First Continental Congress.

Then, in May 1776, while Virginians were writing their state constitution while Jefferson was in Philadelphia. He included a list of grievances against King George III in his proposed Virginia Constitution. Within days, he used that list (much was word-for-word) while drafting *The Declaration of Independence*.

Most are familiar with the opening words of the Declaration, but did you know that 65% of the Declaration is a list of grievances—a "full train of abuses" (a phrase borrowed from John Locke) against the King?

Understanding these grievances helps us see why the American Revolution happened and why the Founders believed freedom was worth fighting for.

As Long as the Sun Shall Shine
Lessons from the Iroquois Confederacy

On May 27, 1776, a group of twenty-one Iroquois leaders from four different tribes arrived in Philadelphia to meet with the Continental Congress. They stayed for over a month, lodging on the second floor of the Pennsylvania Statehouse—the same building where the Founders were preparing to declare independence.

On June 11, 1776, an Onondaga chief addressed the delegates, calling them "Brothers," and shared a message of unity and friendship. They expressed hope that the bond between the Iroquois and the American colonists would last "as long as the sun shall shine and the waters run." [2]

John Hancock, president of the Congress, was given a special honor—an Iroquois name: Karanduawn, meaning "The Great Tree."

The very day the Iroquois addressed Congress, June 11, 1776, Thomas Jefferson began writing *The Declaration of Independence*—inspiring words that would soon give birth to a nation.[3]

How the Iroquois Inspired America

For many centuries, the Haudenosaunee (Iroquois) Confederacy has united different tribes under a system of shared leadership, peace, and cooperation. This idea fascinated the Founding Fathers, who were trying to unite the thirteen colonies.

In 1744, an Iroquois leader named Chief Canassatego of the Onondaga Nation met with colonial leaders. He warned them that unless they learned to work together, they would remain weak.

To prove his point, he picked up a single arrow and snapped it in half. Then, he bundled multiple arrows together and tried again. This time, they would not break.[4] His message was clear: Divided, the colonies would fall. Together, they would be strong.

Later, this powerful symbol inspired the Founding Fathers as they created a government for the United States. Even today, the Great Seal of the United States carries this message—the eagle holds a bundle of arrows in one talon, not as a symbol of war, but of the strength that comes from unity.[5]

The Great Law of Peace

The Haudenosaunee Confederacy (People of the Longhouse) was created long before the United States even existed. Their laws were passed down through oral tradition and recorded on wampum belts.

The **Great Law of Peace** includes many important ideas, including:

- **Leaders should serve the people, not rule over them.** Chiefs (called sachems) were chosen by the people and could be **removed** if they failed to lead with wisdom and fairness.
- **Decisions should be made by consensus.** Instead of one person making all the choices, leaders discussed issues and worked together to find solutions that benefited everyone.
- **Peace is stronger than war.** The Haudenosaunee believed in resolving conflicts through discussion instead of fighting. This is why they buried their weapons of war beneath the Great Tree of Peace.
- **Future generations matter.** Leaders were expected to think seven generations ahead—making decisions not just for themselves, but for their children, grandchildren, and beyond.
- **Unity makes a nation strong.** Just like a bundle of arrows is harder to break than a single arrow, the Iroquois knew that when people stand together, they are much stronger.[6]

THE IROQUOIS NATION'S GREAT LAW OF PEACE
The World's Oldest Constitution

SENECA NATION — CAYUGA NATION — ONONDAGA NATION — ONEIDA NATION — MOHAWK NATION

Wampum belts—intricately woven, beaded memory belts—recorded treaties, laws, and agreements. One of these belts tells the story of the Great Tree of Peace, a sacred white pine where former enemies buried their weapons of war beneath its roots and agreed to live together in harmony.[7]

America 250

As we celebrate 250 years of *The Declaration of Independence*, history still has important lessons to teach us. How can we bury our "weapons of war"—hate and envy—and become more united as a people?

The fight for freedom and equality is not over. But by learning from the past, we can protect those liberties for the future—**as long as the sun shall shine.**

America's Charters of Freedom

The Charters of Freedom are three of the most important documents in American history. They helped shape the United States and define the rights and freedoms that Americans have today.

These documents are displayed in a special room called the "Rotunda for the Charters of Freedom" at the National Archives in Washington, D.C.

The Charters of Freedom include:
- *The Declaration of Independence* – The document that declared America's freedom from British rule.
- **Constitution of the United States** – A set of rules that created our government and explains how it works.
- **Bill of Rights** – The first ten amendments to the Constitution that protect our rights.

Thomas Jefferson believed these documents should always guide our country. He called them:

*"The creed of our political faith;
the text of civic instruction."*

Jefferson warned that if America ever strayed from these principles, we should quickly return to them:

> "These principles form the bright constellation which has gone before us and guided our steps through an age of revolution and reformation… and should we wander from them in moments of error or of alarm, let us hasten to retrace our steps, and to regain the road which alone leads to peace, liberty, and safety."
>
> — Thomas Jefferson, First Inaugural Address, March 4, 1801[8]

Why This Book Matters

This book will help you understand why these documents were written and how they shaped our country. We'll take a close look at *The Declaration of Independence*, breaking it down to understand its meaning, and how the Constitution and Bill of Rights protect the liberties it declares.

The Three Charters of Freedom

These documents were created during a time of great struggle and change. The people who wrote them wanted to build a fair government and protect individual rights.

1. The Declaration of Independence (1776)

Written mostly by Thomas Jefferson, this document was America's way of saying, "We are no longer part of Great Britain!" But it was more than just a breakup letter to King George III—it laid out big ideas about freedom, equality, and human rights. The Declaration states that:

- **All people are created equal.**
- **Everyone has rights that can't be taken away, like life, liberty, and the pursuit of happiness.**
- **Governments must protect these rights, and if they don't, people have the right to change or replace them.**

These ideas were inspired by the Enlightenment, a time when philosophers like John Locke argued that rulers should only have power if the people agree to it. *The Declaration of Independence* took these ideas and put them into action!

2. The Constitution (1787)

Once the colonies won their independence, they needed a plan for running their new country. The first plan, called the Articles of Confederation, wasn't strong enough. In 1787, leaders gathered to write the Constitution, which created:

- **A government with three branches:** Executive, Legislative, and Judicial divide power so no one person or group controls everything.
- **A system of checks and balances:** To make sure the government followed the rules.
- **A federal system:** Where power is shared between the national government and the states.

The Constitution is still the law of the land today, and it begins with the words "We the People"—showing that the government's power comes from its citizens.

3. The Bill of Rights (1791)

When the Constitution was first written, many Americans were deeply concerned. They feared it gave too much power to the federal government without protecting individual rights. George Mason had fought hard to include a declaration of rights during the Federal Convention but was overruled—leading him to refuse to sign the final document. Other states, especially Massachusetts and Virginia, refused to support the Constitution unless a Bill of Rights was added.

The pressure was too great to ignore. James Madison, who had strongly opposed adding a Bill of Rights at the convention, promised to introduce amendments during the first Congress to secure ratification. It was only because of relentless demands from the states that Congress finally drafted and passed the Bill of Rights, which was ratified in 1791. The first ten amendments protect our fundamental liberties, including:

- **Freedom of speech, religion, and the press**
- **The right to protest and gather peacefully**
- **Protection from unfair searches and arrests**
- **The right to a fair trial**

Living Documents: Why the Charters of Freedom Still Matter

The Charters of Freedom aren't just old pieces of paper locked away in a museum—they are living documents that continue to shape our country every day. When we talk about fair laws, voting rights, free speech, or justice, we are talking about ideas that started with *The Declaration of Independence*, the Constitution, and the Bill of Rights. These documents connect the past, present, and future—reminding us that freedom isn't something we receive once and forget about. It has to be protected, defended, and passed down to future generations.

Without clear guidelines, chaos would prevail. Power would be concentrated in the hands of a few, and others would be marginalized. The Constitution provides the framework that ensures fairness, balance, and representation for all. It is the foundation our government must follow to function properly.[9]

The Constitution: A Plan That Adapts

One of the forward thinking things about the Constitution is that it can be changed. The Founding Fathers knew they weren't perfect, and they knew the country would face new challenges in the future. That's why they included a way to amend (change) the Constitution when needed. For example:

- **The 13th Amendment ended slavery.**
- **The 19th Amendment gave women the right to vote.**
- **The 26th Amendment lowered the voting age to 18.**

Because of the system they created, America can grow and improve while still staying true to its original values.

The Power of the Bill of Rights

The Bill of Rights is a fundamental safeguard of freedom. It protects every American by guaranteeing rights that the government cannot infringe upon.

- It guarantees the right to free speech, allowing you to voice your opinions, even if they challenge authority.
- It ensures the freedom to practice your religion or live without religious constraints.
- It safeguards you from unjust treatment by the government or law enforcement.

The Bill of Rights ensures that all individuals are treated equally under the law, regardless of their background or beliefs.

The Bill of Rights ensures that laws apply equally to everyone—no matter who they are. These rights are so important that people fought and died to defend them. Every time you hear about a court case, a protest, or a new law being debated, you are seeing the Bill of Rights in action. It affects your daily life in ways you might not even realize—from what you post online to how you express your opinions at school or in public.

It's because of the Bill of Rights that newspapers can report on the government without fear, why people can gather to demand change, and why no one can be arrested without a reason. It even protects your right to defend yourself if you're accused of a crime, making sure trials are fair and just.

But rights are only as strong as the people willing to defend them. If we take them for granted, we risk losing them. The Bill of Rights is more than just words and lofty ideals—it's a promise that **freedom will always have a protector—the Constitution**. And that promise only holds if every generation understands and values it.[10]

Your Role in Protecting Freedom

The Charters of Freedom weren't written just for the people in 1776, 1787, or 1791—they were written for YOU and for future generations. Every American has a responsibility to understand these documents, defend their principles, and ensure that freedom remains strong.

You don't have to be a president, a judge, or a politician to make a difference. You can:

- **Learn about your rights** so you understand how they protect you.
- **Speak up** if something seems unfair or unjust.
- **Respect other people's rights**, even if you don't agree with them.
- **Stay informed** about how the government works and vote when you're old enough.

These simple actions help keep the ideas of *The Declaration of Independence*, the Constitution, and the Bill of Rights alive and strong.

Moving Forward

As we move forward in this book, we will take a deeper look at *The Declaration of Independence*. We'll uncover the meaning behind its powerful words, the struggles that led to its creation, and how its message still echoes through history.

> **Think About It:** How can you protect freedom—not just for yourself, but for those who will follow?

The Golden Apple in a Silver Frame

President Abraham Lincoln described *The Declaration of Independence* as the **"Golden Apple in a silver frame of the Constitution and Union."** Lincoln's analogy offered a profound interpretation of the relationship between these Charters of Freedom and the broader structure of the nation.[11]

The Golden Apple: The Declaration of Independence

The Declaration of Independence, likened to a golden apple, symbolizes its precious and revered status. At its core, the Declaration is a statement of principles, ideals, and aspirations. It articulates the fundamental notions of liberty, equality, and the pursuit of happiness as unalienable rights. These principles are seen as golden because they are valuable and serve as the moral and ethical foundation upon which the United States was established.

The Silver Frame: The Constitution and Union

The Constitution and the Union are the silver frame that encloses and protects the golden apple. The silver frame is more than a protective barrier; it's a structure that enables the golden apple to be displayed, appreciated, and actualized. The Constitution, with its system of checks and balances, separation of powers, and the Bill of Rights, operationalizes the ideals of the I. It sets up the practical mechanisms through which the rights and principles of the Declaration are upheld and enforced. The Union, representing the collective agreement of the states to form a nation of united states, gives physical and political form to the ideals.[12]

Modern Interpretation

In the modern context, this analogy reminds us that while the Declaration provides the moral compass, the Constitution offers the legal and structural means to realize these ideals. The Union underpins these principles' practical and political viability as a collective agreement of diverse states. It reminds us that principles without a structure to implement them can become hollow, while a structure without moral principles can become oppressive.

Therefore, this analogy beautifully encapsulates the symbiotic relationship between America's founding ideals and governing framework. It highlights the importance of preserving foundational principles, having a robust structure to give them life, and providing safeguards to protect them.

From Hope to Reality: Building a Framework for Liberty

The Declaration of Independence, penned with fervor and adopted unanimously in 1776, represented more than a list of grievances or a bold statement of self-governance. It was a profound pledge, where the Founding Fathers committed their lives, fortunes, and sacred honor to ideals that would redefine human history. Yet, as the ink dried on this revolutionary document, it was evident that these lofty declarations of unalienable rights—life, liberty, and the pursuit of happiness—were not self-executing. At that moment, they were little more than a hope, an aspiration. The test lay ahead: to win a war for independence against a formidable British force to actualize the ideals they so valiantly proclaimed.

The First Step Was to Win the War

The American Revolutionary War, a grueling conflict that tested the resolve and resourcefulness of a developing nation, was a crucible in which the determination and courage of its people were forged. The victory in this conflict was a military triumph and the first crucial step in transforming the Declaration's ideals from abstract concepts into tangible realities. However, the end of the war did not automatically grant the promises of the Declaration. It merely provided the opportunity, the fertile ground upon which a nation committed to these principles could grow.

Weakly United Under the Articles of Confederation:

As the newly independent states embarked on this journey, the Articles of Confederation initially served as the governing document. However, it soon became apparent that this first attempt at unifying the states under a joint government fell short of the robust framework needed to sustain and protect the liberties for which so much had been sacrificed. The Articles, though well-intentioned, needed more provisions to ensure a strong Union, effective governance, and, importantly, the protection of the individual liberties proclaimed in the Declaration. The Articles of Confederation had no executive or judicial branches and provided no facility to tax or regulate trade (including regulating or banning the slave trade). This confederation was, in a word, impotent.

A Government that Endures

Recognizing these shortcomings, the young nation's leaders convened to address the failures of the Articles of Confederation. This soon changed to become a Constitutional Convention, and **the "silver frame" was on its way to becoming a reality**. The transition from *The Declaration of Independence* to the Constitution and the Bill of Rights represents the maturation of **the** American experiment: from declaring noble principles to instituting a practical and enduring framework that would uphold and protect those principles.[13]

Opening Line of The Declaration of Independence
"The unanimous Declaration of the thirteen united States of America."

The Power of a Single Word: "united"

At first glance, this opening line might seem simple, but have you ever noticed something unusual? The word ***"united"*** is lowercase. Today, we always write **"United States of America"** with a capital **"U,"** but in 1776, that wasn't always the case. It's because, at the time, the States were independent governments, each with its own leaders and laws. They weren't a single nation yet—they were thirteen separate states that had chosen to unite for the common causes of liberty and independence from Great Britain.

The capitalized word 'States' stood preeminent over the lowercase 'united,' signaling that individual states held the ultimate authority at that time. They guarded this power fiercely, having witnessed firsthand the dangers of an all-powerful central government.

Thirteen Separate Colonies, One Common Goal

The Articles of Confederation (approved by the Congress November 15, 1777, ratified March 1, 1781) explicitly stated that "each state retains its sovereignty, freedom, and independence" (Articles of Confederation, Art. II). This was not merely a formality—it reflected the deep mistrust the states had for centralized power. Having just fought a war against a distant, overreaching government, they were determined to preserve their autonomy.

When drafting the Constitution, this wariness remained. The states agreed to form a stronger national government, but only with safeguards in place to protect their authority. This led to the Tenth Amendment, which explicitly affirmed that any powers not delegated to the federal government were reserved to the states or the people (U.S. Const., amend. X). The Founders understood that a centralized government, if left unchecked, could easily grow beyond its intended limits.

Power Sharing Between States and the Federal Government

James Madison, in Federalist No. 45, sought to reassure those who feared this shift toward a stronger union. He emphasized that **the powers granted to the federal government were "few and defined,"** limited primarily to national defense, foreign affairs, and interstate matters. By contrast, **the powers left to the states were "numerous and indefinite,"** covering nearly all aspects of daily life, from commerce and justice to education and local governance. This balance of power between state and federal authority remains a fundamental principle of American constitutionalism.[14]

Before declaring independence, the colonies had their own governments, laws, and currencies. The Articles of Confederation, America's first governing document, reinforced this independence. *The Declaration of Independence* called for unity, but not at the expense of state sovereignty.

Today, debates over issues like the Electoral College highlight the Founders' careful balance of power. The Electoral College ensures that smaller states still have a voice, preventing the most populous regions from dominating national elections. Eliminating it would shift power toward urban centers, weakening federalism—the system that divides power between states and the national government.

The Challenge of Staying United

Even after winning the war, unity was fragile. The Articles of Confederation left the states too independent, leading to chaos:
- Some printed their own money, while others used different currencies.
- Trade disputes and border conflicts arose.
- The national government couldn't collect taxes, leaving war debts unpaid.
- Nor could it regulate commerce between states or internationally—including the Slave Trade.

The Constitution Strengthened the Union And Protected the States

The balance between state and federal power remains a key debate today. Understanding the Declaration's opening line helps us understand why our government works the way it does—and why the United States remains strong when it is truly united.

Constitutional Safeguards

- **The Tenth Amendment** guarantees that powers not granted to the federal government belong to the states or the people. They do not "revert" to the states because they were never the federal government's to begin with.

    - **The Founders designed a system where the national government had specific, limited powers**, while the states retained authority over most aspects of daily life.

    - **The federal government cannot grant rights it does not possess**—it can only respect rights that are already the people's or the states'. Our natural rights come from God, not a government.

- **The Thirteenth Amendment supports this with its language** of: **"Neither slavery nor involuntary servitude…shall exist within the United States,** or any place **subject to <u>their jurisdiction</u>"**—**"their" jurisdiction** (the states, plural), not "<u>its</u>" **jurisdiction** (the federal government, singular)—reflecting the recognition and standing of states within the federal system.

When, In the Course of Human Events

"When, in the course of human events, it becomes necessary for one people to dissolve the political bands which have connected them with another, and to assume, among the powers of the earth, the separate and equal station to which the laws of nature and of nature's God entitle them, a decent respect to the opinions of mankind requires that they should declare the causes which impel them to the separation."

Historical Background

The American colonists thought of themselves as British citizens, but they had no real voice in how they were governed. British laws and taxes were forced on them without their consent, and they had no representatives in Parliament to speak for them.

Over time, this felt deeply unfair. The colonists were treated as second-class citizens, denied the same rights as people in Britain. Each new law and tax made things worse, leaving them frustrated and powerless. When they tried peaceful petitions and protests, British soldiers were sent to keep order and enforce unpopular rules.

Eventually, the colonists realized they had to make a choice: stay silent under unfair control or stand up for their rights. They knew the world would ask why they were breaking away, so they wrote a clear explanation to show they weren't acting out of anger, but out of duty.

That is why *The Declaration of Independence* begins with such a strong statement—sometimes people must separate from a government that no longer protects their rights, but they must give good and honest reasons.

How Did This Shape America?

This bold opening made it clear that America's Revolution was not just a fight against a king—it was a fight for a new idea of government. The Founders believed that leaders should only have power if the people agree to it. This is called "consent of the governed."

By declaring independence, the Founders showed the world that people have the right to choose their own government. Their example inspired later revolutions for freedom in France, Haiti, Latin America, and other parts of the world.[15]

A Decent Respect to the Opinions of Mankind

Jefferson wrote that the colonies should show "a decent respect to the opinions of mankind." He meant that America needed to explain its reasons clearly and fairly. The world was watching, and the colonists wanted others to see that they weren't just rebelling—they were standing up for what was right. They wanted freedom, but also the world's respect.

Summary

The Declaration of Independence declared that people have a right to govern themselves. But freedom isn't automatic—it must be protected by laws that make sure people's rights are respected. The Constitution later provided that framework, keeping power in the people's hands.

Modern Interpretation

The idea that government should serve the people is still vital today. When people feel their government is unfair, they have the right to speak up, vote, and work to make things better—just like the colonists did in 1776.

Every debate over laws, justice, or elections connects back to these same founding ideas. From peaceful protests to Supreme Court rulings, Americans still rely on the principles of the Declaration to protect freedom and fairness.

Constitutional Safeguards

- **The government serves the people:** The Constitution begins with "We the People," showing that power comes from citizens, not rulers.
- **The government can't take total control:** The three branches of government—Legislative, Executive, and Judicial—share power so no one group dominates.
- **Rights are protected:** he Bill of Rights guarantees freedoms like speech, religion, and fair trials.
- **The people can change laws:** Amendments and elections let citizens fix unfair rules and improve their government.
- **Laws must be fair and applied equally:** The Fourteenth Amendment ensures equal protection under the law.
- **Leaders must follow the rules:** The Constitution is the highest law of the land, keeping even government officials accountable.

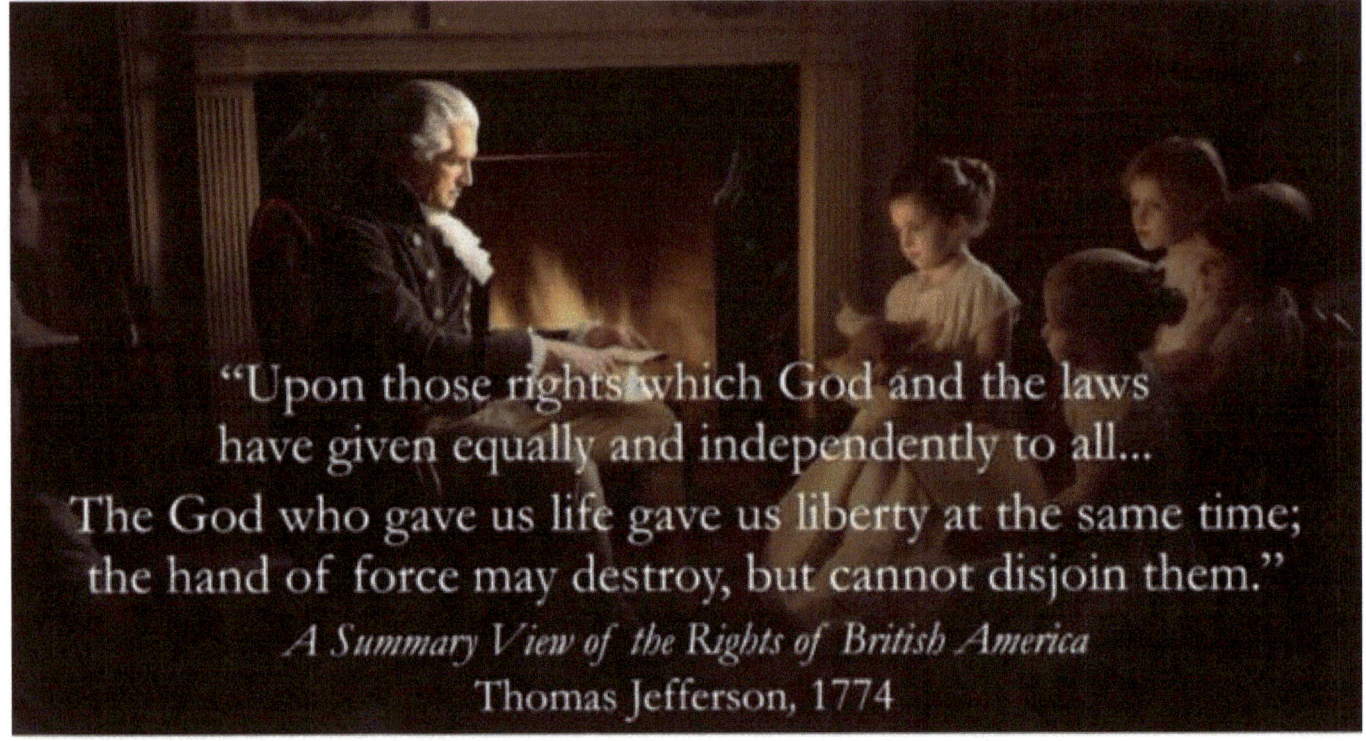

"Upon those rights which God and the laws
have given equally and independently to all...
The God who gave us life gave us liberty at the same time;
the hand of force may destroy, but cannot disjoin them."
A Summary View of the Rights of British America
Thomas Jefferson, 1774

We Hold These Truths

"We hold these truths to be self-evident, that all men are created equal, that they are endowed by their Creator with certain unalienable Rights, that among these are Life, Liberty and the pursuit of Happiness.—That to secure these rights, Governments are instituted among Men, deriving their just powers from the consent of the governed,—That whenever any Form of Government becomes destructive of these ends, it is the Right of the People to alter or to abolish it, and to institute new Government, laying its foundation on such principles and organizing its powers in such form, as to them shall seem most likely to affect their Safety and Happiness."

From Jefferson's 1774 *Summary View of the Rights of British America*

The God who gave us life gave us liberty at the same time; the hand of force may destroy, but cannot disjoin them… Kings are the servants, not the proprietors, of the people.

Franklin's change to Jefferson's phrase **"sacred and undeniable"** to **"self-evident,"** shifted the Declaration from theology to reason—turning belief into proof. Yet what was said to be self-evident—that all men are created equal—was not self-evident in practice. Enslaved Africans and Native peoples stood outside the circle of equality Jefferson described. Even so, those words lit a fuse that generations would carry forward, forcing America to measure its conduct, even today, against its own immortal claim.

Historical Background

The Declaration was born in an age when reason challenged kings and priests alike. Thinkers like Locke, Montesquieu, and Newton had redefined truth as something that could be discovered, not decreed. Jefferson carried their torch into politics, turning philosophy into action. The ideas that shaped the Declaration came from the Enlightenment's great conversation about human nature and moral law:

- **Natural Rights:** Every person is born with rights that come not from rulers but from God.
- **Consent of the Governed:** Legitimate government arises only from the consent of the people. Power without consent is tyranny.
- **Right to Revolution:** When a government becomes destructive of those rights, the people the right and duty to alter or abolish it. Locke taught that this duty is a safeguard of liberty, not a threat to order.
- **Reason and Moral Law:** Truth can be known through observation and reason. Newton revealed the laws of nature; Jefferson and his peers believed those same laws governed human conduct and justice.
- **Life, Liberty, and the Pursuit of Happiness:** Locke wrote that the pursuit of happiness is the aim of human conduct, and that life and liberty are essential to that pursuit. Jefferson joined these ideas, blending Locke's moral psychology with natural law to create something uniquely American. In his hands, happiness became the fulfillment of one's potential within a just and free society.

Together, these ideas made the Declaration both a philosophical and spiritual charter—asserting that freedom is not granted by men but discovered by the light of reason.

Modern Interpretation

Every generation must decide whether truth remains self-evident. If liberty is neglected, its loss will not be sudden—it will be reasoned away. The Declaration reminds us that rights do not depend on rulers, majorities, or even time. They depend on the same eternal law Jefferson saw reflected in nature and conscience, needing no king, priest, or permission. The Declaration is therefore not only a statement of independence but a call to vigilance—reminding us that liberty endures only when reason and faith are joined in moral purpose.

Summary

The Declaration of Independence united ancient faith with Enlightenment reason. Jefferson's words drew deeply from John Locke and other philosophers who taught that life, liberty, and the pursuit of happiness are natural rights. In his *Essay Concerning Human Understanding*, Locke wrote **that "the highest perfection of intellectual nature lies in a careful and constant pursuit of true and solid happiness."** Jefferson carried that truth from moral philosophy into political form, declaring that these rights are the foundation of all just government. When government becomes destructive of them, the people have both the right and the duty to replace it.

Through the Declaration, Jefferson transformed Enlightenment ideals into civic architecture. **The Constitution later completed that vision—strong enough to defend liberty, yet limited enough to preserve it.**

Constitutional Safeguards

- **Article I:** Creates a Congress that represents the people, making laws with their consent—ensuring the government serves, not rules over, the people, and that all are treated equally.
- **Article II:** Establishes a president who takes an oath to "preserve, protect, and defend the Constitution," ensuring life, liberty, and happiness are safeguarded.
- **The Bill of Rights:** The first ten amendments guarantee freedoms such as speech, religion, and fair trials, protect the rights the Declaration calls unalienable, and limit federal power by reserving undelegated authority to the states and the people. Together they reinforce Jefferson's conviction that liberty is a natural right safeguarded by law.

Did George Mason Inspire Jefferson's Preamble?

For over a century, historians and institutions have assumed that Thomas Jefferson drew inspiration for the Declaration's Preamble from George Mason's Virginia Declaration of Rights. This belief is reflected in the National Archives[16] and the National Constitution Center,[17] both of which claim that Mason's work was the foundation for Jefferson's famous words about unalienable rights, the consent of the governed, and the right to alter or abolish an unjust government. But does the evidence support this claim?

The assumption that Jefferson relied on Mason's text comes from the fact that Mason's Virginia Declaration of Rights was adopted by Virginia on June 12, 1776, and published in Philadelphia newspapers at the same time. However, there is no direct evidence that Jefferson used Mason's text. In fact, the timeline suggests otherwise—Jefferson was already drafting *The Declaration of Independence* on June 11, the day before Mason's document was adopted, and his ideas had been in circulation for years. That means Mason's version followed Jefferson's—not the other way around. What if we've been looking at this backward? What if Mason was actually influenced by Jefferson's earlier work?

Jefferson's Ideas Were Already in Print

Jefferson did not need to borrow from Mason because he had already written these concepts himself—most clearly in his *Summary View of the Rights of British America* (1774), two years before the Declaration. This document, published and widely circulated, contains strikingly similar language to both Mason's Virginia Declaration of Rights and Jefferson's own *Declaration of Independence*. Jefferson did not claim his ideas were original—he was stating principles that were well known to the colonists, drawn from mutual experiences and great thinkers like John Locke.

Comparing the Texts

Below are three excerpts from *The Declaration of Independence*, Jefferson's *Summary View of the Rights of British America*, the Jefferson draft of the June 1775 *Declaration of the Causes and Necessity of Taking Up Arms*, and Mason's *Virginia Declaration of Rights*. When viewed side by side, the similarities between Jefferson's *Summary View of the Rights of British America* and *The Declaration of Independence* are undeniable—while Mason's language, though similar, appears less like a source and more like a parallel reflection.

1. Natural Rights & the Creator's Gift of Liberty

Declaration of Independence (Jefferson, June 1776)

"We hold these truths to be self-evident, that all men are created equal, that they are endowed by their Creator with certain unalienable Rights, that among these are Life, Liberty and the pursuit of Happiness."

Summary View of the Rights of British America (Jefferson, July 1774)

"Upon those rights which God and the laws have given equally and independently to all… The God who gave us life gave us liberty at the same time; the hand of force may destroy, but cannot disjoin them."

Declaration of the Causes and Necessity of Taking Up Arms (Jefferson's draft, June 1775)

Exerting to the utmost energies all those powers which our creator hath given us, to preserve that liberty which he committed to us in sacred deposit, & to protect from every hostile hand our lives & our properties.

Virginia Declaration of Rights, (Mason, May–June 1776)

"That all men are by nature equally free and independent and have certain inherent rights…namely, the enjoyment of life and liberty, with the means of acquiring and possessing property, and pursuing and obtaining happiness and safety."

2. The Purpose of Government & the Consent of the Governed

Declaration of Independence (Jefferson, June 1776)

"That to secure these rights, Governments are instituted among Men, deriving their just powers from the consent of the governed."

Summary View of the Rights of British America (Jefferson, July 1774)

"They know, and will therefore say, that kings are the servants, not the proprietors of the people… And this his majesty will think we have reason to expect when he reflects that he is no more than the chief officer of the people, appointed by the laws."

Declaration of the Causes and Necessity of Taking Up Arms (Jefferson's draft, June 1775)

The persons assuming these powers are not chosen by us, are not subject to our controul or influence are exempted by their situation from the operation of these laws.

Virginia Declaration of Rights, (Mason, May–June 1776)

"That all power is vested in, and consequently derived from, the people; that magistrates are their trustees and servants and at all times amenable to them."

3. The Right to Replace an Unjust Government

Declaration of Independence (Jefferson, June 1776)
"That whenever any Form of Government becomes destructive of these ends, it is the Right of the People to alter or to abolish it, and to institute new Government."

Summary View of the Rights of British America (Jefferson, July 1774)
"When the representative body have lost the confidence of their constituents… their continuing in office becomes dangerous to the state, and calls for an exercise of the power of dissolution."

Declaration of the Causes and Necessity of Taking Up Arms (Jefferson's draft, June 1775)
"We are reduced to the alternative of choosing an unconditional submission to the tyranny of irritated ministers, or resistance by force," and "Our cause is just. Our union is perfect. Our internal resources are great… we have counted the cost of this contest, and find nothing so dreadful as voluntary slavery."

Virginia Declaration of Rights, (Mason, May–June 1776)
"When any government shall be found inadequate or contrary to these purposes, a majority of the community has an indubitable, inalienable, and indefeasible right to reform, alter, or abolish it."

Evidence does not support the assumption that Mason's *Virginia Declaration of Rights* was Jefferson's primary inspiration. Jefferson had already articulated these ideas in 1774. His *Summary View of the Rights of British America* contains nearly all the major themes that appear in *The Declaration of Independence*, written two years before Mason's document was even drafted.

Historians have assumed that Jefferson read Mason's work in the newspaper while drafting the Declaration—but this is just that, an assumption. Jefferson never cited Mason as an influence. Instead, his previous writings and Enlightenment philosophy provide the most clear and direct lineage for the ideas in the Declaration.

Historical Background

The Declaration of Independence was not created in isolation, nor was it copied from a single source. Thomas Jefferson had already been writing about these principles long before June 1776. His *Summary View of the Rights of British America* shows that he, like many of his peers, was deeply engaged in the debates about natural rights, self-governance, and the role of government long before Mason's Virginia Declaration of Rights was even written.

Many historians point to comparisons between the Declaration and Mason's work as proof that Jefferson borrowed from Mason. One history book even follows this pattern—lining up three sections of text from both documents to make the case. However, in the very next paragraph, it admits that Mason was familiar with Jefferson's *Summary View* but fails to compare Mason's text to Jefferson's earlier writings. It then claims that, while Jefferson's writing was superior, he certainly introduced no new ideas but merely reworded Mason's text.

Perhaps a better approach is to compare original source documents and let the evidence speak for itself, rather than writing to prove a theory. The reality is that Jefferson had already put these ideas to paper two years before Mason's draft existed. *The Declaration of Independence* remains one of the greatest political documents in history because it captured and perfected ideas that had been evolving for decades. Jefferson did not copy Mason—he expressed the will of a people determined to be free, and he'd been doing so for years.

Summary

For centuries, historians have claimed that Jefferson borrowed his ideas from Mason, but the evidence tells a different story. True history comes to life when we connect the dots using original sources rather than relying on assumptions. Instead of assuming Jefferson needed Mason's text, we can recognize that both men drew from the same well of Enlightenment thought. Rather than assuming Jefferson needed Mason's text, we should recognize that both men were drawing from a deep well of Enlightenment thought, influenced by philosophers like John Locke. More importantly, Jefferson had already articulated these ideas in his *Summary View of the Rights of British America*—two years before Mason's Declaration of Rights was written.

However, none of this diminishes George Mason's importance in shaping America's founding principles. While James Madison is credited as the Father of the Constitution, it was Mason who first insisted on a declaration of rights at the federal convention. Mason rose 136 times to speak, advocating for the inclusion of protections for individual liberties. When the final draft lacked a Bill of Rights, he refused to sign the Constitution. Madison initially opposed adding one, but when Massachusetts and other states made ratification conditional upon future amendments, he finally agreed to push for a in the first Congress. Seven of the ten amendments in the Bill of Rights came directly from Mason's work, cementing his legacy as the true Father of the Constitution.

By examining Jefferson and Mason's contributions side by side, we can appreciate the unique roles both men played—Jefferson as the voice of the Declaration and Mason as the champion of individual rights that would later shape the Constitution's Bill of Rights.

More Food For Thought

Comparing the writings of Mason and Jefferson reveals even more common ground. Thomas Jefferson's 1776 draft of a Virginia Constitution was not merely a list of grievances but a visionary outline for the government he believed America should build. It foreshadowed elements of both the U.S. Constitution and the Bill of Rights. It arrived in Williamsburg too late to be considered, but its depth and structure reflected Jefferson's vision for a government designed to protect liberty and prevent tyranny.

Jefferson's draft established a clear separation of powers among the executive, legislative, and judicial branches—principles later enshrined in the U.S. Constitution. He proposed a bicameral legislature to check tyranny, with both houses elected by the people.

Among his boldest provisions were term limits (to prevent a new aristocracy among the political class). Even more striking, his draft contained a list of fundamental rights, anticipating later constitutional protections:

- **Equal inheritance laws** – He proposed Gavelkind, ensuring equal land distribution, but uniquely included women in inheritance rights.
- **A ban on slavery for future arrivals** – "No person hereafter coming into this county shall be held within the same in slavery under any pretext whatever."
- **Religious freedom** – "All persons shall have full and free liberty of religious opinion; nor shall any be compelled to frequent or maintain any religious institution."
- **Right to bear arms** – "No freeman shall be debarred the use of arms [within his own lands]."
- **Opposition to standing armies** – "There shall be no standing army but in time of actual war."
- **Press freedom** – "Printing presses shall be free, except so far as by commission of private injury cause may be given of private action."

When a Long Train of Abuses

"Prudence, indeed, will dictate, that governments long established, should not be changed for light and transient causes; and accordingly, all experience hath shown, that mankind are more disposed to suffer, while evils are sufferable, than to right themselves by abolishing the forms to which they are accustomed. But when a long train of abuses and usurpations, pursuing invariably the same object, evinces a design to reduce them under absolute despotism, it is their right, it is their duty, to throw off such government, and to provide new guards for their future security. Such has been the patient sufferance of these Colonies; and such is now the necessity which constrains them to alter their former systems of government."

NOTE: Jefferson's words remind us that liberty is not lost in a moment—it erodes when people endure abuse for too long. The colonies had pleaded, reasoned, and petitioned, but each attempt was met with new injury. Only after years of patience did they resolve to act. Jefferson's earlier writing, *A Summary View of the Rights of British America*, had already declared that rulers who betray the trust of the people forfeit their right to demand obedience. The passage that follows shows how he transformed that belief into a universal principle of resistance.

From Thomas Jefferson's 1774 Summary View of the Rights of British America

When the representative body has lost the confidence of their constituents, when they have notoriously made sale of their most valuable rights, when they have assumed to themselves powers which the people never put into their hands, then indeed their continuing in office becomes dangerous to the state, and calls for an exercise of the power of dissolution.

Breaking down the phrases

"Prudence, indeed, will dictate, that governments long established, should not be changed for light and transient causes"

>Jefferson opens by invoking "prudence," or wise judgment, to argue that stable, long-standing governments should not be overthrown for trivial or short-lived reasons. He acknowledges that stability is valuable and that rash actions can be detrimental.

"…and accordingly, all experience hath shown, that mankind are more disposed to suffer, while evils are sufferable, than to right themselves by abolishing the forms to which they are accustomed."

>Jefferson notes that human history has shown people generally put up with "evils" or injustices as long as they can bear them, rather than take the risky step of overthrowing an established system. This is an appeal to the natural human tendency to stick with the familiar, even if it's flawed.

"But when a long train of abuses and usurpations, pursuing invariably the same object, evinces a design to reduce them under absolute despotism, it is their right, it is their duty, to throw off such government, and to provide new guards for their future security."

>This is the crux of the argument. Jefferson says that when a government consistently abuses its power with the clear intention of establishing tyrannical rule, the people not only have the right but also the moral obligation to revolt and establish a new form of governance that ensures their future safety. John Locke used this same phrase, "long train of abuses," in his reasoning a century before.

"Such has been the patient sufferance of these Colonies; and such is now the necessity which constrains them to alter their former systems of government."

>Here, Jefferson directly applies his preceding philosophical points to the American colonies, saying that they have patiently endured abuses and now find it necessary to change their governmental system. Invoking the term 'necessary' in the parlance of the day, meant that it was virtually ordained or inevitable this action take place. This transition serves to legitimize the colonial struggle by aligning it with the broader principles he just outlined.

Each sentence in this portion of the preamble carefully lays out the conditions under which revolt is justifiable and why the American colonies met those conditions. Jefferson's text moves from general principles to the specific case of the colonies, linking the two to build a compelling case for independence.

Overview

This second half of the Preamble to *The Declaration of Independence* serves as a nuanced addendum to the bold claims of the first part. It addresses when it is appropriate to take the drastic measure of overthrowing a government. Jefferson argues that long-standing governments should not be overthrown for trivial reasons; however, when a government systematically undermines the rights of its people, then it becomes not just a right but a moral imperative for the people to revolt and establish a new government. The key distinction he makes is that people will generally endure oppression unless it becomes so systematic and intolerable that there is no other recourse. This argument provides the philosophical backbone for the list of grievances that follows, demonstrating that the colonies had exhausted all other means before taking up the mantle of revolution.

The language of this passage is deliberately structured to appeal to reason, morality, and history. By establishing that the colonists had long endured these grievances and had no other option but to break free, Jefferson and the other Founders made their case not only to the British government but also to the world, seeking legitimacy in the eyes of European powers and potential allies.

Historical Background

The ideas expressed in this part of the preamble had roots in Enlightenment philosophy, notably the works of John Locke and other thinkers who espoused the concept of a "social contract" between the governed and their government. This section was crucial for convincing domestic and international audiences that the colonies acted appropriately and with just cause. Given that the colonies were part of the British Empire for over a century, it was essential to establish that their move towards independence was a last resort, precipitated by a series of unaddressed grievances. It is interesting to note that **John Locke** used the phrase, "a long train of abuses" in his **1690** *Second Treatise on Government*, Section 225:

> But if a long train of abuses, prevarications, and artifices, all tending the same way, make the design visible to the people, and they cannot but feel what they lie under, and see whither they are going, it is not to be wondered that they should then rouse themselves, and endeavour to put the rule into such hands which may secure to them the ends for which government was at first erected.[18]

Jefferson and many others had addressed this long train of abuses for years leading up to the Revolution. Perhaps the most comprehensive was Jefferson's *Summary View of the Rights of British America*, written for Virginia Delegates to the First Continental Congress in 1774. It was considered too radical by those conventioneers but was distributed as a pamphlet throughout the colonies and even in Great Britain. This document will be discussed in detail on the following pages, as it was foundational to the concepts adopted and declared by the Second Continental Congress of 1776. We cannot discount Jefferson's familiarity with the long history of intolerable acts perpetrated upon the colonies by the Crown and how the colonies responded to such treatments.

Additionally, the Founders were aware of previous struggles against tyranny, including the English Civil War (1642–1651) and the Glorious Revolution of 1688, which set precedents for challenging unjust rulers. *The Declaration of Independence*, therefore, was not an unprecedented act, but rather the culmination of historical and philosophical ideas about the necessity of revolution in the face of persistent tyranny.

The Colonial Charters

In the dawn of colonial America, each colony was established under a charter—a solemn contract granted by the English Crown. These charters defined the scope of governance, the liberties of the settlers, and the obligations owed to the King. Whether royal, proprietary, or joint-stock in nature, each charter created a unique balance between authority and autonomy, shaping the political landscape of early America.

To many colonists, however, the charters represented something even more sacred than self-government: the right of private ownership in land. Within their parchment boundaries lay both liberty and livelihood. The charters did not merely authorize local assemblies; they conveyed the power to hold and dispose of land, to draw borders, and to govern free from arbitrary interference by the King or Parliament.

Early Troubles and Restrictions

The nascent colonies faced early troubles and restrictions imposed by the mother country. The Crown's jealousy and desire for subjection led to a series of restrictive measures, particularly targeting colonial manufacturing and trade. Acts from the Navigation Acts of 1651 and the Molasses Act of 1733 to the Royal Proclamation of 1763, and the Quebec Act of 1774 stifled colonial independence and fueled resentment among colonists.

Diverging Views on Charters

A profound schism emerged between the Crown and the colonists regarding the nature and obligations of the colonial charters. While the Crown viewed them as revocable governance instruments, the colonists saw them as sacred compacts, guaranteeing their rights and liberties, as well as their borders. This dissonance laid the groundwork for future conflicts and paved the path for colonial resistance.

Rising Tensions and Committees of Correspondence

As tensions between the colonies and the Crown reached a boiling point, colonial assemblies took proactive measures to coordinate resistance. Committees of Correspondence, like the one established by Virginia in 1773, became conduits of unity and defiance, fostering communication and solidarity among the colonies.

List of British Acts and Colonial Responses

The British Parliament, seeking to assert control over its colonial possessions, passed a series of acts that further antagonized the colonies. From the Royal Proclamation of 1763, the Stamp Act of 1765 to the Intolerable Acts of 1774, each measure tightened the grip of British authority and fueled colonial discontent. In response, colonists staged acts of resistance, from boycotts and protests to the iconic Boston Tea Party of 1773.

The "long train of abuses" was about much, much more than a two percent tax on tea, as illustrated below:

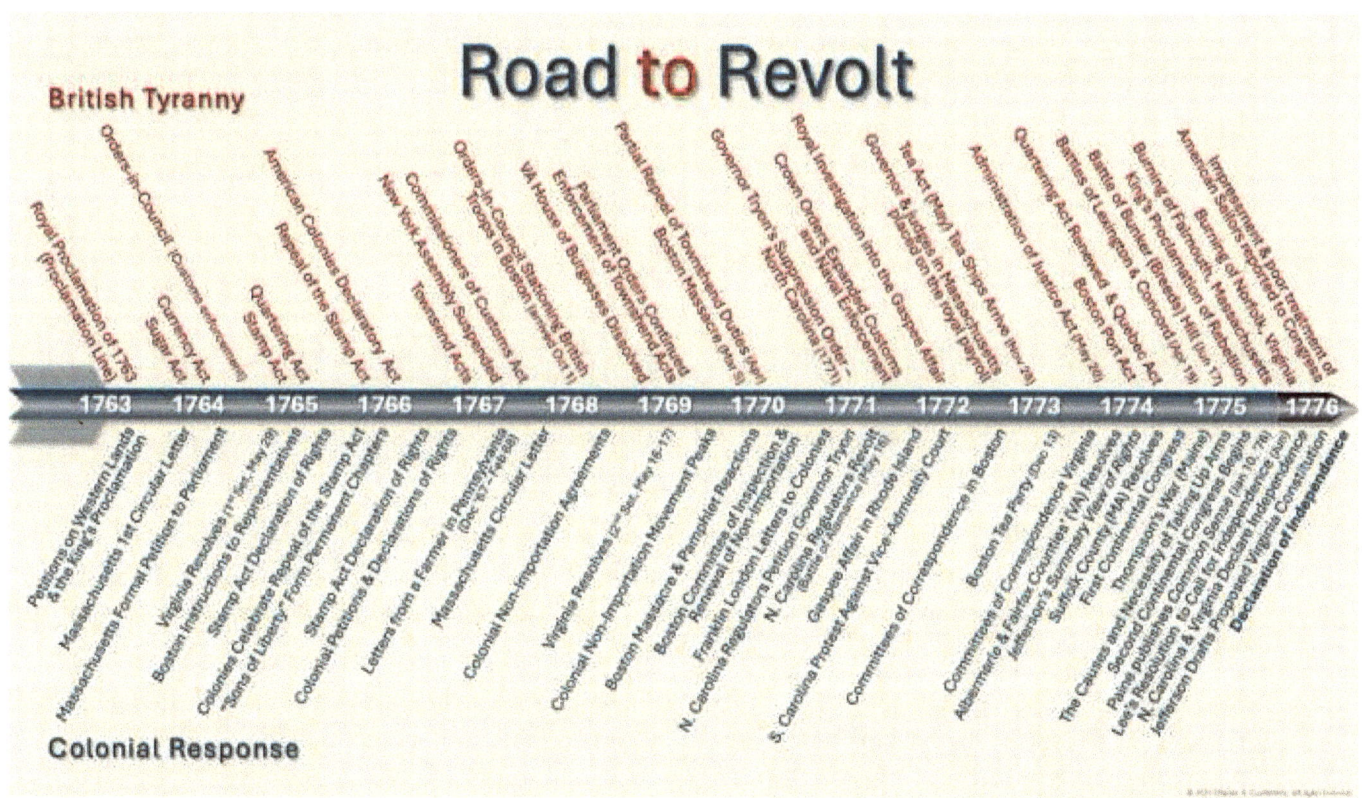

Each act of British tyranny provoked a colonial response—and the clash of wills led to the birth of a nation.

The Spread of Resistance

The spirit of resistance spread like wildfire across colonial America, transcending geographical boundaries. From the bustling streets of Boston to the tranquil shores of Charleston, colonists united in defiance against British oppression. "Tea Parties," symbolic acts of protest echoing from Maine to South Carolina, exemplified the fervent resolve of a people determined to safeguard their liberties.

The Road to Revolt: British Acts and Colonial Responses

The British government passed law after law trying to control the American colonies and raise money. Each new act made life harder and fueled growing resentment. These weren't just taxes on tea—they were signs that the colonists were losing control over their own lives. As tensions between the colonies and the Crown escalated, the British Parliament passed a series of punitive measures known as the Intolerable Acts in response to the Boston Tea Party. These acts further inflamed colonial grievances and set the stage for open rebellion. Following is a partial list of abusive acts and some responses that propelled the colonies towards declaring independence:

Navigation Acts (1651)
- **Purpose:** These Acts were a series of laws passed by the British Parliament to regulate colonial trade and commerce, primarily with the goal of ensuring that trade benefited England.
- **Significance:** The Navigation Acts required colonial goods to be transported on English ships, restricted certain colonial exports to England, and imposed duties on certain imports. These acts contributed to colonial resentment towards British economic control and played a role in the lead-up to the American Revolution.[19]

Molasses Act (1733)
- **Purpose:** This Act imposed a tax on molasses, rum, and sugar imported into the American colonies from non-British Caribbean sources.
- **Significance:** The Molasses Act was widely evaded by colonial merchants, who engaged in smuggling to avoid the high duties. It contributed to colonial opposition to British taxation without representation and set the stage for future conflicts over taxation policies.[20]

Currency Act (1751)
- **Purpose:** This Act prohibited the American colonies from issuing their own paper currency as legal tender.
- **Significance:** The Currency Act disrupted colonial economies and hindered their ability to conduct trade and commerce. It was viewed as another instance of British economic control over the colonies and further strained colonial relations with the mother country.[21]

Albany Congress (1754)
- **Purpose:** The Albany Congress was a meeting of colonial representatives convened to discuss and coordinate defense efforts against French expansion in North America during the French and Indian War.
- **Significance:** Although the Albany Plan of Union proposed at the Congress was not adopted, it laid the groundwork for future discussions of colonial unity and cooperation, foreshadowing the later Continental Congresses.[22]

Proclamation Line of 1763 (Royal Proclamation)
- **Purpose:** This proclamation, issued by King George III, prohibited colonial settlement west of the Appalachian Mountains. It aimed to avoid conflicts with Native American tribes and maintain British control over Western territories.
- **Significance:** The Proclamation of 1763 angered many colonists who had fought in the French and Indian War and sought to claim land in the Ohio Valley. It was seen as an infringement on colonial land rights and contributed to growing colonial resentment towards British policies.[23]

Sugar Act (1764)
- **Purpose:** This Act lowered the duty on molasses imported into the colonies but increased enforcement of customs regulations and expanded the list of taxable goods.
- **Significance:** The Sugar Act was part of a series of revenue-raising measures by the British government aimed at reducing colonial smuggling and raising revenue to pay for the cost of colonial defense. It was met with resistance from colonists, who viewed it as another form of taxation without representation.[24]

Currency Act (1764)
- **Purpose:** This Act extended the prohibition on colonial paper currency as legal tender and further restricted colonial monetary practices.
- **Significance:** The Currency Act further hindered colonial economic development and exacerbated colonial grievances against British economic policies.[25]

Stamp Act (1765)
- **Purpose:** The Stamp Act imposed a direct tax on various paper goods in the colonies, including newspapers, legal documents, and playing cards.
- **Significance:** The Stamp Act was met with widespread protests and boycotts by colonists, who saw it as an unconstitutional and oppressive tax imposed without their consent. It galvanized colonial opposition to British taxation policies and laid the groundwork for organized resistance.[26]

Quartering Act (1765)
- **Purpose:** This act required colonial assemblies to provide housing and provisions for British troops stationed in the colonies.
- **Significance:** The Quartering Act was another source of colonial resentment towards British military presence and contributed to growing tensions between soldiers and civilians in the colonies. Additionally, it highlighted the hypocrisy of Parliament in Great Britain, which had previously passed laws in the 1628 Petition of Right and the 1689 Bill of Rights prohibiting such quartering of troops among the king's subjects in England. This apparent double standard further fueled colonial opposition, as colonists saw their rights being trampled upon in ways that British citizens would not tolerate.[27]

Declaratory Act (1766)
- **Purpose:** This Act asserted the British Parliament's authority to legislate for the colonies "in all cases whatsoever," including taxation.
- **Significance:** The Declaratory Act was passed alongside the repeal of the Stamp Act and affirmed Parliament's sovereignty over the colonies, setting the stage for future conflicts over colonial autonomy and self-government.[28]

Townshend Revenue Act (1767)
- **Purpose:** These Acts imposed duties on various imported goods, including tea, glass, paper, and lead, with the revenue used to pay colonial officials and support British troops in America.
- **Significance:** The Townshend Acts reignited colonial opposition to British taxation policies and led to renewed boycotts and protests. The suspension of the New York Assembly for refusing to comply with the Quartering Act further escalated tensions.[29]

Boston Massacre (March 5, 1770)
- **Event:** A confrontation between British soldiers and a mob of colonists in Boston led to the soldiers firing into the crowd, killing five colonists.
- **Significance:** The Boston Massacre further inflamed anti-British sentiment in the colonies and was used as propaganda by colonial leaders to rally support for resistance efforts.[30]

Tea Act (1773)
- **Purpose:** This Act granted the British East India Company a monopoly on tea sales in the American colonies and allowed the company to sell surplus tea directly to colonial merchants.
- **Significance:** The Tea Act was seen as another attempt by the British government to assert its authority and maintain the principle of parliamentary taxation. It led to the Boston Tea Party and further heightened tensions between Britain and the colonies.[31]

Boston Tea Party (1773)
- **Event:** Colonists disguised as Mohawk Indians boarded British ships in Boston Harbor and dumped chests of tea into the water in protest against the Tea Act.
- **Significance:** The Boston Tea Party was a dramatic act of colonial defiance against British taxation policies and monopoly control over colonial trade. It led to harsh reprisals by the British government and the passage of the Intolerable Acts.[32]

Intolerable or Coercive Acts (1774)
- **Purpose:** These Acts were a series of punitive measures passed by the British Parliament in response to the Boston Tea Party. They aimed to punish Massachusetts and assert British authority in the colonies.
- **Significance:** The Intolerable Acts included the Boston Port Act, the Massachusetts Government Act, the Administration of Justice Act, and the Quartering Act, among others. They further escalated tensions between Britain and the colonies, significantly galvanizing colonial opposition and unity.[33]

The Boston Port Act (March 31, 1774)
- **Purpose:** Closed the port of Boston until damages from the Boston Tea Party were paid for.
- **Attitude in the Colonies:** This was seen as an egregious attack on the rights of the colonists and a blatant act of retaliation by the British government.[34]

The Massachusetts Government Act (May 20, 1774)
- **Purpose:** Altered the Massachusetts charter of government, granting the British-appointed governor significant power and restricting town meetings.
- **Significance:** Viewed as an assault on colonial self-government and an attempt to undermine representative institutions.[35]

The Administration of Justice Act (May 20, 1774)
- **Purpose:** Allowed British officials accused of crimes in the colonies to be tried in Great Britain or another colony, where it was believed they would receive a more sympathetic trial.
- **Significance:** This was seen as a violation of the principle of trial by jury and an affront to colonial legal rights.[36]

Sugar Act (1764)

- **Purpose:** This Act lowered the duty on molasses imported into the colonies but increased enforcement of customs regulations and expanded the list of taxable goods.
- **Significance:** The Sugar Act was part of a series of revenue-raising measures by the British government aimed at reducing colonial smuggling and raising revenue to pay for the cost of colonial defense. It was met with resistance from colonists, who viewed it as another form of taxation without representation.[24]

Currency Act (1764)

- **Purpose:** This Act extended the prohibition on colonial paper currency as legal tender and further restricted colonial monetary practices.
- **Significance:** The Currency Act further hindered colonial economic development and exacerbated colonial grievances against British economic policies.[25]

Stamp Act (1765)

- **Purpose:** The Stamp Act imposed a direct tax on various paper goods in the colonies, including newspapers, legal documents, and playing cards.
- **Significance:** The Stamp Act was met with widespread protests and boycotts by colonists, who saw it as an unconstitutional and oppressive tax imposed without their consent. It galvanized colonial opposition to British taxation policies and laid the groundwork for organized resistance.[26]

Quartering Act (1765)

- **Purpose:** This act required colonial assemblies to provide housing and provisions for British troops stationed in the colonies.
- **Significance:** The Quartering Act was another source of colonial resentment towards British military presence and contributed to growing tensions between soldiers and civilians in the colonies. Additionally, it highlighted the hypocrisy of Parliament in Great Britain, which had previously passed laws in the 1628 Petition of Right and the 1689 Bill of Rights prohibiting such quartering of troops among the king's subjects in England. This apparent double standard further fueled colonial opposition, as colonists saw their rights being trampled upon in ways that British citizens would not tolerate.[27]

Declaratory Act (1766)

- **Purpose:** This Act asserted the British Parliament's authority to legislate for the colonies "in all cases whatsoever," including taxation.
- **Significance:** The Declaratory Act was passed alongside the repeal of the Stamp Act and affirmed Parliament's sovereignty over the colonies, setting the stage for future conflicts over colonial autonomy and self-government.[28]

Townshend Revenue Act (1767)

- **Purpose:** These Acts imposed duties on various imported goods, including tea, glass, paper, and lead, with the revenue used to pay colonial officials and support British troops in America.
- **Significance:** The Townshend Acts reignited colonial opposition to British taxation policies and led to renewed boycotts and protests. The suspension of the New York Assembly for refusing to comply with the Quartering Act further escalated tensions.[29]

Boston Massacre (March 5, 1770)
- **Event:** A confrontation between British soldiers and a mob of colonists in Boston led to the soldiers firing into the crowd, killing five colonists.
- **Significance:** The Boston Massacre further inflamed anti-British sentiment in the colonies and was used as propaganda by colonial leaders to rally support for resistance efforts.[30]

Tea Act (1773)
- **Purpose:** This Act granted the British East India Company a monopoly on tea sales in the American colonies and allowed the company to sell surplus tea directly to colonial merchants.
- **Significance:** The Tea Act was seen as another attempt by the British government to assert its authority and maintain the principle of parliamentary taxation. It led to the Boston Tea Party and further heightened tensions between Britain and the colonies.[31]

Boston Tea Party (1773)
- **Event:** Colonists disguised as Mohawk Indians boarded British ships in Boston Harbor and dumped chests of tea into the water in protest against the Tea Act.
- **Significance:** The Boston Tea Party was a dramatic act of colonial defiance against British taxation policies and monopoly control over colonial trade. It led to harsh reprisals by the British government and the passage of the Intolerable Acts.[32]

Intolerable or Coercive Acts (1774)
- **Purpose:** These Acts were a series of punitive measures passed by the British Parliament in response to the Boston Tea Party. They aimed to punish Massachusetts and assert British authority in the colonies.
- **Significance:** The Intolerable Acts included the Boston Port Act, the Massachusetts Government Act, the Administration of Justice Act, and the Quartering Act, among others. They further escalated tensions between Britain and the colonies, significantly galvanizing colonial opposition and unity.[33]

The Boston Port Act (March 31, 1774)
- **Purpose:** Closed the port of Boston until damages from the Boston Tea Party were paid for.
- **Attitude in the Colonies:** This was seen as an egregious attack on the rights of the colonists and a blatant act of retaliation by the British government.[34]

The Massachusetts Government Act (May 20, 1774)
- **Purpose:** Altered the Massachusetts charter of government, granting the British-appointed governor significant power and restricting town meetings.
- **Significance:** Viewed as an assault on colonial self-government and an attempt to undermine representative institutions.[35]

The Administration of Justice Act (May 20, 1774)
- **Purpose:** Allowed British officials accused of crimes in the colonies to be tried in Great Britain or another colony, where it was believed they would receive a more sympathetic trial.
- **Significance:** This was seen as a violation of the principle of trial by jury and an affront to colonial legal rights.[36]

Sugar Act (1764)
- **Purpose:** This Act lowered the duty on molasses imported into the colonies but increased enforcement of customs regulations and expanded the list of taxable goods.
- **Significance:** The Sugar Act was part of a series of revenue-raising measures by the British government aimed at reducing colonial smuggling and raising revenue to pay for the cost of colonial defense. It was met with resistance from colonists, who viewed it as another form of taxation without representation.[24]

Currency Act (1764)
- **Purpose:** This Act extended the prohibition on colonial paper currency as legal tender and further restricted colonial monetary practices.
- **Significance:** The Currency Act further hindered colonial economic development and exacerbated colonial grievances against British economic policies.[25]

Stamp Act (1765)
- **Purpose:** The Stamp Act imposed a direct tax on various paper goods in the colonies, including newspapers, legal documents, and playing cards.
- **Significance:** The Stamp Act was met with widespread protests and boycotts by colonists, who saw it as an unconstitutional and oppressive tax imposed without their consent. It galvanized colonial opposition to British taxation policies and laid the groundwork for organized resistance.[26]

Quartering Act (1765)
- **Purpose:** This act required colonial assemblies to provide housing and provisions for British troops stationed in the colonies.
- **Significance:** The Quartering Act was another source of colonial resentment towards British military presence and contributed to growing tensions between soldiers and civilians in the colonies. Additionally, it highlighted the hypocrisy of Parliament in Great Britain, which had previously passed laws in the 1628 Petition of Right and the 1689 Bill of Rights prohibiting such quartering of troops among the king's subjects in England. This apparent double standard further fueled colonial opposition, as colonists saw their rights being trampled upon in ways that British citizens would not tolerate.[27]

Declaratory Act (1766)
- **Purpose:** This Act asserted the British Parliament's authority to legislate for the colonies "in all cases whatsoever," including taxation.
- **Significance:** The Declaratory Act was passed alongside the repeal of the Stamp Act and affirmed Parliament's sovereignty over the colonies, setting the stage for future conflicts over colonial autonomy and self-government.[28]

Townshend Revenue Act (1767)
- **Purpose:** These Acts imposed duties on various imported goods, including tea, glass, paper, and lead, with the revenue used to pay colonial officials and support British troops in America.
- **Significance:** The Townshend Acts reignited colonial opposition to British taxation policies and led to renewed boycotts and protests. The suspension of the New York Assembly for refusing to comply with the Quartering Act further escalated tensions.[29]

Boston Massacre (March 5, 1770)
- **Event:** A confrontation between British soldiers and a mob of colonists in Boston led to the soldiers firing into the crowd, killing five colonists.
- **Significance:** The Boston Massacre further inflamed anti-British sentiment in the colonies and was used as propaganda by colonial leaders to rally support for resistance efforts.[30]

Tea Act (1773)
- **Purpose:** This Act granted the British East India Company a monopoly on tea sales in the American colonies and allowed the company to sell surplus tea directly to colonial merchants.
- **Significance:** The Tea Act was seen as another attempt by the British government to assert its authority and maintain the principle of parliamentary taxation. It led to the Boston Tea Party and further heightened tensions between Britain and the colonies.[31]

Boston Tea Party (1773)
- **Event:** Colonists disguised as Mohawk Indians boarded British ships in Boston Harbor and dumped chests of tea into the water in protest against the Tea Act.
- **Significance:** The Boston Tea Party was a dramatic act of colonial defiance against British taxation policies and monopoly control over colonial trade. It led to harsh reprisals by the British government and the passage of the Intolerable Acts.[32]

Intolerable or Coercive Acts (1774)
- **Purpose:** These Acts were a series of punitive measures passed by the British Parliament in response to the Boston Tea Party. They aimed to punish Massachusetts and assert British authority in the colonies.
- **Significance:** The Intolerable Acts included the Boston Port Act, the Massachusetts Government Act, the Administration of Justice Act, and the Quartering Act, among others. They further escalated tensions between Britain and the colonies, significantly galvanizing colonial opposition and unity.[33]

The Boston Port Act (March 31, 1774)
- **Purpose:** Closed the port of Boston until damages from the Boston Tea Party were paid for.
- **Attitude in the Colonies:** This was seen as an egregious attack on the rights of the colonists and a blatant act of retaliation by the British government.[34]

The Massachusetts Government Act (May 20, 1774)
- **Purpose:** Altered the Massachusetts charter of government, granting the British-appointed governor significant power and restricting town meetings.
- **Significance:** Viewed as an assault on colonial self-government and an attempt to undermine representative institutions.[35]

The Administration of Justice Act (May 20, 1774)
- **Purpose:** Allowed British officials accused of crimes in the colonies to be tried in Great Britain or another colony, where it was believed they would receive a more sympathetic trial.
- **Significance:** This was seen as a violation of the principle of trial by jury and an affront to colonial legal rights.[36]

The Quartering Act (June 2, 1774)
- **Purpose:** Expanded the scope of the Quartering Act of 1765, allowing British troops to be quartered in private homes, including unoccupied buildings and barns, if necessary.
- **Significance:** It was perceived as an infringement on colonial property rights and personal liberties, further fueling resentment towards the British military presence.

The Quebec Act (June 22, 1774)
- **Purpose:** Expanded Quebec's boundaries and granted religious freedoms to French Catholics while extending Quebec's jurisdiction into the Ohio Valley.
- **Significance:** This was a direct threat to colonial land claims and religious freedoms, exacerbating fears of British tyranny and Catholic dominance.[37]

Modern Interpretation
In the modern context, this part of the preamble is often cited in discussions about the legitimacy of protest movements, civil disobedience, and even revolution. It posits that people must revolt only when a government's actions make it evident that its goal is authoritarian rule. This nuanced perspective offers a framework for evaluating historical and contemporary movements that seek to change or overthrow existing governance systems.

Summary
The second half of the preamble establishes that the colonies did not decide to seek independence lightly. It acknowledges that a threshold of suffering must be crossed to justify overthrowing a long-established government. This section provides the rationale for American independence and outlines relevant principles for assessing governmental change or revolution legitimacy. The ideas presented in the second half of the preamble are far-reaching and continue to be pertinent in conversations about the nature of government, civil disobedience, and the rights and duties of the citizenry. The Declaration does not glorify revolution for its own sake but treats it as a last resort when all other avenues for redress have been exhausted. This principle has remained foundational in American political philosophy and has influenced democratic movements across the globe.

Constitutional Safeguards

The U.S. Constitution weaves the Enlightenment principles underpinning the Declaration's Preamble into the governance framework. The Constitution establishes a government empowered and constrained by the rule of law. The system of checks and balances among the three branches of government ensures that no single entity can become tyrannical, reflecting the Declaration's caution against despotism.

- **Article IV, Section 4:** Guarantees to every state a republican form of government, ensuring that the principles of our republic are enshrined in the nation's fabric.
- **Article V:** Provides a mechanism for amending the Constitution, allowing for the orderly and lawful evolution of governance in response to "a long train of abuses and usurpations" without resorting to revolution.
- **The Bill of Rights:** Provides specific protections for individuals and states against federal overreach, directly addressing the concern that a government must not violate the people's unalienable rights. It embodies the Declaration's insistence on "new guards for their future security" against tyranny.

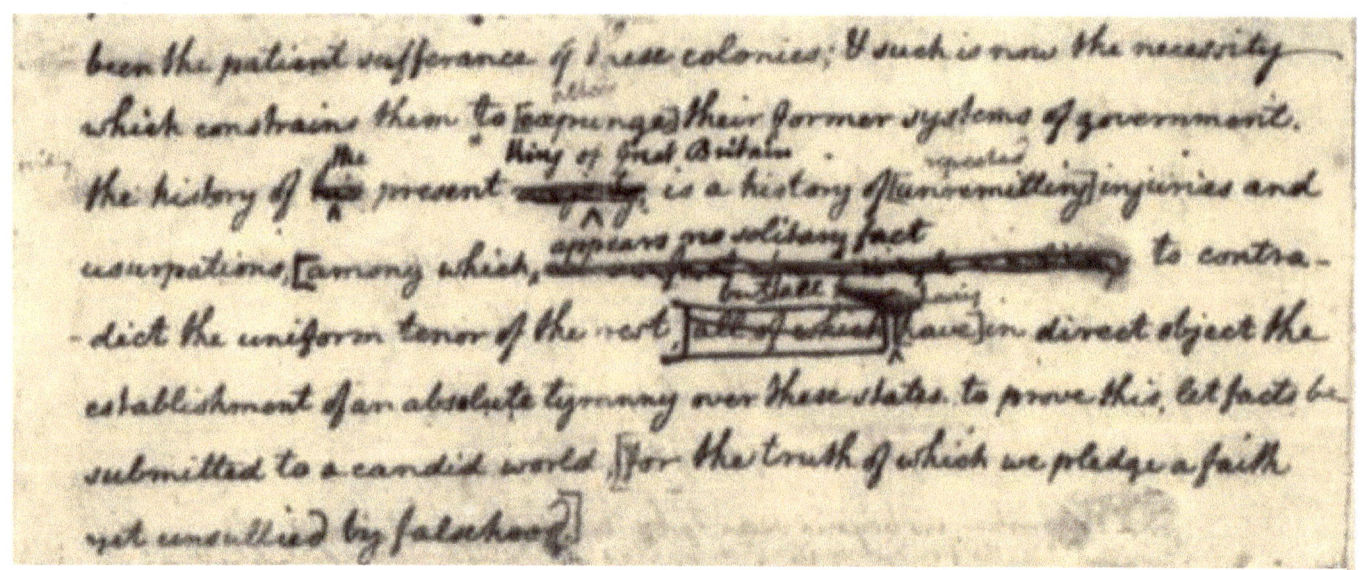

Portion of page 1 of Jefferson's Rough Draft of the Declaration of Independence, courtesy of the Library of Congress

Let Facts Be Submitted to a Candid World

"The history of the present King of Great Britain is a history of repeated injuries and usurpations, all having in direct object the establishment of an absolute tyranny over these States. To prove this, let facts be submitted to a candid world."

NOTE: Reviewing the last two sentences of the preamble is essential to set the stage for understanding the reasons for and importance of these grievances. We will also discuss why Jefferson was tasked to author the Declaration and how his former study and writings, particularly his 1774 *Summary View of the Rights of British America*, was, quite literally, an enlarged first draft of *The Declaration of Independence*. It could be argued that *The Declaration of Independence* is a condensed version of Jefferson's *Summary View of the Rights of British America*.

Breaking Down the Phrases

"The history of the present King of Great Britain is a history of repeated injuries and usurpations, all having in direct object the establishment of an absolute tyranny over these States."

> Jefferson indicts King George III, summarizing the king's actions as a series of abuses aimed at establishing absolute rule over the colonies. This acts as a transition into the list of grievances that make up the bulk of the Declaration.

"To prove this, let facts be submitted to a candid world."

> Jefferson concludes this section by stating that he will present factual evidence to the world to substantiate his claims against the British Crown. This appeals to rationality and indicates that the American case is not just emotional but based on observable, objective, and prolonged wrongs.

The Indictment: Leading to a List of Grievances

Reviewing the last two sentences of the preamble, "The history of the present King of Great Britain is a history of repeated injuries and usurpations, all having in direct object the establishment of an absolute tyranny over these States. To prove this, let facts be submitted to a candid world" is vital to set the stage for understanding the reasons and importance of these grievances.

These final lines of the preamble are pivotal because they transition from the philosophical framework that justifies rebellion to the specific list of grievances against King George III. This transition ensures that readers understand that the colonies aren't revolting on a whim but are instead taking a measured, justified action based on **a *"long train of abuses and usurpations."*** By stating that these grievances will be submitted ***"to a candid world,"*** Jefferson emphasizes the intent to expose these injustices globally for judgment, thereby bolstering their legitimacy.

The choice of Thomas Jefferson as the author of *The Declaration of Independence* was no accident. An accomplished writer and thinker, his previous works had laid the intellectual and historical groundwork for the Declaration. Jefferson's 1774 *Summary View of the Rights of British America* can be seen as a precursor to the Declaration, exploring nearly all of the themes, historical background, and arguments laid out in the initial and final drafts of *The Declaration of Independence*. Additionally, Jefferson wrote the preamble to the 1776 Virginia Constitution, which included nearly the exact wording as the twenty-seven grievances in *The Declaration of Independence*. Reading Jefferson's prior work helps us understand how the Declaration did not spontaneously arise but resulted from years of intellectual and political evolution. Jefferson, more than any other man, was prepared for that moment.[38]

Constitutional Safeguards

While crafted a decade later, the Constitution of the United States can be seen as the practical implementation of the principles and grievances laid out in the Declaration. In direct response to the "history of repeated injuries and usurpations," the Constitution establishes a government whose authority is derived from the people. It outlines a structure that prevents the emergence of a despotic power.

- **Article III:** Establishes an independent judiciary to protect against King George III's abuses. It ensures that justice is administered based on a fair and transparent legal process rather than the whims of a monarch.

- **Article I, Section 9:** Places clear limits on the powers of Congress, prohibiting the kind of arbitrary rule and "injuries and usurpations" the colonies experienced under British rule. This includes limitations on suspending the writ of habeas corpus and passing bills of attainder and ex post facto laws.

- **The First Amendment:** Ensures that grievances can be freely expressed, allowing for the "facts to be submitted to a candid world" without fear of retribution.

Presenting The Grievances

Thomas Jefferson ended the Preamble with these strong words:

> "The history of the present King of Great Britain is a history of repeated injuries and usurpations, all having in direct object the establishment of an absolute tyranny over these States. **To prove this, let facts be submitted to a candid world.**"

With these words, Jefferson began listing the many ways King George III had mistreated the American colonies. These weren't just complaints—they were proof that the king had abused his power again and again. The colonists had tried to fix things peacefully, but the king refused to listen. Now, they were explaining to the world why they had no choice but to separate.

Besides, the British had already attacked Lexington and Concord, and Bunker Hill had been fought. It was time.

The left-side pages generally include

- **Illustration** – A visual aid to help readers see or imagine the issue.
- **Short Title** – A simple label for quick reference.
- **Declaration Grievance** – The exact text from *The Declaration of Independence*, followed by a short introduction.
- **Jefferson's *Summary View of the Rights of British America* (1774)** – A forerunner to the Declaration, this document listed similar complaints against British rule. Jefferson even wrote several Grievances.
  - **Jefferson's Draft of The Causes and Necessity of Taking Up Arms (1775)** – This or other sources were used to inspire the text for the few Grievances not covered in Jefferson's *Summary View*.
  - **Jefferson's Preamble to the Virginia Constitution (May-early June 1776)** – He copied from this to write the Grievances in the Rough Draft of the Declaration, already written, nearly word-for-word.
- **Benson J. Lossing's *Our Country: A Household History* (1877)** – A historian's look at the Revolution, drawn from firsthand accounts and original documents. Lossing's words are kept as they were written to preserve the historical record.

The right-side pages generally include

- **Historical Background** – What was happening in the colonies, and how did this Grievance arise?
- **Modern Interpretation** – How these same ideas still affect freedom today.
- **Summary** – A short reflection about power, freedom, or government.
- **This Means**: *(Youth Version only)* A shaded callout box that restates the meaning of each Grievance in clear, simple language, helping readers grasp its meaning and importance at a glance.
- **Constitutional Safeguards** – How lessons from each Grievance helped shape the U.S. Constitution to prevent similar abuses.

By studying Jefferson's words, the writings of his time, and historians like Lossing, we see that these Grievances weren't just about the past—they became the blueprint for America's freedom. They show how courage, reason, and persistence shaped a new kind of government, one built to protect liberty for all.

Each Grievance reveals a real story of struggle and courage. Some are dramatic, others surprising—but every one of them shows why freedom had to be declared, and defended.

Grievance 1	He Refuses to Assent to Necessary Laws
Grievance 2	He Forbids Passing Laws of Pressing Importance
Grievance 3	He Suppresses Representation
Grievance 4	He Burdens Legislatures with Fatiguing Measures
Grievance 5	He Dissolves Parliaments & Opposes Rights
Grievance 6	He Endangers Us by Neglecting Elections
Grievance 7	He Controls Settlement of Lands & Naturalization
Grievance 8	He Blocks Local Administration of Justice
Grievance 9	He Has Made Our Judges Dependent on His Will
Grievance 10	He Erected New Offices & Sent Swarms of Officers
Grievance 11	He Keeps Armies Among Us in Times of Peace
Grievance 12	His Military is Superior to Our Civil Authority
Grievance 13	He Subjects Us to Foreign Jurisdiction
Grievance 14	For Quartering Large Bodies of Troops
Grievance 15	He Protects Foreign Soldiers by Mock Trials
Grievance 16	For Cutting Off from Global Trade
Grievance 17	Taxation Without Representation
Grievance 18	Deprived of Trial by Juries
Grievance 19	Transporting Us Beyond Seas for Trial
Grievance 20	Enlarging the Borders of a Neighboring Province
Grievance 21	Taking Away Charters and Valuable Laws
Grievance 22	Suspends Legislatures & Assumes Power
Grievance 23	Abdicating Governance and Protection
Grievance 24	He Plundered, Ravaged, Burnt & Destroyed
Grievance 25	Foreign Mercenaries Terrorize Our People
Grievance 26	Taken Captive to Bear Arms Against Fellow Citizens
Grievance 27	Inciting Insurrections & Unleashing Merciless Forces
The Slavery Clause	

Grievance 1

He Refuses to Assent to Necessary Laws

"He has refused his assent to laws the most wholesome and necessary for the public good."

NOTE: Before revolution came frustration. The colonies could not pass even the simplest local laws without royal approval. Britain's king withheld assent again and again, stifling reform and denying self-government.

From Jefferson's 1774 *Summary View of the Rights of British America*

It is now, therefore, the great office of his majesty, to resume the exercise of his negative power…. which we have seen his majesty practice on the laws of the American legislatures. For the most trifling reasons, and sometimes for no conceivable reason at all, his majesty has rejected laws of the most salutary tendency.

From *Our Country, A Household History*, Volume 3, by Benson J. Lossing, 1877

The Colonial Assemblies, from time to time, made enactments touching their commercial operations, the emission of a colonial currency, and concerning representatives in the imperial Parliament, but the assent of the sovereign to these laws was withheld. After the Stamp-Act excitements, Secretary Conway informed the Americans that the tumults should be overlooked, provided the Assemblies would make provision for full compensation for all public property which had been destroyed. In complying with this demand, the Assembly of Massachusetts thought it would be "wholesome and necessary for the public good," to grant free pardon to all who had been engaged in the disturbances, and passed an act accordingly. It would have produced quiet and good feeling; but the royal assent was refused.

Historical Background

The refusal of royal assent was a critical issue during the colonial period, as it symbolized the overarching control of the British monarchy over the American colonies. The British king's denial of laws, which the colonies deemed essential for their well-being, was seen as an abuse of power and a violation of the rights of self-governance. In his *Summary View of the Rights of British America*, Thomas Jefferson highlighted this grievance, emphasizing the arbitrary nature of the king's refusals.

The Framers of the Constitution were acutely aware of the grievances laid out in *The Declaration of Independence*, including the refusal to assent to necessary laws, and they structured the government in such a way as to prevent this from happening in the United States. The system of checks and balances, federalism, and the separation of powers were all designed to avoid the tyranny of a single ruler and ensure that the legislative body had the means to pass laws for the welfare of the people.[39]

Modern Interpretation

In today's context, this Grievance underscores the importance of having a system that prevents the concentration of decision-making power in a single individual. The modern interpretation of this Grievance advocates for democratic processes and systems of checks and balances to enact laws without undue obstruction to best serve the public interest.

Summary

Grievance 1 reflects the colonial frustration with the British monarchy's refusal to approve laws passed by colonial legislatures. It has informed the structure of the American government, which is designed to prevent such abuses of power. The Constitution ensures that lawmaking remains a legislative process, with checks and balances to prevent any single branch of government, including the executive, from having unchecked power.

Constitutional Safeguards for Grievance 1

- **Article I, Section 1:** All legislative powers are vested in Congress, which consists of a Senate and a House of Representatives. This ensures that the power to make necessary laws is held by a representative body, not a monarch.

- **Article I, Section 7:** Outlines how a bill becomes a law. It requires both houses of Congress to pass a bill before it is sent to the President. If the President vetoes a bill, Congress can override the veto with a two-thirds majority in both the House and Senate, thus preventing the executive from having an absolute negative on legislation.

- **Article I, Section 8:** Enumerates Congress's powers, ensuring it has the authority to pass laws in areas deemed necessary for the public good, such as taxation, defense, commerce, and more.

- **The Bill of Rights (Amendments 1–10):** Added to the Constitution to ensure individual freedoms and state rights. Although they don't directly address the power to pass laws, they protect against the abuses that could result from the concentration of energy the colonists experienced under British rule.

- **The Tenth Amendment:** Reserves powers not delegated to the United States by the Constitution, nor prohibited by it to the States, to the States respectively, or to the people. This further decentralizes power, ensuring local and state governments can make laws for the public good in areas not covered by federal law.

Grievance 2

He Forbids Passing Laws of Pressing Importance

"He has forbidden his governors to pass laws of immediate & pressing importance, unless suspended in their operation till his assent should be obtained; and when so suspended, he has neglected utterly to attend to them."

NOTE: Colonial governors could not act without royal permission. Even urgent laws waited months or years for approval from London, leaving local crises unresolved and communities powerless.

From Jefferson's 1774 *Summary View of the Rights of British America*

With equal inattention to the necessities of his people here has his majesty permitted our laws to lie neglected in England for years, neither confirming them by his assent, nor annulling them by his negative; so that such of them as have no suspending clause we hold on the most precarious of all tenures, his majesty's will, and such of them as suspend themselves till his majesty's assent be obtained, we have feared, might be called into existence at some future and distant period, when time, and change of circumstances, shall have rendered them destructive to his people here. And to render this Grievance still more oppressive, his majesty by his instructions has laid his governors under such restrictions that they can pass no law of any moment unless it have such suspending clause; so that, however immediate may be the call for legislative interposition, the law cannot be executed till it has twice crossed the Atlantic, by which time the evil may have spent its whole force.

From *Our Country, A Household History*, Volume 3, by Benson J. Lossing, 1877

In 1764, the Assembly of New York took measures to conciliate the Six NATIONS, and other Indian tribes. The motives of the Assembly were misconstrued, representations having been made to the king that the colonies wished to make allies of the Indians, so as to increase their physical power and proportionate independence of the British crown. The monarch sent instructions to all his governors to desist from such alliances, or to suspend their operations until his assent should be given. He then "utterly neglected to attend to them." The Massachusetts Assembly passed a law in 1770, for taxing officers of the British government in that colony. The governor was ordered to withhold his assent to such tax-bill. This was in violation of the colonial charter, and the people justly complained. The Assembly was prorogued from time to time, and laws of great importance were "utterly neglected."

Historical Background

This Grievance reflects a profound struggle with bureaucracy and an unresponsive central government. At the heart of the complaint was systemic inefficiency and neglect. The king's governors in the colonies were in a bind: they were forbidden from passing essential, immediate laws without royal permission. Worse yet, the king must attend to these laws, leaving them in an administrative limbo. This was an arduous process; laws had to cross the Atlantic not just once but twice, subject to the whims of a distant monarch. Jefferson's 1774 *Summary View* articulates this frustration clearly, revealing a profound sense of vulnerability.[40]

Modern Interpretation

The themes of this Grievance continue to resonate strongly today. In our modern context, delays in governance aren't just an inconvenience; the delays can lead to significant societal damage. Whether it's stalling emergency funding during a natural disaster or delaying public health measures during a pandemic, the consequences of inaction or slow action can be dire. Slow action can lead to government shutdowns and even cost lives. And this isn't just an American concern; think of the European Union grappling with individual member states' rights versus centralized control or countries trying to coordinate international efforts to tackle climate change. The essence of the Grievance reflects a contemporary tension between the agility of localized control and the caution of centralized oversight. In a world of instant communication and emerging crises that require swift action, this Grievance provides food for thought on the importance of creating governmental systems that can respond effectively and ethically to immediate needs.

Summary

Grievance 2 brings to light the crippling effects of a sluggish, unresponsive governance system. It serves as a potent reminder of the perils of centralized control that's out of touch with localized, immediate needs. While this Grievance was rooted in the colonial struggle for autonomy and efficient governance, it poses timeless questions about how any society—whether an eighteenth-century colony or a twenty-first-century republic —balances quick, effective decision-making with the complexities and due diligence required in a centralized system.

Constitutional Safeguards for Grievance 2

- **Article I, Section 1:** Vests all legislative powers in Congress, ensuring that lawmaking is in elected representatives who can act on pressing matters quickly and efficiently without waiting for executive assent.

- **Article I, Section 7:** Outlines a transparent, time-bound process for the passage of laws. If the President does not sign a bill within ten days while Congress is in session, it automatically becomes law without his signature, thus preventing indefinite suspension.

- **Article I, Section 8:** Grants Congress the authority to make all laws necessary and proper for carrying into execution its powers, enabling swift action when needed.

- **The 10th Amendment:** Empowers the states to act independently on matters not constitutionally reserved for the federal government, ensuring that local legislatures can respond to immediate concerns without undue delay.

Grievance 3

He Suppresses Representation

"He has refused to pass other laws for the accommodation of large districts of people unless those people would relinquish the right of representation, a right inestimable to them, formidable to tyrants alone."

NOTE: Britain's rulers sought to weaken liberty by silencing local voices. Colonists were told no new laws would pass unless they surrendered their right of representation—the foundation of self-government itself.

From Jefferson's 1774 *Summary View of the Rights of British America*

Their western counties, therefore, are of indefinite extent; some of them are actually seated many hundred miles from their eastern limits. Is it possible, then, that his majesty can have bestowed a single thought on the situation of those people, who, in order to obtain justice for injuries, however great or small, must, by the laws of that colony, attend their county court, at such a distance, with all their witnesses, monthly, till their litigation be determined? Or does his majesty seriously wish, and publish it to the world, that his subjects should give up the glorious right of representation, with all the benefits derived from that, and submit themselves the absolute slaves of his sovereign will?

From *Our Country, A Household History,* Volume 3, by Benson J. Lossing, 1877

A law was passed by [the British] Parliament in the spring of 1774, by which the popular representative system in the province of Quebec (Canada) was annulled, and officers appointed by the crown had all power as legislators, except that of levying taxes. The Canadians being Roman Catholics were easily pacified under the new order of things, by having their religious system declared the established religion of the province. But "large districts of people" bordering on Nova Scotia felt this deprivation to be a great grievance. Their humble petitions concerning commercial regulations were unheeded because they remonstrated against the new order of things, and Governor Carleton plainly told them that they must cease their clamor about representatives before they should have any new commercial laws. A [British] bill for "better regulating the government in the province of Massachusetts Bay," passed that year, provided for the abridgment of the privileges of popular elections, to take the government out of the hands of the people, and vest the nomination of judges, magistrates, and even sheriffs, in the crown. When thus deprived of "free representation in the Legislature," and the governor refused to issue warrants for the election of members of the Assembly, they called a convention of the freemen, and asked for the passage of "laws for the accommodation of large districts of people." These requests were disregarded, and they were told that no laws should be passed until they should quietly "relinquish the right of representation in the Legislature—a right inestimable to them, and formidable to tyrants only."

Historical Background

Look at the map to the right. Can you imagine traveling from Northern Massachusetts, now Maine, to somewhere near Boston to attend court? Or how would it be to travel from western Connecticut (below Lake Erie) in present-day Ohio to attend to a matter at the county seat hundreds of miles away?

Jefferson's words were deeply rooted in the Enlightenment values of the time, which emphasized individual liberty and democratic governance. His references to the far-flung Western counties were not just logistical grievances; they represented an early awareness of what would become a significant issue in American governance.[41]

Modern Interpretation

Today, equal representation is a cornerstone of our American republic, ensuring citizens from all districts can elect representatives to voice their concerns and interests. The notion that representation is "formidable to tyrants alone" is central to the system of governance in the United States, as it empowers the populace and provides a mechanism to hold the government accountable through the election process.

Summary

The Constitution provides multiple layers of protection for the right of representation, from the federal to the state level. These provisions ensure that large districts and diverse populations can participate in the democratic process, directly responding to the tyranny of disenfranchisement experienced under British rule.

Constitutional Safeguards for Grievance 3

- **Article I, Sections 2 and 3:** Ensures proportional representation in the House of Representatives and equal representation in the Senate, guaranteeing that all districts and states have a voice in the federal legislative process.

- **The 14th Amendment:** Includes the Equal Protection Clause, which has been interpreted to require states to provide equal representation in their legislatures, reinforcing the right to representation on a more local level.

- **The 17th Amendment:** Provides for the direct election of Senators, further ensuring that state legislatures or political machinations do not suppress the people's right to representation.

Grievance 4

He Burdens Legislatures with Fatiguing Measures

"He has called together legislative bodies at places unusual, and also uncomfortable, and distant from the depository of their Public Records, for the sole purpose of fatiguing them into compliance with his measures."

NOTE: When the King wanted to punish colonial leaders, he made their work as hard as possible. He forced them to meet far away from their records—hoping to wear them down.

Virginia House of Burgesses Resolution (May 24, 1774)

When the British closed Boston's port and punished Massachusetts for resisting unfair taxes, Virginia lawmakers stood with them. As a delegate, Jefferson helped write a resolution expressing sympathy and support.

> "This House, being deeply impressed with the deplorable condition of our sister colony of Massachusetts Bay, whose Assembly is now held in a place at a distance from their records and from the body of their constituents, are desirous to testify their sympathy with their sufferings, and to express their firmest resolve to support them in every constitutional measure for the redress of the grievances under which they labor."

Two days later, the royal governor dissolved the Virginia Assembly. But the delegates refused to stop. Meeting at the Raleigh Tavern in Williamsburg, they called for a general meeting of all the colonies. That led to the formation of the First Continental Congress—the first united step on the road to American independence.[42]

From *Our Country, A Household History*, Volume 3, by Benson J. Lossing, 1877

In consequence of the destruction of tea in Boston harbor in 1773, the inhabitants of that town became the special objects of royal displeasure, The Boston Port Bill was passed as a punishment. The custom-house, courts, and other public operations were removed to Salem, while the public records were kept in Boston and so well guarded by two regiments of soldiers, that the patriotic members of the Colonial Assembly could not have referred to them. Although compelled to meet at a place "distant from the repository of the public records," and in a place extremely "uncomfortable," they were not fatigued into compliance, but in spite of the efforts of the governor, they elected delegates to a general Congress, and adopted other measures for the public good.

Historical Background

By forcing colonial legislatures to convene in inconvenient or distant locations, royal governors sought to weaken resistance to British policies. The goal was to exhaust legislators physically and logistically, making them more likely to acquiesce to Crown-imposed measures rather than fight them. The closure of Boston's port and the relocation of government operations to Salem exemplified this grievance. Colonial lawmakers, cut off from their records and central meeting places, faced deliberate obstacles meant to diminish their effectiveness. However, rather than succumbing, they organized resistance, culminating in the First Continental Congress.[43]

The Crown's disruption of legislative assemblies was not limited to Massachusetts or Virginia—it was part of a broader imperial pattern. Governors in North Carolina, South Carolina, and New York likewise dissolved or relocated assemblies whenever the people's representatives resisted taxation or questioned royal authority. In each case, the strategy was the same: to weary the lawmakers, scatter their influence, and force submission through inconvenience rather than argument. Jefferson recognized these tactics as deliberate assaults upon civil order—proof that despotism need not roar to be effective; it could whisper through weariness.[44]

Legislative Control as a Tool of Power

Throughout history, authoritarian rulers have used similar tactics to hinder legislative bodies, whether by relocating meetings, delaying sessions, or restricting access to essential resources. These actions are designed to frustrate and weaken the ability of representatives to organize opposition.

Modern Safeguards Against Government Manipulation

Laws governing where and when legislative bodies convene prevent the type of interference that colonial legislatures faced. United States Congressional sessions occur at designated times, and state legislatures follow predetermined schedules, shielding them from external efforts to obstruct governance.

Summary

Ensuring that lawmakers can meet without undue burden remains a cornerstone of our republic. Today, even in crises, governments provide secure and functional meeting places, recognizing that an accessible legislature is essential for the rule of law and responsive governance.

Constitutional Safeguards for Grievance 4

The Declaration of Independence raises concerns about the deliberate inconveniences imposed on colonial legislatures, which were tactics used by the Crown to wear down resistance to unpopular measures. The United States Constitution addressed this Grievance with several provisions that establish the logistics and operations of legislative bodies to protect them from such manipulation.

- **Article I, Section 4:** Declares that each state can regulate the times, places, and manner of elections for Senators and Representatives. However, it also allows Congress to make or alter such regulations, except in the areas of senators' choice.

- **Article I, Section 5:** Stipulates that each House of Congress may determine the rules of its proceedings, punish its members for disorderly behavior, and expel a member with the concurrence of two-thirds.

- **The 20th Amendment:** Sets the terms of the President, vice President, and Congress, preventing unnecessary delays in the legislative process and ensuring a regular and orderly transition of government authority.

Grievance 5

He Dissolves Parliaments & Opposes Rights

"He has dissolved Representative houses repeatedly & continually, for opposing with manly firmness his invasions on the rights of the people."

NOTE: When colonial leaders spoke up for their rights, the King punished them by shutting down their assemblies. But every time he silenced one, another rose to take its place.

From Jefferson's 1774 *Summary View of the Rights of British America*

After dissolving one house of representatives, they have refused to call another, so that, for a great length of time, the legislature provided by the laws has been out of existence.

From *Our Country, A Household History*, Volume 3, by Benson J. Lossing, 1877

When the British government became informed of the fact that the Assembly of Massachusetts in 1768 had issued a circular to other Assemblies, inviting their co-operation in asserting the principle that Great Britain had no right to tax the colonists without their consent, Lord Hillsborough, the Secretary for Foreign Affairs, was directed to order the governor of Massachusetts to require the Assembly of that province to rescind its obnoxious resolutions expressed in the circular. In case of their refusal to do so, the governor was ordered to dissolve them immediately. Other Assemblies were warned not to imitate that of Massachusetts, and when they refused to accede to the wishes of the king, as expressed by the several royal governors, they were repeatedly dissolved. The Assemblies of Virginia and North Carolina were dissolved for denying the right of the king to tax the colonies, or to remove offenders out of the country for trial. In 1774, when the several Assemblies entertained the proposition to elect delegates to a general Congress, nearly all of them were dissolved.

Historical Background

The British Crown had the power to dissolve Parliament, a practice that was sometimes used to silence opposition. Colonial legislatures mirrored the British system and were vulnerable to dissolution when their actions displeased royal governors. Dissolving Parliament in Great Britain in 1688–89 led to the "Glorious Revolution" and the British Bill of Rights in 1689, as part of the abdication of King James in favor of William and Mary. Interestingly, the same principles that led to the revolution in England were trampled in America by the king and Parliament.[45]

Beyond taxation issues, these dissolutions sought to suppress colonial resistance to British policies. By eliminating legislatures before they could coordinate responses, the Crown aimed to weaken unity and prevent organized opposition. However, these actions had the opposite effect, leading colonies to establish extralegal assemblies, such as the Committees of Correspondence and the First Continental Congress, which ultimately laid the groundwork for the Revolution.[46]

Modern Interpretation

In the modern United States, the Constitution's provisions prevent any single branch of government from having the power to dissolve the legislative branch. This ensures that the people's representatives can conduct their duties without the threat of arbitrary dismissal.

Summary

The Framers of the Constitution, informed by grievances like this one, created a system of government that safeguards against the dissolution of legislative bodies. By doing so, they ensured that the legislature could resist "invasions on the rights of the people" and maintain continuous representation.

Constitutional Safeguards for Grievance 5

Grievance 5 expresses the colonists' frustration with the Crown's practice of dissolving representative houses to silence opposition. The Constitution of the United States directly addresses this grievance by establishing a stable legislative process and ensuring that the people's right to representation cannot be arbitrarily suspended.

- **Article I, Section 2:** Establishes the House of Representatives and ensures the people of the states choose its members every second year. This provision guarantees a regular and consistent legislative body and protects against arbitrary dissolution.

- **Article I, Section 3:** Provides that two Senators represent each state, elected on staggered six-year terms, ensuring a continuous legislative body in which only one-third of its members are replaced every two years.

- **Article I, Section 5:** Grants each House the power to determine the rules of its own proceedings, preventing outside forces—including the executive—from dissolving or interfering with its operations.

- **Article I, Section 7:** Outlines the complete legislative process, including how a bill becomes law, which cannot be disrupted by unilateral executive action.

- **Twentieth Amendment:** Establishes the dates for congressional sessions and limits any external power from suspending or dissolving them capriciously, thereby ensuring continuity in legislative governance as prescribed by the Constitution.

Grievance 6
He Endangers Us by Neglecting Elections

"He has refused for a long space of time to cause others to be elected, whereby the legislative powers, incapable of annihilation, have returned to the people at large for their exercise, the state remaining in the mean time exposed to all the dangers of invasion from without, & convulsions within."

NOTE: When the King shut down local elections, he left whole colonies without leaders or laws. Without government, chaos grew—and people had to govern themselves to survive.

From Jefferson's 1774 *Summary View of the Rights of British America*

From the nature of things, every society must at all times possess within itself the sovereign powers of legislation…The feelings of human nature revolt against the supposition of a state so situated as that it may not in any emergency provide against dangers which perhaps threaten immediate ruin. While those bodies are in existence to whom the people have delegated the powers of legislation, they alone possess and may exercise those powers; but when they are dissolved by the lopping off one or more of their branches, the power reverts to the people, who may exercise it to unlimited extent, either assembling together in person, sending deputies, or in any other way they may think proper.

From *Our Country, A Household History*, Volume 3, by Benson J. Lossing, 1877

When the Assembly of New York, in 1766, refused to comply with the provisions of the Mutiny Act, its legislative functions were suspended by royal authority, and for several months the State remained "exposed to all the dangers of invasion from without and convulsions within." The Assembly of Massachusetts after its dissolution in July, 1768, was not permitted to meet again until the last Wednesday of May, 1769, and then they found the place of meeting surrounded by a military guard, with cannons pointed directly at their place or meeting. They refused to act under such tyrannical restrains and their legislative powers "returned to the people."

Historical Background

The Crown's refusal to allow for proper legislative elections, which was seen as a direct threat to self-governance and the protection of the colonies continued to fester. The absence of a functional legislature, caused by the king's refusal to authorize elections left the colonies without a local government, exposing them to potential chaos and external threats.

By suspending or delaying elections, the British government created power vacuums that disrupted governance and left colonies vulnerable to lawlessness, economic instability, and external threats from hostile nations or Native American tribes. The failure to convene legislatures meant that critical decisions regarding defense, taxation, and infrastructure could not be made, exacerbating tensions between the colonies and the Crown.

A striking example occurred in New York in 1766, when the colony's refusal to comply with the Mutiny Act led to the suspension of its Assembly. Without a functioning legislature, the colony struggled to maintain order, enforce laws, and manage relations with neighboring territories. Similarly, in Massachusetts in 1768, the legislature was dissolved and prevented from meeting for nearly a year, further escalating tensions that led to increased British military presence and ultimately the Boston Massacre.

Jefferson's *Summary View of the Rights of British America* makes a crucial point: when legislative bodies are prevented from functioning, their powers revert to the people. In practice, this principle played out in the formation of alternative institutions, such as the Committees of Correspondence and the Continental Congress. These grassroots efforts demonstrated that when the Crown failed to provide governance, the people would take matters into their own hands, setting the stage for the Revolution.[47]

Modern Interpretation

In modern governance, these constitutional provisions ensure that legislative power remains with elected officials, preventing an executive from negating the people's will by refusing to hold elections. The structure of government established by the Constitution prevents any single entity from having too much power and ensures representation for the populace.

Summary

Grievance 6 reflects the colonists' demand for representative government and the protection of their legislative rights. The Framers of the Constitution crafted a system that safeguards against the concentration of power and neglect of elections that the colonists experienced under British rule.

Constitutional Safeguards for Grievance 6

- **Article I:** Establishes a bicameral legislature (Congress) with representatives elected by the people.
- **Article I, Section 2:** Mandates that members of the House of Representatives be elected every two years by the people of the several states.
- **Article I, Section 4:** Gives Congress the power to regulate the times, places, and manner of elections for Senators and Representatives to each state's legislature. Only Congress can alter such regulations.
- **The 17th Amendment:** Democratized the process, electing Senators by a vote of the people rather than state legislatures appointing Senators.

Grievance 7

He Controls the Settlement of Lands & Naturalization

"He has endeavored to prevent the population of these states; for that purpose, obstructing the laws for naturalization of foreigners; refusing to pass others to encourage their migrations hither; & raising the conditions of new appropriations of lands."

NOTE: The King wanted to control who could live in America and where they could settle. By blocking land grants and immigration, he slowed the colonies' growth and tried to keep them weak. This was very troubling because the colonies owned western lands that King George III now claimed following the French and Indian War.

From Jefferson's 1774 *Summary View of the Rights of British America*

But his majesty has lately taken on him to advance the terms of purchase [of land], and of holding to the double of what they were; by which means the acquisition of lands being rendered difficult, the population of our country is likely to be checked. It is time, therefore, for us to lay this matter before his majesty, and to declare that he has no right to grant lands of himself. From the nature and purpose of civil institutions, all the lands within the limits which any particular society has circumscribed around itself are assumed by that society, and subject to their allotment only.

From *Our Country, A Household History*, Volume 3, by Benson J. Lossing, 1877

Secret agents were sent to America soon after the accession of George the Third to the throne of England, to spy out the condition of the colonists. A large influx of liberty-loving German emigrants was observed, and the king was advised to discourage these immigrations. Obstacles in the way of procuring lands, and otherwise, were put in the way of all emigrants, except from England, and the tendency of French Roman Catholics to settle in Maryland was also discouraged. The British government was jealous of the increasing power of the colonies; and the danger of having that power controlled by democratic ideas, caused the employment of restrictive measures. The easy conditions upon which actual settlers might obtain lands on the Western frontier, after the peace of 1763, were so changed, that toward the dawning of the Revolution, the vast solitudes west of the Alleghanies were seldom penetrated by any but the hunter from the seaboard provinces. When the War for Independence broke out, immigration had almost ceased. The king conjectured wisely, for almost the entire German population in the colonies were on the side of the patriots.

Challenging the Boundaries of Empire and Sovereignty

After the French and Indian War, the Royal Proclamation of 1763 redrew the geography of empire—and rewrote the constitutional order that had defined the English colonies for more than a century. Issued under the pretext of "preserving peace" with Indigenous nations, the proclamation was in fact a royal seizure of authority over territory already secured by colonial charter and defended by colonial blood.

The King declared that all lands west of the Appalachian Mountains were "reserved to Our Crown," erasing boundaries long guaranteed under law. By treating these lands as newly conquered territory—a bounty of war wrested from the French—the Crown nullified the prior legal title of the colonies themselves. What Jefferson called the "power of dividing and dismembering a country" had now become imperial policy.[48]

Charter Rights Long Preceded French Claims

The British colonies' legal title to western lands was older and superior to any claim made by France.

- The Virginia Charter of 1609 granted territory extending from the Atlantic "up into the Land throughout from Sea to Sea, West and Northwest," encompassing the entire Ohio and Illinois country.[49]

- Maryland (1632), Connecticut (1662), and Carolina (1663) charters echoed these sweeping westward grants, defining America as a transcontinental dominion of English settlement.[50]

By contrast, France's claim arose only in the 1670s and 1680s, when René-Robert Cavelier, Sieur de La Salle descended the Mississippi and proclaimed "Louisiana" for the French Crown. His act of possession was not settlement, but declaration—a paper claim laid upon territory already embraced within English patents and, in several regions, already occupied by English traders and surveyors.[51]

Thus, when Britain later spoke of "acquiring" the Ohio Valley from France, it accepted French pretensions that had never held lawful weight. The King's recognition of those claims as legitimate spoils of conquest placed French usurpation above English law and voided the colonies' chartered inheritance.

Curtailing Immigration and Colonial Growth

Benson J. Lossing observed that King George III and his ministers viewed the influx of liberty-minded German immigrants with alarm. Restrictive naturalization laws, new land-purchase fees, and obstructive licensing schemes were deliberately imposed to discourage immigration and settlement beyond the royal line.

> "The king conjectured wisely," wrote Lossing, "for almost the entire German population in the colonies were on the side of the patriots."

Jefferson condemned these same manipulations:

> "But his majesty has lately taken on him to advance the terms of purchase [of land]… by which means the acquisition of lands being rendered difficult, the population of our country is likely to be checked."

The King wanted the colonies to remain distinctly British. Having tolerated enough German settlement, he weaponized immigration control—stalling growth, discouraging migration, and keeping the frontier under royal supervision.

Royal Bounty Lands and the Seizure of Charter Rights

While forbidding colonial expansion, the King simultaneously granted himself power to distribute conquered lands as rewards for military service. This made the Ohio and Illinois territories instruments of patronage rather than the rightful extension of colonial self-government.

Bounty Land Promises under the Royal Proclamation of 1763

- **Field Officer**: 5,000 acres
- **Captain**: 3,000 acres
- **Subaltern or Staff Officer**: 2,000 acres
- **Non-Commissioned Officer**: 200 acres
- **Private Soldier**: 50 acres

These bounties were not drawn from Crown land on the islands of Great Britain but from colonial soil in the Ohio Country—land that was guaranteed by charter. By redefining that soil as a royal bounty of war, the King converted lawful colonial territory into his own spoils, to be sold or gifted at will. In Jefferson's eyes, this was not merely unlawful—it was despotic. A monarch who could dispose of chartered lands at pleasure could, by the same logic, dispose of liberty itself.

Accepting French Territorial Claims Nullifies Colonial Charters

The King's great offense was that he claimed France's territorial claims for the Crown as bounties of war after the French and Indian War. By adopting France's claim to the Ohio and Illinois country as "spoils of victory," he nullified 154 years of colonial charters. Before La Salle's expedition of 1679–1682, France's reach had been confined to the Maritime Provinces and the St. Lawrence seaway to the Great Lakes. Later claim to the Mississippi basin—land long included within colonial charters—was never recognized by English law. Yet the Proclamation of 1763 treated this ancient English domain as newly conquered spoils of war, subject to royal control.

> "The lands which were conquered by the joint arms of Great Britain and America are declared to be their conquest, and subject to their disposal."—Jefferson, 1775

This was the colonists' Grievance in its sharpest form: what had preserved Colonial claims at the expense of British and American blood was then seized solely as British bounty.

The Ohio Company as a Precursor to War

The **Ohio Company of Virginia,** formed in 1748 by Lawrence and Augustine Washington, George Mason, and others, received a royal charter to settle 200,000 acres along the upper Ohio River—territory long secured by Virginia's Royal Charter. When France began building a chain of forts from Lake Erie to the Ohio in 1753, the Company's lands were directly challenged. Governor Dinwiddie dispatched young **George Washington** to demand French withdrawal, an event that ignited the **French and Indian War**. Colonists believed they fought to defend their own chartered inheritance; yet the **Royal Proclamation of 1763** redefined those victories as the King's "bounty of war." Thus, what the colonies won through their joint arms became the Crown's spoils of conquest.[52]

The Fiction of Protection

The Royal Proclamation of 1763 claimed to shield Native nations from colonial intrusion, but its protection was fiction. The King alone could grant or sell land, license trade, and decide who might cross the mountains. What was framed as defense became dominion. Indigenous sovereignty served as a royal pretext; colonial self-government became the casualty. By claiming the Ohio and Illinois territories as spoils of war, the Crown turned inheritance into property and subjects into tenants.

Colonial vs Royal Territorial Claims

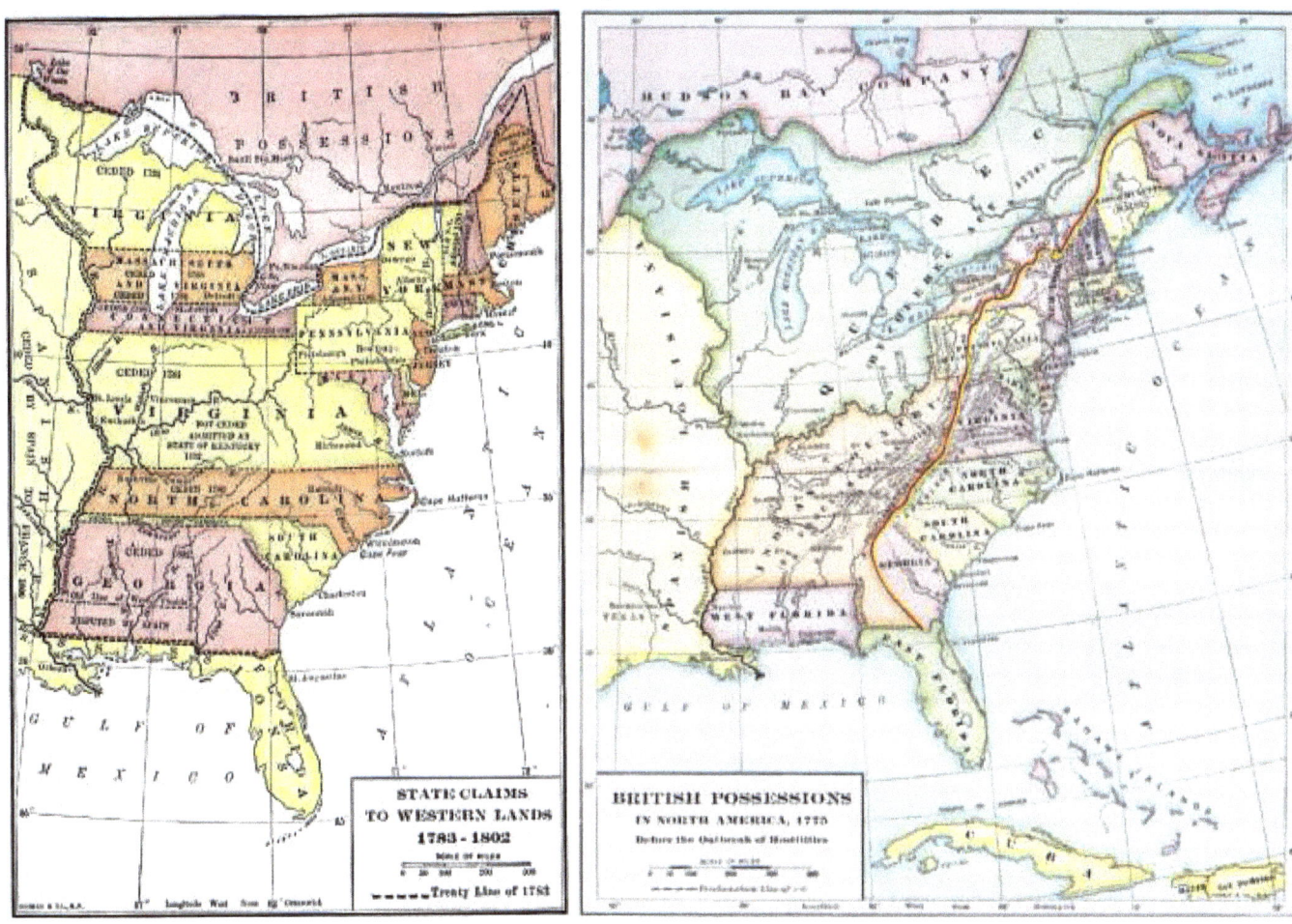

State Claims to Western Lands, 1783–1802. From Matthew H. Bowman, An Atlas of American History (New York: Charles Scribner's Sons, 1911). Map engraved by C. S. Hammond & Company. Public Domain, courtesy of the United States Library of Congress and the Perry-Castañeda Library Map Collection, University of Texas at Austin.

Albert Bushnell Hart, LL.D., The American Nation Vol 14 (New York, NY: Harper and Brothers, 1906)

The red and yellow Proclamation Line of 1763, was colored by the author to represent the new western boundaries of the colonies, as designated by the Royal Proclamation of 1763.

(The map on the left approximates accepted colonial claims prior to the 1763 proclamation)

Summary

The Royal Proclamation of 1763 clothed empire in moral language. By accepting France's territorial claims as his own, the King nullified colonial charters, converted their lands into a royal bounty. The seizure of the Ohio Company's holdings exposed the deception. Jefferson, Washington, and their peers saw the truth: this was not protection, but confiscation—a violation of law, liberty, and birthright.

Constitutional Safeguards for Grievance 7

- **Article IV, Section 3, Clause 2:** This is the **"Property Clause,"** which grants Congress the power to dispose of and make rules and regulations respecting the territory or other property belonging to the United States. This ensures federal management of land acquisition and disposition.

- **Article I, Section 8, The Naturalization Clause:** Gives Congress the power to establish a uniform rule of naturalization, ensuring a standardized, federal approach to becoming a U.S. citizen, as opposed to the arbitrary restrictions imposed by the Crown.

- **The Fifth Amendment:** Includes the **"Takings Clause,"** which provides that private property cannot be taken for public use without compensation, protecting landowners' rights and ensuring fair treatment in cases of eminent domain.

Grievance 8

He Blocks Local Administration of Justice

"He has suffered the administration of justice totally to cease in some of these colonies, refusing his assent to laws for establishing judiciary powers."

NOTE: The King took control of local courts, making judges serve him instead of the people. Without fair judges or juries, colonists could no longer trust the law to protect their rights.

Albemarle County Resolves: Jefferson, July 26, 1774

"We will ever maintain the legal and constitutional power of our own courts of justice, and protest against any attempt by the King or Parliament of Great Britain to suspend their operation or prevent the due course of justice within this colony."[53]

From *Our Country, A Household History*, Volume 3, by Benson J. Lossing, 1877

By an act of Parliament in 1774, the judiciary was taken from the people of Massachusetts. The judges were appointed by the king, were dependent on him for their salaries, and were subject to his will. Their salaries were paid from moneys drawn from the people by the commissioners of customs, in the form of duties. The same act deprived them, in most cases, of the benefit of trial by jury, and the "administration of justice" was effectually obstructed. The rights for which Englishmen so manfully contended in 1688 were trampled under foot. Similar grievances concerning the courts of law existed in other colonies; and throughout the Anglo-American domain there was but a semblance of justice left. The people met in conventions when assemblies were dissolved, and endeavored to establish "judiciary powers," but in vain; and were finally driven to rebellion.

Historical Background

Grievance 8 addresses King George III's refusal to approve laws establishing judiciary powers in the colonies. This action led to a significant obstruction in the administration of justice. The colonists perceived this as a direct attack on their rights to a fair and functional legal system, critical for maintaining order and resolving disputes.

The judiciary was a cornerstone of colonial governance, but the British government increasingly used judicial control as a means of maintaining dominance over the colonies. One of the most egregious examples occurred in Massachusetts in 1774, when Parliament passed the Massachusetts Government Act, part of the Coercive (Intolerable) Acts. This law stripped Massachusetts citizens of their ability to elect judges, transferring judicial appointments to the Crown and ensuring that judges were financially and politically dependent on the king. Additionally, the act removed key legal protections, such as trial by jury in many cases, making colonial courts functionally ineffective. This move paralleled earlier actions taken against New York, where colonial courts had been suspended due to legislative resistance to royal directives.[54]

Without functional courts, colonial leaders found themselves unable to uphold contracts, resolve legal disputes, or prosecute crimes. This judicial void led to the emergence of extralegal assemblies and conventions, where colonists attempted to administer justice themselves. These alternative legal structures, often referred to as "shadow governments," were among the first acts of open defiance against British rule. They signaled that the colonies were willing to take judicial matters into their own hands when the Crown refused to act justly.[55]

Modern Interpretation

Today, the Constitution's provisions ensure that the judiciary operates independently of the executive's whims. Establishing a robust federal court system under the Constitution and the rights guaranteed by the Sixth Amendment have been fundamental in maintaining a fair and effective judicial system in the United States.

Summary

Grievance 8 reflects the colonists' frustration with the interruption of judicial processes by the executive branch. The Constitution's establishment of an independent judiciary and the rights enshrined in the Bill of Rights represent a direct response to this grievance, ensuring the consistent and fair administration of justice.

Constitutional Safeguards for Grievance 8

- **Article III:** Establishes the federal government's judicial branch, ensuring an independent judiciary separate from the executive and legislative branches. This structure prevented the kind of executive interference in judicial matters that the colonists experienced under British rule.

- **The first section of Article III:** States, "The judicial Power of the United States shall be vested in one supreme Court, and in such inferior Courts as the Congress may from time to time ordain and establish." This clause ensures a federally managed judiciary system, preventing the executive branch from ceasing its operation.

- **The Sixth Amendment:** Guarantees the right to a speedy and public trial, impartial juries, and the right to counsel. These rights ensure that justice is administered and done fairly and transparently.

Grievance 9

He Has Made Our Judges Dependent on His Will

"He has made our judges dependent on his will alone,
for the tenure of their offices, and amount of their salaries."

NOTE: Although Jefferson didn't write directly about this issue in *Summary View*, the problem was well known in his time. In 1774, the Massachusetts Government Act—one of the Intolerable Acts—put judges under the King's control by letting him decide how long they served and how much they were paid. Many colonists saw this as destroying fair and independent justice.

From Jefferson's 1774 *Summary View of the Rights of British America*

That these exercises of usurped power have not been confined to instances alone, in which themselves were interested, but they have also intermeddled with the regulation of the internal affairs of the colonies. The act of the 9th of Anne* for establishing a post office in America seems to have had little connection with British convenience, except that of accommodating his majesty's ministers and favourites with the sale of a lucrative and easy office.[56]

* Post Office Revenues Act of 1710, the Queen Anne 10th Act in 9th year of her reign. Though Jefferson did not name the judiciary specifically, he denounced the Crown's intrusion into colonial civil offices, a principle that soon extended to the courts themselves." [57]

From *Our Country, A Household History*, Volume 3, by Benson J. Lossing, 1877

As we have observed, judges were made independent of the people. Royal governors were placed in the same position. Instead of checking their tendency to petty tyranny, by having them depend upon the Colonial Assemblies for their salaries, these were paid out of the national treasury. Independent of the people they had no sympathies with the people, and thus became fit instruments of oppression, and ready at all times to do the bidding of the king and his ministers. The Colonial Assemblies protested against the measure, and out of the excitement which it produced, grew that power of the Revolution, the Committees of Correspondence. When, in 1774, Chief Justice Oliver, of Massachusetts, declared it to be his intention to receive his salary from the crown, the Assembly proceeded to impeach him, and petitioned the governor for his removal. The governor refused compliance, and great irritation ensued.

Historical Background

Concerns over judicial independence, which they saw as fundamental to a just legal system was deeply troubling. In the colonies, judges were appointed by the king and served at his pleasure, meaning they could be dismissed if their rulings displeased the Crown. Their salaries were controlled by the monarchy, creating financial dependence that could pressure judges to rule in favor of British interests.

This issue became particularly alarming after the Judiciary Act of 1761, which reaffirmed that judicial salaries in the colonies would be paid by the crown, rather than by colonial legislatures. The shift in financial control further solidified British dominance over judicial proceedings, making judges more susceptible to coercion. As resistance to British rule grew, royal officials used this control to crack down on dissenters, ensuring that court rulings favored the monarchy in disputes over taxation, property seizures, and resistance to British military actions.

In response, colonial leaders increasingly called for independent courts, where judges could not be arbitrarily removed or have their pay withheld for issuing rulings that challenged British authority. The colonists saw an impartial judiciary as essential to protecting individual rights, preventing governmental overreach, and ensuring the rule of law. The Constitutional safeguards that would later be enshrined in Article III of the U.S. Constitution were a direct response to these colonial grievances.[58]

Modern Interpretation

In modern governance, judicial independence is a bedrock principle of the republic, preventing judges from being subjected to political pressure or executive control. Unlike the colonial system, federal judges in the United States serve for life (barring impeachment for misconduct), and their salaries cannot be reduced during their tenure, ensuring that their rulings remain impartial and uninfluenced by external pressures.

This protection is crucial in landmark cases where the judiciary must check executive or legislative overreach. Decisions such as Marbury v. Madison (1803), which established judicial review, and Brown v. Board of Education (1954), which ended legal segregation, demonstrate the importance of a judiciary free from political coercion. Without these safeguards, judges might be swayed by changing political tides rather than interpreting the law based on constitutional principles.

Summary

Grievance 9 underscores the importance of an independent judiciary, free from executive influence. The Constitution's response to this Grievance is a cornerstone of the republic, ensuring that judges can make decisions without fear of losing their jobs or facing salary cuts for unpopular rulings.

Constitutional Safeguards for Grievance 9

- **Article III, Section 1:** States, "The Judges, both of the supreme and inferior Courts, shall hold their Offices during good Behaviour, and shall, at stated Times, receive for their Services a Compensation, which shall not be diminished during their Continuance in Office." This clause establishes that federal judges serve for life (unless impeached and removed for misconduct) and that their salaries cannot be reduced while in office, protecting them from political pressures.

    This structure contrasts sharply with the colonial system, where judges depended on the Crown for their positions and income, potentially influencing their decisions to favor the monarchy.

Grievance 10
He Erected New Offices & Sent Swarms of Officers

"He has erected a multitude of new offices by a self-assumed power, & sent hither swarms of officers to harass our people & eat out their substance."

NOTE: The phrase is Jefferson's own invention—appearing first in his Fair Copy of the Declaration—but the complaint it expresses was rooted in colonial outrage over the enforcement of the Sugar Act (1764), Townshend Duties (1767), and later the Intolerable Acts (1774). Each expanded royal customs and tax enforcement, filling the colonies with swarms of officers to collect taxes.[59] Jefferson transformed this long-festering economic Grievance into one of the Declaration's most memorable indictments. This phrase or concept is not found in any writings of other members of the Committee of Five. Jefferson did refer slightly to this in his *Summary View*.

From Jefferson's 1774 *Summary View of the Rights of British America*
Accordingly, that country, which had been acquired by the lives, the labours, and the fortunes, of individual adventurers, was by these princes, at several times, parted out and distributed among the favourites and followers of their fortunes, and, by an assumed right of the crown alone, were erected into distinct and independent governments.

From *Our Country, A Household History*, Volume 3, by Benson J. Lossing, 1877
After the passage of the Stamp-Act, stamp distributers were appointed in every considerable town. In 1766 and 1767, acts for the collection of duties created "swarms of officers," [unreadable] of whom received high salaries; and when, in 1768, admiralty and vice-admiralty courts who established on a new basis, an increase in the number of officers was made. The high salaries and extensive perquisites [a thing regarded as a special right or privilege enjoyed as a result of one's position (perks)] of all of these, were paid with the people's money, and thus "swarms of officers" "eat out their substance."

Historical Background

Frustration with the British monarchy's establishment of numerous offices and appointment of officials without the people's consent was a great affront to the colonists. These officials often acted in the interests of the Crown rather than the colonies, leading to widespread resentment. The colonists saw this as an abuse of power and an infringement on their autonomy, particularly when these officials enforced unpopular laws and collected taxes without colonial representation in Parliament.

One of the most notorious examples was the expansion of customs officials following the Townshend Acts (1767), which imposed duties on goods such as glass, lead, paint, and tea. To enforce these taxes, Britain stationed revenue officers in colonial ports and empowered them to conduct warrantless searches under "writs of assistance." These broad, unchecked search powers infuriated colonists, as they violated traditional English protections against unlawful searches and seizures.[60]

Additionally, Britain expanded the network of vice-admiralty courts—which lacked juries—to prosecute smugglers and tax resisters. The colonists viewed these courts as biased in favor of the Crown, since judges and officials were financially rewarded for ruling in favor of the British government. The increased number of tax collectors, customs agents, and court officers represented the very "swarms of officers" that Jefferson described in the Declaration, as these bureaucrats were often corrupt, intrusive, and financially burdensome to the colonies.[61]

Modern Interpretation

In today's context, these constitutional provisions ensure a balance of power between the branches of government in creating offices and appointing officials. It prevents the executive branch from unilaterally expanding its power and influence, as was the case under British rule.

Summary

Grievance 10 reflects the colonial opposition to the Crown's unilateral creation of offices and appointment of officials. The Constitution's mechanisms for appointments and office creation, including checks and balances and the role of Congress, address this Grievance by preventing such unilateral actions by the President and ensuring broader representation in these decisions.

Constitutional Safeguards for Grievance 10

The U.S. Constitution addresses the concern of unchecked executive power in creating offices and appointing officials:

- **Article II, Section 2:** Requires that the Senate confirm primary presidential appointments, including ambassadors, public ministers, consuls, and Supreme Court Justices. This provides a check on the President's power to appoint officials unilaterally.

- **Article I, Section 8:** Allows Congress to create and abolish federal offices. This decentralizes the power of office creation and ensures it's not solely in the hands of the executive.

- **The Tenth Amendment:** Reserves powers not delegated to the federal government to the states or the people, further restricting the federal government's ability to impose unwanted officials on state governments.

Grievance 11
He Keeps Armies Among Us in Times of Peace

"He has kept among us, in times of peace, Standing Armies without the Consent of our legislatures."

NOTE: After the French and Indian War, Britain kept a permanent army in the American colonies—even during peacetime. The King used these troops to enforce taxes and silence protest, without the colonies' consent. To the colonists, this was not protection—it was intimidation.

From Jefferson's 1774 *Summary View of the Rights of British America*

That in order to enforce the arbitrary measures before complained of his majesty has from time to time sent among us large bodies of armed forces, not made up of the people here, nor raised by the authority of our laws: Did his majesty possess such a right as this, it might swallow up all our other rights whenever he should think proper. But his majesty has no right to land a single armed man on our shores, and those whom he sends here are liable to our laws made for the suppression and punishment of riots, routs, and unlawful assemblies; or are hostile bodies, invading us in defiance of law.

From *Our Country, A Household History*, Volume 3, by Benson J. Lossing, 1877

After the treaty of peace with France, in 1763, Great Britain left quite a large number of troops in America, and required the colonists to contribute to their support. There was no use for this standing army, except to repress the growing spirit of Democracy among the colonists, and to enforce compliance with taxation laws. The presence of troops was always a cause of complaint; and when, finally, the colonists boldly opposed the unjust measures of the British government, armies were sent hither to awe the people into submission. It was one of those "standing armies" kept here "without the consent of the Legislature," against which the patriots at Lexington, and Concord, and Bunker Hill so manfully battled in 1775.

Historical Background

Deep unease with the British practice of maintaining standing armies in the colonies during peacetime without the consent of local legislatures was very troubling, especially to the people of Massachusetts. This practice was seen as a tool for enforcing unpopular laws and threatening the colonists' liberties. The presence of these armies heightened tensions and contributed significantly to the sense of alienation and injustice felt by the colonists.

Following the French and Indian War (1754–1763), Britain left a large standing army in North America, arguing that it was necessary to protect the colonies from external threats. However, with no immediate war at hand, many colonists suspected that the real purpose of these troops was to enforce British rule and suppress colonial dissent. The Quartering Act of 1765 further inflamed tensions by forcing colonists to house and supply British troops, reinforcing the view that the army was an instrument of control rather than protection.

The presence of British soldiers also led to violent confrontations, most notably the Boston Massacre of 1770, when British troops fired on an unarmed crowd, killing five colonists. This tragic event became a rallying cry against the occupation, proving that standing armies in times of peace could lead to oppression and bloodshed. By 1775, as British military presence increased, colonial resistance escalated, culminating in the Battles of Lexington and Concord, where the British army attempted to seize colonial military supplies. These battles marked the beginning of the Revolutionary War and confirmed the colonists' fears that standing armies could be used against their own people.[62]

Modern Interpretation

Today, these constitutional provisions emphasize civilian control over the military and protect citizens' rights against military intrusion in everyday life. The idea of consent and regular civilian oversight ensures that the military is accountable to the people through their elected representatives.

Summary

Grievance 11 responded to the British Crown's imposition of standing armies in the colonies without legislative consent. The Constitution's provisions for congressional control over military funding, the Third Amendment's protection against quartering troops, and the Second Amendment's emphasis on a well-regulated militia all address and rectify this concern, embedding the principles of civilian oversight and consent into US governance.

Constitutional Safeguards for Grievance 11

- **Article I, Section 8:** Grants Congress the power to raise and support armies but requires that appropriations for this purpose be limited to two years, ensuring civilian control and regular review.

- **The Third Amendment:** Part of the Bill of Rights, which specifically prohibits the quartering of soldiers in private homes without the owner's consent, reflecting a direct response to colonial grievances about British troops.

- **The Second Amendment:** Provides for a well-regulated militia to counterbalance a standing army, ensuring that local, decentralized forces controlled by the states and the people are available for defense.

Grievance 12

His Military is Superior to Our Civil Authority

"He has affected to render the military, independent of & superior to the civil power."

NOTE: The colonists were deeply alarmed when British generals began ruling over civilian leaders. This grievance shows their fear that the army—acting on the King's command—could overrule local laws and take control of everyday life.

From Jefferson's 1774 *Summary View of the Rights of British America*

To render these proceedings still more criminal against our laws, instead of subjecting the military to the civil powers, his majesty has expressly made the civil subordinate to the military. But can his majesty thus put down all law under his feet? Can he erect a power superior to that which he erected himself? He has done it indeed by force; but let him remember that force cannot give right.

From *Our Country, A Household History*, Volume 3, by Benson J. Lossing, 1877

General Gage, commander-in chief of the British forces in America, was appointed governor of Massachusetts in 1774: and to put the measures of the Boston Port Bill into execution, he encamped several regiments of soldiers upon Boston Common. The military there, and also in New York, was made independent of, and superior to, the civil power, and this, too, in a time of peace, before the Minute-men were organized.

Historical Background

The colonists were greatly concerned over the British military's dominance over civilian authority. This Grievance reflects the fear that the army, acting under the king's orders, could override local laws and civil governance, eroding the colonies' autonomy and the rule of law.

One of the most glaring examples of this occurred in Massachusetts in 1774, when General Thomas Gage, commander-in-chief of British forces in North America, was appointed as military governor of the colony. This move placed both executive and military power in his hands, rendering civilian authorities effectively powerless. Gage's presence was meant to enforce the Coercive Acts, particularly the Boston Port Act, which sought to punish Massachusetts for the Boston Tea Party. However, rather than restoring order, his heavy-handed military rule intensified colonial resistance and further alienated the population.

In Boston and New York, British troops were stationed in civilian areas, and military tribunals often bypassed local courts. Colonists were subjected to arbitrary arrests, intimidation, and show-of-force tactics that undermined their legal rights. British officers acted with near-total impunity, knowing they were backed by a military force that was answerable only to the Crown. This practice violated longstanding English constitutional traditions, including those enshrined in the Magna Carta (1215) and the English Bill of Rights (1689), which sought to keep military power subordinate to civilian law.[63]

This Grievance was not just about the presence of soldiers—it was about the fundamental principle of civilian control over government and the judiciary. By placing military officers above civilian authorities, the British government disregarded local self-governance and replaced it with martial law in all but name. The colonists saw this as a direct path to tyranny, reinforcing their belief that independence was necessary to preserve their liberties.

Modern Interpretation

The principle that military power is subordinated to civilian leadership is a fundamental tenet of the American republic. This structure ensures accountability and prevents military overreach, protecting the nation's democratic institutions and the rule of law.

Summary

Grievance 12 addresses the concern over the military's dominance over civil authority. The US Constitution and subsequent laws like the Posse Comitatus Act establish explicit civilian control over the military, preventing abuses feared by the colonists and ensuring that democratically established rules and principles exercise military power.

Constitutional Safeguards for Grievance 12

- **Article II, Section 2:** Designates the President as the Commander in Chief of the armed forces, firmly placing military leadership under an elected civilian.
- **Article I, Section 8:** Grants Congress the power to declare war, raise and support armies, make rules for the government, regulate the land and naval forces, and distribute military oversight powers across the civilian government.
- **Posse Comitatus Act of 1878,**[64] although not part of the Constitution, limited the use of the U.S. military in domestic law enforcement, reinforcing the separation between military and civilian spheres.

Grievance 13

He Subjects Us to Foreign Jurisdiction

"He has combined with others to subject us to a jurisdiction foreign to our constitutions and unacknowledged by our laws; giving his assent to their pretended acts of legislation."

NOTE: The colonists were angered when British officials forced them under foreign laws and courts that ignored local rights. They believed this stripped them of justice and placed them under powers they had never agreed to obey.

From Jefferson's 1774 *Summary View of the Rights of British America*

That these are the acts of power, assumed by a body of men, foreign to our constitutions, and unacknowledged by our laws, against which we do, on behalf of the inhabitants of British America, enter this our solemn and determined protest; and we do earnestly entreat his majesty, as yet the only mediatory power between the several states of the British empire, to recommend to his parliament of Great Britain the total revocation of these acts, which, however nugatory [worthless] they be, may yet prove the cause of further discontents and jealousies among us.

From *Our Country, A Household History*, Volume 3, by Benson J. Lossing, 1877

The establishment of a Board of Trade, to act independent of colonial legislation through its creatures (resident commissioners of customs) in the enforcement of revenue laws, was altogether foreign to the constitution of any of the colonies, and produced great indignation. The establishment of this power, and the remodeling of the admiralty courts so as to exclude trial by jury therein, in most cases rendered the government fully obnoxious to the charge in the text. The people felt their degradation under such petty tyranny, and resolved to spurn it. It was effectually done in Boston, as we have seen, and the government, after all its bluster, was obliged to recede. In 1774, the members of the council of Massachusetts (answering to our Senate), were, by a Parliamentary enactment, chosen by the king, to hold the office during his pleasure. Almost unlimited power was also given to the governor, and the people were indeed subjected to "a jurisdiction foreign to their constitution" by these creatures of royalty.

Historical Background

This Grievance reflects the colonists' frustration with British legislative control that was perceived as foreign and illegitimate, particularly regarding the imposition of laws and governance structures unfamiliar and often contrary to established colonial practices. The Grievance is rooted in the belief that the legislative acts imposed by the British Parliament violated the colonial charters and the traditional rights of Englishmen, as the colonists saw themselves.

One of the most egregious examples of this was the remodeling of the admiralty courts, which stripped colonists of their right to trial by jury and placed judicial authority in the hands of British-appointed judges who enforced trade and tax laws without local oversight. These courts, which operated under British maritime law rather than traditional English common law, were seen as a direct violation of colonial legal norms. Colonists accused of smuggling or violating trade restrictions were often tried in Nova Scotia or other distant locations, where British officials—rather than local peers—determined their fate.[65]

Similarly, the establishment of the Board of Trade and Customs Commissioners, who enforced British taxation without input from colonial legislatures, was viewed as another example of Britain subjecting the colonies to a jurisdiction foreign to their own. These unelected officials had the power to override local decisions, seize property, and levy fines, further alienating colonists from their own legal and political institutions.[66]

Modern Interpretation

This underlines the importance of sovereignty in legislative and judicial matters. The US has built a legal system where laws are created and interpreted by domestically elected or appointed officials, reflecting the nation's values and legal traditions. This framework protects against foreign interference in the nation's legal and political systems.

Summary

Grievance 13 addresses concerns over foreign legislative and judicial control. The Constitution's establishment of an independent judiciary and reserving powers to the states (per the Tenth Amendment) ensure that laws and their interpretation align with American values and legal traditions, free from foreign influence.

Constitutional Safeguards for Grievance 13

- **Article III:** Establishes an independent judicial system for the United States, ensuring that legal matters are adjudicated under U.S. law, not foreign influence.

- **The Tenth Amendment:** Reinforces this by reserving powers not delegated to the federal government to the states, ensuring that external authorities do not override local laws and practices.

- **Article II, Section 2:** Requires Senate confirmation of federal judges and justices, ensuring that elected representatives approve those interpreting laws.

Grievance 14

For Quartering Large Bodies of Troops

"For quartering large bodies of armed troops among us."

NOTE: The colonists were furious when British soldiers were forced into their towns and homes without permission. They had to feed and house them—turning private life into military duty.

From Jefferson's 1774 *Summary View of the Rights of British America*

Every state must judge for itself the number of armed men which they may safely trust among them, of whom they are to consist, and under what restrictions they shall be laid.

From *Our Country, A Household History*, Volume 3, by Benson J. Lossing, 1877

In 1774 seven hundred troops were landed in Boston, under cover of the cannons of British armed ships in the harbor; and early the following year, Parliament voted ten thousand men for the American service, for it saw the wave of rebellion rising high under the gale of indignation which unrighteous acts had spread over the land. The tragedies at Lexington and Concord soon followed, and at Bunker Hill the War for Independence was opened in earnest.

Historical Background

The Quartering Acts of 1765 and 1774 demanded that colonies accommodate British soldiers by providing food, fuel, and transportation, placing a heavy financial burden on colonial legislatures and communities. This symbolized British infringement on colonial self-governance, as it allowed the Crown to station troops in the colonies without their explicit consent and forced the population to support an occupying military force.

While the Quartering Acts did not initially mandate the housing of soldiers in private homes, they required public buildings, inns, and empty properties to be used to accommodate troops. However, in practice, when suitable locations were unavailable, soldiers were often housed in civilian areas, creating friction between British troops and colonists. The standoff at Boston's Manufactory House in 1768 exemplified this growing tension, as residents refused to vacate the building to accommodate British troops. The presence of these soldiers—not for defense but for law enforcement and suppression of protests—was seen as a direct threat to colonial liberties and a means of intimidation.

The Quartering Acts' impact in America starkly contrasts with England's own legal protections, including the 1628 Petition of Right and the Bill of Rights of 1689, which prohibited the quartering of troops in private homes without consent during peacetime. The hypocrisy of Parliament—applying restrictions in Britain but disregarding them in the colonies—deepened colonial resentment. Colonists saw this as further evidence that they were being treated as second-class subjects, subject to laws that British citizens would never tolerate.[67]

Additionally, resistance to these acts led to direct confrontations between the colonies and the Crown. The New York Assembly's refusal to fund troop quartering in 1767 resulted in Parliament suspending the Assembly until compliance was met. This escalated tensions and demonstrated how Britain would override colonial governance to enforce unpopular laws, fueling broader opposition to British rule. By the time the 1774 Quartering Act expanded the law's reach and allowed troops to be housed in occupied dwellings, it further reinforced colonial fears that British soldiers were not there for protection, but to control and suppress dissent.

This issue became one of the most tangible symbols of British oppression, contributing significantly to the growing revolutionary sentiment and shaping the Founders' resolve to ensure permanent protections against military intrusion in civilian life in the U.S. Constitution.

Modern Interpretation

This Grievance and its response to the Constitution underscore the American value of civilian control over the military and the importance of respecting individual rights and property. The limitations on military powers and the protections against forced quartering are fundamental to a free society where the military serves under civilian leadership and is not used to oppress or control the populace.

Summary

Grievance 14 highlights colonial opposition to the Quartering Acts, which forced them to accommodate British troops, symbolizing military occupation and suppression. The hypocrisy of Parliament, enforcing restrictions in Britain but not in the colonies, fueled resentment and resistance.

Constitutional Safeguards for Grievance 14

- **The Third Amendment:** Explicitly prohibits the quartering of soldiers in private homes without the owner's consent, reflecting a direct response to the colonial grievances about British troops.
- **Article I, Section 8:** Gives Congress the power to raise and support armies, but with significant limitations, including the requirement that appropriations for the military cannot be for more than two years, ensuring civilian control over the military.
- **The Second Amendment:** Provides for a well-regulated militia, reflecting the founders' preference for local defense forces over standing armies.

Grievance 15

He Protects Foreign Soldiers by Mock Trials

"For protecting them by a mock Trial from punishment for any
Murders they should commit on the Inhabitants of these States."

NOTE: The colonists were outraged that British soldiers could escape punishment for crimes against Americans. Even when they killed colonists, the King's system let them be tried back in England—or not at all.

The Crown's Administration of Justice Act (May 20, 1774)

If a British officer was accused of a serious crime, like murder, the governor could send him to another colony or even back to England to be tried. That trial would still count as legal, even though it did not happen where the crime took place.

From *Our Country, A Household History*, Volume 3, by Benson J. Lossing, 1877

In 1768, two citizens of Annapolis, in Maryland, were murdered by some marines belonging to a British armed ship. The trial was a mockery of justice; and in the face of clear evidence against them, the criminals were acquitted. In the difficulties with the Regulators in North Carolina, in 1771, some of the soldiers who had shot down citizens when standing up in defence of their rights, were tried for murder and acquitted; while Governor Tryon mercilessly hung six prisoners. who were certainly entitled to the benefits of the laws of war if his own soldiers were.

Historical Background

British soldiers receiving legal immunity for crimes committed against colonists. The most infamous example was the Boston Massacre of 1770, where British troops fired into a crowd, killing five civilians. While John Adams provided a legal defense that resulted in the acquittal of most of the soldiers involved, many colonists saw the trial as a symbol of British bias, believing that the soldiers were protected from real consequences for their actions.

Beyond Boston, similar instances fueled distrust. In 1768, two citizens of Annapolis, Maryland, were murdered by British marines, yet the soldiers were acquitted despite clear evidence against them. Likewise, during the Regulator Rebellion in North Carolina (1771), Governor Tryon's troops killed protesting citizens, and those soldiers were cleared of wrongdoing. However, Tryon executed six colonial prisoners, treating them as criminals rather than granting them the rights of lawful combatants. These events reinforced the belief that British authorities prioritized protecting their own soldiers over delivering justice for colonists.

The situation worsened with the Administration of Justice Act of 1774, one of the Intolerable Acts, which allowed British officials accused of capital crimes to be tried in Britain rather than in colonial courts. This effectively removed accountability, as colonial witnesses often could not travel to Britain, making convictions nearly impossible. This act was seen as a direct attempt to shield British officials and soldiers from colonial justice, further inflaming revolutionary sentiment.[68]

Modern Interpretation

This underscores the importance of judicial impartiality and accountability, regardless of an individual's status or position. Today, the U.S. Constitution guarantees that all accused persons—whether civilians or military personnel—are entitled to due process and a fair trial.

Under the Uniform Code of Military Justice (UCMJ), U.S. military personnel are subject to strict legal oversight, ensuring that crimes committed by soldiers, whether in wartime or peacetime, do not go unpunished. Additionally, the Posse Comitatus Act (1878) limits the military's role in civilian law enforcement, reducing the likelihood of military personnel being placed in positions where they might come into conflict with civilians.

Summary

Colonial fears that British soldiers were shielded from accountability, reinforcing the perception of an unjust legal system favoring the Crown was an underlying factor for this Grievance. Events like the Boston Massacre trials, the Regulator Rebellion, and the Administration of Justice Act demonstrated that British military personnel often received unfair protections.

Constitutional Safeguards for Grievance 15

- **The Sixth Amendment:** Guarantees the right to a speedy and public trial by an impartial jury in the district where the crime was committed.
- **The Third Amendment:** Prohibits the quartering of troops in private homes without the owner's consent, reducing the likelihood of conflicts between soldiers and civilians.
- **The Fifth Amendment:** Ensures due process rights, preventing any person from being deprived of life, liberty, or property without due process of law. It applies to all within the U.S. jurisdiction, including military personnel.

Grievance 16

For Cutting Off Global Trade

"For cutting off our trade with all parts of the world."

NOTE: This grievance is about a basic idea of freedom—the right to work, make things, and trade freely.

Britain's trade laws did more than control business. They were used to control the colonies. Colonists were not allowed to trade with other countries, so prices went up, and people often had to buy lower-quality goods.

Families—not just merchants—felt the effects.

Some British officials and merchants made money from these rules by controlling trade and collecting fees. This created a system where people benefited from keeping the colonies under control.

To Jefferson, this was not just about money—it was about right and wrong. When a government controls what people can buy, sell, and earn, it takes away their freedom.

The fight for free trade was really a fight for dignity—the belief that people should be free to earn a living and provide for their families.

From Jefferson's 1774 *Summary View of the Rights of British America*

That the exercise of a free trade with all parts of the world, possessed by the American colonists as of natural right, and which no law of their own had taken away or abridged, was next the object of unjust incroachment.

From *Our Country, A Household History*, Volume 3, by Benson J. Lossing, 1877

The navigation laws were always oppressive in character: and in 1764, the British naval commanders having been clothed with the authority of custom-house officers, completely broke up a profitable trade which the colonists had long enjoyed with the Spanish and French West Indies, notwithstanding it was in violation of the old Navigation Act of 1660, which had been almost ineffectual. Finally, Lord North concluded to punish the refractory colonists of New England, by crippling their commerce with Great Britain, Ireland, and the West Indies. Fishing on the banks of Newfoundland was also prohibited, and thus, as far as Parliamentary enactments could accomplish it, their "trade with all parts of the world" was cut off.

Historical Background

Britain regarded her colonies not as partners in commerce but as instruments of a mercantilist system—suppliers of raw materials and captive markets for finished goods. American harvests flowed outward, while British manufactures returned at inflated prices, ensuring the mother country profited at both ends of the exchange—buying low and selling high. Parliament's Navigation Acts barred Americans from selling freely or developing competing industries, binding colonial trade to British interests alone. This system reached most clearly into staple crops that sustained colonial economies.

> **In his *Summary View*, Jefferson described the system plainly:**
> "That these acts prohibit us from carrying in quest of other purchasers the surplus of our tobaccoes remaining after the consumption of Great Britain is supplied; so that we must leave them with the British merchant for whatever he will please to allow us, to be by him reshipped to foreign markets, where he will reap the benefits of making sale of them for full value."

What resulted was not merely regulation but subordination. Colonists produced the goods, but Great Britain:

- Fixed the price—buying American goods low and selling finished goods high
- Controlled every point of exchange
- Claimed the profits at home and abroad—a complete system of mercantilist control

By forcing Americans to buy and sell only through British channels, Parliament transformed commerce into an instrument of control. What began as economic policy became political and economic servitude—reducing free producers to tenants of imperial will.

Modern Interpretation

Jefferson's warning against monopoly and coerced dependency remains as relevant now as in 1774. His grievance speaks not only to prosperity but to principle—the right of a people to enjoy the rewards of their own labor. Economic servitude, whether imposed by kings, concentrated power, or distant systems, erodes freedom as surely as political tyranny. In every age, when control of markets replaces freedom of exchange, independence withers. Jefferson's call was not for unchecked commerce, but for dignity—the conviction that no people should be compelled to enrich others at the expense of their own liberty.

Summary

By cutting off American trade with the world, the empire sought not only revenue but obedience. Jefferson transformed commerce into a question of human dignity: to trade freely was to live freely. In defending that right, he elevated merchants, farmers, artisans, and housewives alike into the ranks of patriots. What began as a protest against economic control became a declaration that liberty could neither be bought, restricted, nor shipped at the command of Parliament—not even King George III.

Constitutional Safeguards for Grievance 16

- **Article I, Section 8, Clause 3, the Commerce Clause:** Grants Congress the power to regulate commerce with foreign nations, among the states, and with Indian tribes. This ensures a federal approach to trade policy and prevents the arbitrary and restrictive trade practices imposed by the British Parliament.
- **Article I, Section 9:** Limits Congress's power to give preference to the ports of one state over another, ensuring equal trade among states under a unified federal commercial policy and preventing the grievances Jefferson described from recurring within the new Republic.
- **Article I, Section 10:** States are prohibited from regulating foreign commerce, ensuring a unified commercial system and preventing both federal and state-level trade discrimination.

That the exercise of a free trade with all parts of the world, possessed by the American colonists, as of natural right, and which no law of their own had taken away or abridged, was next the object of unjust encroachment… the [British] parliament… assumed upon themselves the power of prohibiting their trade with all other parts of the world, except the island of Great Britain.

"Summary View of the Rights of British America" – Jefferson, 1774

(The British) have raised their commodities, called for in America, to the double and treble of what they sold for before such exclusive privileges were given them, and of what better commodities of the same kind would cost us elsewhere, and at the same time give us much less for what we carry thither than might be had at more convenient ports.

"Summary View of the Rights of British America" – Jefferson, 1774

By one other act, passed in the 23d year of the same reign, the iron which we make we are forbidden to manufacture, and heavy as that article is, and necessary in every branch of husbandry, besides commission and insurance, we are to pay freight for it to Great Britain, and freight for it back again, for the purpose of supporting not men, but machines, in the island of Great Britain.

"Summary View of the Rights of British America" – Jefferson, 1774

By an act passed in the 5th Year of the reign of his late majesty king George the second, an American subject is forbidden to make a hat for himself of the fur which he has taken perhaps on his own soil.

"Summary View of the Rights of British America" – Jefferson, 1774

Grievance 17

Taxation Without Representation

"Or imposing taxes on us without our consent."

NOTE: The colonists were furious when Britain taxed them without letting them have a vote or voice in Parliament. They believed only their own elected assemblies—not a distant king—had the right to decide how they were taxed.

From Jefferson's 1774 *Summary View of the Rights of British America*

Still <u>less</u> let it be proposed that our properties within our own territories shall be taxed or regulated by any power on earth but our own… The Royal Governor in Boston taxing them to the amount of their recognizance, and that amount may be whatever a governor pleases.

From *Our Country, A Household History*, Volume 3, by Benson J. Lossing, 1877

In addition to the revenue taxes imposed from time to time and attempted to be collected by means of writs of assistance, the Stamp Act was passed, and duties upon paper, painters' colors, glass, tea, etc., were levied. This was the great bone of contention between the colonists and the imperial government. It was contention on the one hand for the great political truth that taxation and representation are inseparable, and a lust for power and the means for replenishing an exhausted treasury, on the other. The climax of the contention was the Revolution.

Historical Background

Taxation without representation was a profoundly contentious issue for the colonies. This Grievance stems from various British acts imposing taxes on the colonies without their consent or representation in Parliament. Notably, the Sugar Act (1764), Stamp Act (1765), and Townshend Acts (1767) were pivotal in escalating colonial unrest. Jefferson's *Summary View of the Rights of British America* highlights the unreasonableness and injustice of such taxation, underscoring the colonists' demand for autonomy in managing their fiscal affairs.

The British government justified these taxes by arguing that the colonies benefited from British military protection and should contribute to the empire's financial burdens. Parliament also believed the colonies must be taxed to help offset the enormous debt incurred during the French and Indian War. However, the colonists viewed these measures as a direct violation of their rights as Englishmen, particularly the long-held principle that taxation required the consent of elected representatives. Resistance to these acts took many forms, including boycotts, protests, and even violent confrontations, such as the Stamp Act riots. The repeated imposition of new taxes, even after previous ones had been repealed, convinced many colonists that Britain sought to exert control rather than simply raise revenue. This growing distrust and defiance not only fueled colonial unity but also became the rallying cry that propelled the movement toward full independence: **"No Taxation Without Representation!"**[69]

Modern Interpretation

Today, this Grievance is seen as foundational in forming our republic, emphasizing the principle that citizens should have a say in how they are taxed. It underpins the American ethos of a republic and government accountability to its people. The idea that taxation must be tied to representation remains a core value, influencing contemporary debates about tax policy and fiscal responsibility.

Summary

Grievance 17 encapsulates the colonial frustration with British taxation policies and the lack of colonial representation in the British Parliament. It played a crucial role in shaping the principles of representation and taxation in the US Constitution and continues to influence American political discourse.

Constitutional Safeguards for Grievance 17

The framers of the Constitution, clearly mindful of the historical grievances about taxation without representation, crafted a system ensuring that the people's elected representatives levy taxes. The 16th Amendment further evolved the taxation system to accommodate the complexities of a modern economy while retaining the essential democratic principle of representation in fiscal matters.

- **Article I, Section 2:** Mandates direct representation for taxation, stipulating that taxes should be levied based on population, as determined by the census.

- **Article I, Section 8:** Grants Congress, composed of elected representatives, the power to lay and collect taxes, ensuring that taxation decisions are made by those accountable to the electorate.

- **The 16th Amendment:** Allows Congress to levy an income tax without apportioning it among the states or basing it on the U.S. Census, reflecting the evolution of the American taxation system.

Grievance 18

Deprived of Trial by Juries

"For depriving us of the benefits of trial by jury."

NOTE: When people were accused of breaking a law, they were often denied a fair trial. Instead of being judged by neighbors or local citizens, many colonists had to face royal judges chosen by the King. This meant verdicts were decided by the Crown—not by the local community.

From Jefferson's 1774 *Summary View of the Rights of British America*

And the wretched criminal, if he happen to have offended on the American side, stripped of his privilege of trial by peers of his vicinage, removed from the place where alone full evidence could be obtained, without money, without counsel, without friends, without exculpatory proof, is tried before judges predetermined to condemn. The cowards who would suffer a countryman to be torn from the bowels of their society, in order to be thus offered a sacrifice to parliamentary tyranny, would merit that everlasting infamy now fixed on the authors of the act!

From *Our Country, A Household History*, Volume 3, by Benson J. Lossing, 1877

This was especially the case when commissioners of customs were concerned in the suit. After these functionaries were driven from Boston in 1768, an act was passed which placed violations of the revenue laws under the jurisdiction of the admiralty courts, where the offenders were tried by a creature of the crown, and were deprived "of the benefits of trial by jury."

Historical Background

Trial by jury was a fundamental right long cherished in British common law and considered essential to ensuring fair and impartial justice. The colonists viewed this right as a safeguard against tyranny, ensuring that legal decisions would be made by fellow citizens rather than government-appointed judges loyal to the Crown.

The British government systematically eroded this right through measures like the use of admiralty courts, which handled violations of British trade laws without juries and were overseen by judges loyal to the Crown. These courts presumed guilt, denied local trials, and removed defendants from their communities. The Administration of Justice Act (1774) worsened the situation by allowing British officials accused of crimes to be tried in England, making it nearly impossible for colonial witnesses to testify. The colonists saw these policies as deliberate attempts to deny them the legal protections enjoyed by British citizens, reinforcing their belief that the British legal system had become a tool of oppression rather than justice.

This Grievance was particularly alarming because trial by jury had been considered a cornerstone of English liberty since the Magna Carta of 1215. By stripping this right away, Britain not only disregarded its own legal traditions but also treated the colonies as second-class subjects. The absence of juries in admiralty courts allowed British judges to levy harsh fines, seize property, and imprison colonists without proper legal recourse. Additionally, the policy of moving trials to England left many accused individuals unable to mount a proper defense due to lack of funds, legal counsel, or access to witnesses.

Many colonists saw this as part of a larger pattern of British overreach, where Parliament and the Crown sought to punish dissenters and enforce unpopular laws without fear of resistance. This abuse of judicial power strengthened calls for self-governance and legal protections that would prevent such injustices in an independent America. By the time of the Revolution, the demand for a fair and impartial legal system had become a defining cause, influencing the legal framework of the U.S. Constitution and Bill of Rights.[70]

Modern Interpretation

Today, the right to a trial by jury is considered a cornerstone of the American legal system. This principle reflects the democratic principle that legal judgments should not be the sole purview of the government but involve the citizenry. This Grievance and its constitutional redress highlight the enduring importance of protecting individual rights against potential governmental overreach.

Summary

This underscores the colonial desire to preserve and respect fundamental legal rights, specifically the right to trial by jury. This right was seen as crucial for safeguarding liberty and ensuring justice. Its incorporation into the Constitution and the Bill of Rights reflects its fundamental importance in American legal and political thought.

Constitutional Safeguards for Grievance 18

- **Article III, Section 2:** Guarantees the right to a jury trial in all criminal prosecutions.
- **The Sixth Amendment:** Elaborates on this right, ensuring a speedy and public trial by an impartial jury in the state and district where the crime was committed.
- **The Seventh Amendment:** Extends the right to a jury trial in civil cases.

Grievance 19

Transporting Us Beyond Seas for Trial

"For transporting us beyond Seas to be tried for pretended offences."

NOTE: When colonists were accused of crimes against the British government, some were sent to England to stand trial. That meant leaving behind their families, witnesses, and anyone who could defend them. Facing British judges across the ocean, they had no chance for fairness or truth.

From Jefferson's 1774 *Summary View of the Rights of British America*

By the act for the suppression of riots and tumults in the town of Boston, passed also in the last session of parliament, a murder committed there is, if the governor pleases, to be tried in the court of King's Bench, in the island of Great Britain, by a jury of Middlesex. The witnesses, too, on receipt of such a sum as the governor shall think it reasonable for them to expend, are to enter into recognizance to appear at the trial. This is, in other words, taxing them to the amount of their recognizance, and that amount may be whatever a governor pleases; for who does his majesty think can be prevailed on to cross the Atlantic for the sole purpose of bearing evidence to a fact? His expenses are to be borne, indeed, as they shall be estimated by a governor; but who are to feed the wife and children whom he leaves behind, and who have had no other subsistence but his daily labour?

From *Our Country, A Household History*, Volume 3, by Benson J. Lossing, 1877

A law of 1774 provided that any person in the province of Massachusetts, who should be accused of riot, resistance of magistrates or the officers of customs, murder, "or any other capital offence," might, at the option of the governor, be taken for trial to another colony, or transported to Great Britain for the purpose. The minister pretended that impartial justice could not be administered in Massachusetts; but the facts of Captain Preston's case refuted his arguments in that direction. The bill was violently opposed in Parliament, yet it became a law. It was decreed that Americans might be "transported beyond the seas, to be tried for pretended offences," or real crimes.

Historical Background

Colonists' objected to being transported overseas for trial, which they saw as a direct violation of their rights under British law. The Administration of Justice Act of 1774, one of the Intolerable Acts, allowed British officials or soldiers accused of capital offenses in the colonies to be tried in Britain or another colony rather than in the jurisdiction where the alleged crime occurred. This effectively removed accountability, as colonial witnesses could not afford to travel across the Atlantic, making a fair trial nearly impossible.

Colonists viewed this as a deliberate attempt to shield British officials from justice, particularly in cases where they had used violence or excessive force against civilians. They feared that British judges and juries, far removed from the realities of colonial rule, would favor the Crown's representatives and ensure their acquittal. In contrast, ordinary colonists accused of crimes were still subject to local courts and harsh penalties, creating an unjust double standard in the colonial legal system.

Jefferson's *Summary View of the Rights of British America* vividly illustrates the hardships imposed on the accused and their families, emphasizing that being forcibly removed from their communities meant losing access to legal counsel, witnesses, and any support network. Colonists saw this as an abuse of judicial power designed to suppress dissent and discourage resistance to British authority. This grievance, combined with the denial of trial by jury, reinforced the belief that Britain had abandoned justice in favor of control, strengthening the call for American independence.[71]

Modern Interpretation

This Grievance and its constitutional resolutions underscore the importance of local jurisdiction and the right to be tried within one's community. It reflects a fundamental principle of justice—that one should be tried near the alleged offense and by a jury comprising community members, thereby ensuring a fair and relevant judgment.

Summary

Grievance 19 highlights the colonists' opposition to transporting individuals for trial across seas, which they saw as a form of justice and local jurisdiction. The Framers of the Constitution directly addressed this issue, embedding the right to a regional trial within the fundamental law of the land.

Constitutional Safeguards for Grievance 19

The U.S. Constitution and the Bill of Rights address this Grievance by ensuring that trials are held in the state and district where the alleged crime was committed:

- **Article III, Section 2:** Stipulates that trials for all crimes, except in cases of impeachment, shall be held in the state where said crimes have been committed.
- **The Sixth Amendment:** Mandates a speedy and public trial by an impartial jury of the state and district wherein the crime shall have been committed.

By incorporating provisions for local trials in the Constitution and the Bill of Rights, the framers sought to prevent the injustices and practical hardships highlighted in this grievance. These constitutional safeguards ensure that trials are accessible and fair, conducted within the community familiar with the local context and where the alleged offense occurred. This approach reflects a commitment to justice grounded in the community and responsive to its norms and values.

Grievance 20
Enlarging the Borders of a Neighboring Province

"For abolishing the free System of English Laws in a neighboring Province, establishing therein an Arbitrary government, and enlarging its Boundaries to render it at once an example and fit instrument for introducing the same absolute rule into these Colonies."

NOTE: The King redrew maps and changed laws to tighten his control over the colonies. By expanding Canada's borders and replacing English law with royal rule, he sent a warning to the rest of America: Your freedoms can be taken away too.

Jefferson's July 1775 Draft of *The Declaration of the Causes and Necessity of Taking Up Arms*

"They have erected in a neighbouring province, **acquired by the joint arms of Great Britain and America,** a tyranny dangerous to the very existence of all these colonies."

This was a Grievance adopted by the Second Continental Congress on July 6, 1775. The final version was written edited by John Dickinson in an effort to soften some of Jefferson's fiery complaints against the crown.[72]

Royal Proclamation of 1763
The Proclamation Line of 1763 was a British-produced boundary marked in the Appalachian Mountains at the Eastern Continental Divide. Decreed on October 7, 1763, the Proclamation Line prohibited Anglo-American colonists from settling on lands acquired from the French following the French and Indian War.

Quebec Act of 1774
Eleven years later, the King made things worse with the Quebec Act of 1774. It gave much of the Northwest Territory—land claimed by several colonies—to Quebec and pushed its borders south to the Ohio River. This alarmed leaders like George Washington and George Mason, who had royal permission to settle or invest in that region. It also broke promises made who had fought for Britain in the French and Indian War.

The Act was designed to keep French Canadians loyal to Britain. It allowed the Catholic Church to keep its power, restored old French civil laws, and brought back a feudal land system where tenants had to pay dues to wealthy landowners. These changes pleased some French leaders but angered English-speaking settlers who wanted elected government, English law, and private land ownership. Instead, the King placed Quebec under a 23-member council he appointed himself.

To many Americans, this Act was a warning. If the King could change borders and laws in Canada without consent, he could do the same in the Thirteen Colonies. The Quebec Act became a symbol of how far Britain was willing to go to replace freedom with royal rule.[73]

From *Our Country, A Household History*, Volume 3, by Benson J. Lossing, 1877

This charge is embodied in an earlier one. The British ministry thought it prudent to take early steps to secure a footing in America so near the scene of inevitable rebellion as to allow them to breast, successfully, the gathering storm. The investing of a legislative council in Canada with all powers except levying of taxes, was a great stride toward that absolute military rule which bore sway there within eighteen months afterward. Giving up their political rights for doubtful religious privileges, made them willing slaves, and Canada remained a part of the British empire when its sister colonies rejoiced in freedom.

Historical Background—Proclamation Line of 1763 and the 1774 Quebec Act

The Proclamation Line of 1763 was a British-produced boundary marked in the Appalachian Mountains at the Eastern Continental Divide. Decreed on October 7, 1763, the Proclamation Line prohibited Anglo-American colonists from settling on lands acquired from the French following the French and Indian War.

This Grievance also addresses the British government's Quebec Act of 1774.[74] This further inflamed tensions following the Proclamation Line of 1763. The act extended Quebec's boundaries southward to the Ohio River, alarming the colonies as it impeded westward expansion. Additionally, it replaced English civil law with French civil law and granted religious freedom to Catholics, challenging the predominantly Protestant ethos of the Thirteen Colonies. The colonists perceived these actions as a direct threat to their own governance and legal systems, fearing the imposition of similar arbitrary rule. If the Crown could take land claimed by colonial charters and assign it to another country, what would limit the king from doing similar or worse in the future?[75]

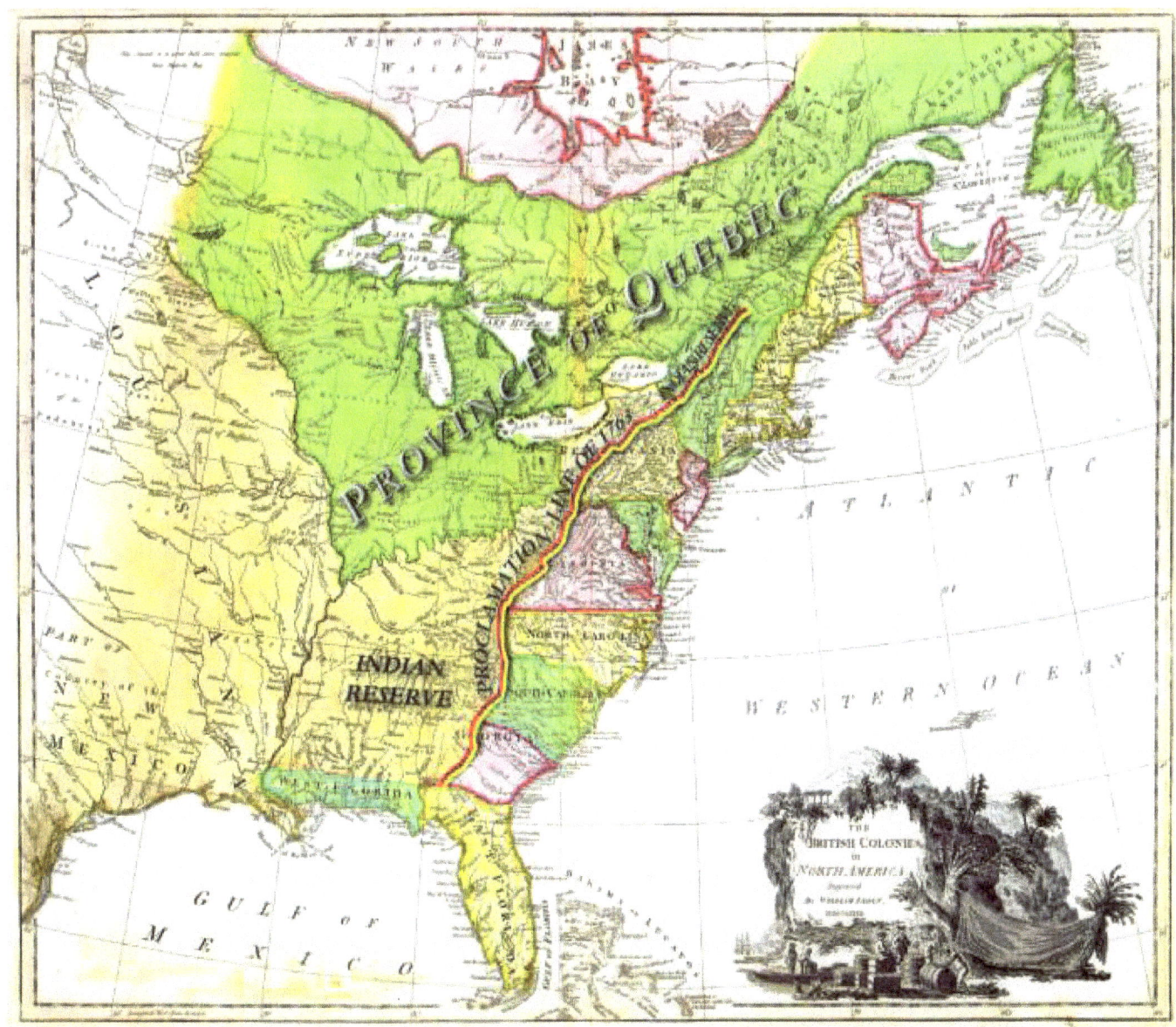

British colonies in North America; Lawrence H. Slaughter Collection of English maps, charts, globes, books and atlases / Charts and maps, 1777, Engraved by William Faden, 1750?–1836
[Proclamation Line of 1763 and enlarged titles of Province of Quebec and Indian Reserve added by author]

French Proposal at The Treaty of Paris

MAP OF
NORTH AMERICA
Showing the Boundaries of
THE UNITED STATES, CANADA, AND
THE SPANISH POSSESSIONS
according to the proposals of the Court of France in 1782

English	Red (Ohio Country and Canada)
United States	Green (Eastern Seaboard)
Spanish	Yellow (Alabama, Mississippi, Tennessee)
Uncolored	Indian Territory

Under Spanish (yellow) or American (white) protection, according as it lies West or East of the Yellow intersecting line.

The French Foreign Minister, Vergennes, proposed, in September 1782, that the United States gain independence but limit it to the area east of the Appalachian Mountains. In his proposal, Britain would retain the land north of the Ohio River (the future Northwest Territory) as part of its Province of Quebec. An independent Indian state was to be established, with the southern part designated as Indian Territory under Spanish control. This would have constrained the United States from the Eastern Seaboard to the crest of the Appalachian Mountains.[76]

Treaty of Paris, September 3, 1783

John Adams, Benjamin Franklin, and John Jay rejected the French proposal and negotiated peace terms directly with the British, resulting in the Treaty of Paris, officially ending the Revolutionary War. Important points included:

1. Great Britain recognized independence for the United States of America.

2. It placed vast Western territories to the Mississippi River within the United States of America, and America recognized British colonies in Canada and Florida.

3. The treaty overturned boundaries of the Proclamation of 1683 and the Quebec Act of 1774.

4. Provisions were made for Loyalists to have their properties returned and prewar debts repaid.

5. America was awarded fishing rights in the waters off of Newfoundland.

6. Britain and the United States each had access to the Mississippi River.

7. The British were to surrender of all posts within the territory of the United States.[77]

Historical Background

The Proclamation Line of 1763 was a British-produced boundary marked in the Appalachian Mountains, decreed on October 7, 1763, to prohibit Anglo-American colonists from settling on lands acquired from the French after the French and Indian War. Intended to prevent conflict with French Canadians and Native nations, it instead angered settlers whose colonial charters already claimed that land. This was just as likely a "land grab" by king to profit from the fur trade and the immense potential of the Ohio territory.

The French had claimed all the territory west of the Appalachian Mountains that drained into the Ohio and Mississippi Rivers, conflicting with existing Colonial charters. The king reneged on promises of land in the Ohio Country made to American veterans of the French and Indian War. Instead of honoring those promises and the historic boundaries of Colonial charters, he recognized the former French land claims, declaring the territory his own royal bounty—a personal prize of conquest. It was like saying, "This land is now mine and anyone who does business here or wishes to acquire land must pay me."

This Grievance also addresses the British government's Quebec Act of 1774, which further inflamed tensions. The act extended Quebec's boundaries southward to the Ohio River, impeding colonial westward expansion and disregarding land claims granted under colonial charters.

To many in the colonies, the Quebec Act was a dangerous precedent—if Britain could alter laws and governance in Quebec, it could do the same elsewhere, introducing arbitrary rule and stripping colonies of their legal traditions. This reinforced fears that Britain sought to impose authoritarian rule across North America, using Quebec as a model for eroding colonial self-governance. The combination of territorial restrictions, legal changes, and religious implications made the Quebec Act one of the most reviled policies leading up to the Revolution.[78]

Modern Interpretation

The concerns raised in this Grievance reflect the importance of self-governance and legal consistency. The Constitution's provisions ensure that the federal government respects state autonomy and established legal frameworks, preventing the kind of arbitrary rule and legal changes imposed in Quebec. The resolution at the Treaty of Paris in 1783 restored vast territories, tripling the size of our nation.

Summary

Colonists feared arbitrary rule and legal inconsistency, like the British government's actions in Quebec. The US Constitution addresses these concerns by ensuring state autonomy, protecting against arbitrary changes in state boundaries or governance, and safeguarding religious freedom and a republican government. In Jefferson's view, this encroachment on lawful charters made the colonies' own governance precarious—for if the Crown could seize land once, it could arbitrarily seize more and more. And with it…our liberties.

Constitutional Safeguards for Grievance 20

The U.S. Constitution ensures that the establishment of arbitrary government and changes in legal systems without representation or consent, as experienced in Quebec, cannot occur within the United States.

- **Article IV, Section 3:** Addresses the administration of territories and the creation of new states, ensuring that any changes in boundaries or governance are under the direct control of Congress, thus preventing unilateral or arbitrary alterations.
- **Article IV, Section 4:** Guarantees every state a republican form of government, preventing the establishment of arbitrary or authoritarian rule.
- **The First Amendment:** Protects religious freedom, preventing the government from imposing religious changes or favoring one religious group.
- **The Tenth Amendment:** Reserves powers not delegated to the federal government to the states or the people, ensuring local autonomy and protection against unwarranted federal encroachment.

Grievance 21

Taking Away Charters and Valuable Laws

"For taking away our Charters, abolishing our most valuable Laws, and altering fundamentally the Forms of our Governments."

NOTE: The King attacked the very foundations of colonial government. By seizing charters and rewriting local laws and maps, he stripped colonies of their right to rule themselves. What had once been free governments were now ruled by royal decree.

From Jefferson's 1774 *Summary View of the Rights of British America*

America was conquered, and her settlements made, and firmly established, at the expence of individuals … for themselves alone they have right to hold. … No exercise of such a power, of dividing and dismembering a country, has ever occurred in his majesty's realm of England, nor could it be justified or acquiesced under there, or in any other part of his majesty's empire.

Jefferson here defined the King's claim over western lands as a violation of the British Constitution itself—a seizure of charters by "right of conquest."

From *Our Country, A Household History*, Volume 3, by Benson J. Lossing, 1877

This is a reiteration of a charge already considered, and refers to the alteration of the Massachusetts charter, so as to make judges and other officers independent of the people, and subservient to the crown. The governor was empowered to remove and appoint all inferior judges, the attorney generals, provost-marshals, and justices of the peace, and to appoint sheriffs independent of the council. As the sheriffs chose jurors, trial by jury might easily be made a mere mockery. The people had hitherto been allowed, by their charter, to select jurors; now the whole matter was placed in the hands of the creatures of government.

Historical Background:

Jefferson's punctuation was deliberate. The commas in this Grievance are, essentially, separations for separate "clauses" in this sentence. Each clause describes a distinct breach of colonial charters and of British constitutional law—territory, law, and government—revealing a coordinated royal effort to dissolve American self-rule. These clauses may be defined as follows:

GRIEVANCE CLAUSES	CONSTITUTIONAL OFFENSE	HISTORICAL EXAMPLE & CONTEXT
Clause 1: For **TAKING** away our Charters,	Revoked territorial and constitutional rights guaranteed by colonial charters.	*Royal Proclamation of 1763 and Quebec Act (1774)* erased long-standing colonial boundaries, seizing the Ohio Country as royal domain secured for the Crown.
Clause 2: ABOLISHING our most valuable Laws,	Nullified colonial self-legislation and the right of local consent.	Parliament's repeated disallowance of colonial acts and veto of assemblies' laws placed governance above local will.
Clause 3 and **ALTERING** fundamentally the Forms of our Governments.	Substituted representative government with royal authority.	*The Massachusetts Government Act (1774) replaced elected councils and judges with Crown appointees, ending jury independence and local self-rule.*

The king assumed, "by right of conquest," the Ohio and Illinois countries claimed by the French. Official French claims on that territory, however, were made decades after the royal colonial charters had been granted for the very same territory LaSalle claimed for France in 1682. The claim was for all of the Mississippi River basin. Under British Constitutional law, colonial charters held precedent over later French claims. When the French began building forts in today's Western Pennsylvania in 1753, that was too much. George Washington was sent to tell them to leave, which sparked the French and Indian War; the Seven Years War that devastated the world.

> **Jefferson's Initial Draft:** *Declaration of the Causes and Necessity of Taking Up Arms*, 1775
> "The British parliament... assumed a right of altering our charters and established laws, and have declared that they may of right make laws to bind us in all cases whatsoever. They have undertaken to give and grant our property without our consent... The lands which were conquered by the joint arms of Great Britain and America are declared to be their conquest, and subject to their disposal."

This Grievance reflects the colonists' frustration with the British Crown's unilateral revocation of colonial charters and alteration of established laws and governmental forms. **Colonial charters were foundational documents, granting settlers the right to self-governance and outlining legal structures**. The British government's decision to alter or revoke these charters was viewed as a direct assault on colonial autonomy and an effort to centralize power under royal authority.[79]

The Massachusetts Charter was revoked in 1684, and tensions escalated further under the Massachusetts Government Act (1774), which stripped the colony of its ability to elect its own officials, making judges and sheriffs accountable only to the Crown. This effectively eliminated fair trials, as sheriffs—appointed by royal governors—held exclusive control over jury selection. The Act also restricted town meetings, limiting the people's ability to govern themselves and voice grievances.[80]

Colonists viewed these actions as fundamental attacks on their rights as Englishmen, violating legal traditions dating back to the Magna Carta (1215). They feared that if Britain could revoke one colony's charter, it could dismantle all colonial governments at will, replacing representative assemblies with arbitrary rule by royal decree. The loss of these self-governing structures further unified resistance across the colonies, fueling the growing demand for independence and constitutional protections against such abuses.[81] American Colonial charters which determined boundary lines were also violated by Crown's arbitrary claims and restrictions in the *Royal Proclamation of 1763* and the *Quebec Act of 1774*.[82]

The Keystone Grievances

A trio of Grievances sum up the rest, with this 21st Grievance perhaps the most important. Together, they trace the full arc of royal overreach—from the seizure of the land that was guaranteed by charters, to the perversion of the laws that governed them, to the destruction of the governments that protected them.

A Triad of Tyranny

Grievances 7, 20, and 21 form a triad—three offenses that together annulled the American system of self-rule.

Grievance 7—Land and Population

The Crown obstructed immigration, controlled settlement, and raised the cost of land to restrict growth. The *Royal Proclamation of 1763* reserved the Ohio and Illinois country as "bounty of war," redefining territory won by the joint arms of Britain and America as the personal estate of the King.

Grievance 20—Law and Boundaries

The *Quebec Act of 1774* extended French civil law into lands secured by English charters, abolishing representative government in that region. This was not protection—it was conversion. Royal prerogative replaced English liberty, setting a precedent for arbitrary rule across the continent.

Grievance 21—Charters and Constitutions

The ultimate act of aggression was the seizure of constitutional authority itself. By "taking away our charters," the Crown denied the legal existence of the colonial governments—the very institutions that had created the settlements, raised the militias, and governed by consent for over a century.

In these three acts—controlling land, altering law, and destroying liberty—the King made himself master over what had been free.

Jefferson's Moral Logic of Rebellion

Jefferson reminded Parliament that the Crown had not invested in the planting of America. The colonies were not royal ventures but private ones—financed by sponsors and emigrants themselves, who paid their own passage or were indentured to clear their own fields and defend their own frontiers.

> "America was conquered, and her settlements made, and firmly established, at the expense of individuals; for themselves alone they have a right to hold, and to dispose of as they please."
> —*A Summary View of the Rights of British America* (1774)

If the King had not planted the seed, he could not claim the harvest. A government that neither plowed nor paid for the soil had no moral title to the fruits of it. To be ruled, taxed, and restrained as dependents under those terms was, in Jefferson's view, slavery in everything but name.

The Ancestral Precedent

Jefferson traced this right of independence to England's own origins.

> "Our ancestors, before their emigration to America, were the free inhabitants of the British dominions in Europe, and possessed a right which nature has given to all men, of departing from the country in which chance, not choice, has placed them…"
> —*A Summary View* (1774)

He reminded his readers that the Saxons had once crossed the sea from Germany to Britain, carrying their laws and liberties with them. When they settled England, they owed no tribute to the princes they had left behind. So too, the Americans owed no allegiance to a king who neither financed their passage nor defended their rights.

The Law of Life and Liberty

To Jefferson, independence was not rebellion—it was renewal. The migration of peoples was a law of nature, like the division of living cells: life perpetuates by separation, not by servitude. The new society inherits the essence of the old, yet lives by its own vitality.

Britain's error was to see the colonies not as kindred growths in the great organism of civilization, but as plantations—property to harvest rather than kindred to honor.

Just as the Angles and Saxons had left their homeland to form England, so the English had crossed the Atlantic to plant new societies in America. The right to depart, to build, and to govern anew was not rebellion against kings, but obedience to the natural laws of creation itself—foremost of which is liberty.

The Restoration of Law

Thus, in the 21st Grievance, Jefferson brings all wrongs into one frame:

- **The taking of land** (Grievance 7)
- **The corrupting of law** (Grievance 20)
- **The destruction of government** (Grievance 21)

These were not political missteps but constitutional thefts—seizures of the people's right to exist as a lawful nation.

When the Americans declared independence, they did not destroy their governments; they rescued them from confiscation. What the King had called rebellion was, in truth, restoration—an act of preservation in obedience to the oldest compact of all: that law, *not power*, is the rightful sovereign of mankind.

> **"Just as the Saxons once became English, the English now became American."**

Summary

Grievance 21 highlights the colonists' concerns over the British Crown's arbitrary interference with their charters and laws. The US Constitution addresses these issues by guaranteeing a republican form of government, protecting states' rights to manage their internal affairs, and preventing the federal government from passing laws retroactively impairing contracts or legal obligations.

Constitutional Safeguards for Grievance 21

The U.S. Constitution provides safeguards against the arbitrary revocation of charters and fundamental laws, ensuring stable governance:

- **Article IV, Section 4:** Guarantees every state a republican form of government, ensuring that the fundamental form of state governments cannot be unilaterally altered.
- **Article I, Sections 9 and 10:** Limit the powers of both the federal government and the states, ensuring that neither can pass ex post facto laws or laws impairing the obligation of contracts, which would include unilateral alterations to charters.

The Tenth Amendment: Reserves to the states all powers not delegated to the federal government, which includes the power to establish and modify their charters and laws within the bounds of the Constitution.

Grievance 22
Suspends Legislatures & Assumes Power

"For suspending our own legislatures & declaring themselves invested with power to legislate for us in all cases whatsoever."

NOTE: When colonial assemblies stood up to the King, he shut them down. Governors dissolved meetings, silenced representatives, and replaced local decision-making with royal command. By suspending colonial legislatures, Britain sent a clear message: the voice of the people no longer mattered.

From Jefferson's 1774 *Summary View of the Rights of British America*

But that one other act, passed in the same 7th year of the reign, having been a peculiar attempt, must ever require peculiar mention; it is intitled "An act for suspending the legislature of New York." One free and independent legislature hereby takes upon itself to suspend the powers of another, free and independent as itself; … Shall these governments be dissolved, their property annihilated, and their people reduced to a state of nature, at the imperious breath of a body of men, whom they never saw, in whom they never confided, and over whom they have no powers of punishment or removal, let their crimes against the American public be ever so great?

From *Our Country, A Household History*, Volume 3, by Benson J. Lossing, 1877

This, too, is another phase of the charge just considered. We have noticed the suppression of the Legislature of New York, and in several cases, the governors, after dissolving Colonial Assemblies, assumed the right to make proclamations stand in the place of statute law. Lord Dunmore assumed this right in 1775, and so did Sir James Wright of Georgia, and Lord William Campbell of South Carolina. They were driven from the country in consequence.

Historical Background

British Parliament's suspension of colonial legislatures was highlighted by the 1767 suspension of the New York Assembly. The British government took this step in retaliation for the colony's refusal to comply with the Quartering Act, which required them to provide housing and provisions for British troops. This act was seen as a blatant usurpation of colonial self-governance, deeply infringing upon the rights and autonomy of the colonies.

Beyond New York, royal governors in multiple colonies dissolved assemblies when they resisted British policies. In 1774, the Massachusetts Government Act nullified the colony's charter and placed it under direct royal control, effectively ending its legislative independence. Governors such as Lord Dunmore in Virginia, Sir James Wright in Georgia, and Lord William Campbell in South Carolina went further—issuing proclamations that substituted royal decrees for local law. These governors often fled their posts as colonial resistance intensified, demonstrating that British efforts to assert control through legislative suppression backfired.

The colonists viewed these actions as direct violations of the English constitutional tradition, which held that legislatures should not be arbitrarily dissolved or overridden. They feared that if Britain could suspend one colonial government, it could do the same to all, effectively nullifying representative rule. This Grievance solidified the belief that only complete independence could safeguard colonial self-government and prevent future legislative overreach by Britain.[83]

Modern Interpretation

This Grievance emphasizes the importance of representative government and legislative autonomy. In a modern context, this Grievance reinforces the principle that the legislative powers of elected bodies cannot be suspended or usurped by another branch of government. This principle is fundamental to the American political system and emphasizes checks and balances, separation of powers, and federalism.

Summary

Grievance 22 reflects the colonists' objection to the British Parliament's suspension of colonial legislatures and assumption of legislative powers. The US Constitution addresses these concerns by guaranteeing a republican form of government, establishing a separate and independent legislative branch, and reserving certain powers to the states.

Constitutional Safeguards for Grievance 22

The U.S. Constitution directly addresses this Grievance by establishing a clear framework for federalism and the separation of powers:

- **Article IV, Section 4:** Guarantees every state in the union a republican form of government, ensuring that the federal government can suspend no state legislature.
- **Article I:** Establishes a bicameral legislature (Congress), ensuring that all legislative powers are vested in an elected body, thus preventing the executive from unilaterally suspending or assuming legislative powers.
- **The Tenth Amendment:** Reserves to the states all powers not delegated to the United States by the Constitution, ensuring state legislative autonomy in matters not under federal jurisdiction.

Grievance 23

Abdicating Governance and Protection

*"He has abdicated Government here, by declaring us
out of his Protection and waging War against us."*

NOTE: When Britain called the colonies rebels, it stopped acting like their protector. The King refused to defend them, then sent armies and hired mercenaries to attack his own subjects. By turning against the colonies, he abandoned his duty to govern and protect.

From Jefferson's 1774 *Summary View of the Rights of British America*

When the representative body have lost the confidence of their constituents, when they have notoriously made sale of their most valuable rights, when they have assumed to themselves powers which the people never put into their hands, then indeed their continuing in office becomes dangerous to the state, and calls for an exercise of the power of dissolution.

From *Our Country, A Household History*, Volume 3, by Benson J. Lossing, 1877

In his message to Parliament early in 1775, the king declared the colonists to be in a state of open rebellion; and by sending armies hither to make war upon them, he really "abdicated government," by thus declaring them "out of his protection," He sanctioned the acts of governors in employing the Indians against his subjects, and himself bargained for the employment of German hirelings. And when, yielding to the pressure of popular will, his representatives (the royal governors) fled before the indignant people, he certainly "abdicated government."

Historical Background

The abandonment of governance and protection by the Crown was especially worrisome for the colonies. This action left the colonies without legitimate leadership and vulnerable to internal strife and external threats. It was perceived as a betrayal by the Crown and a relinquishment of its responsibilities toward the colonies.

By August 23, 1775, King George III issued a Proclamation of Rebellion, officially declaring the colonies in a state of insurrection. This proclamation justified military action against the colonies rather than seeking reconciliation. The Crown's refusal to negotiate reinforced the belief that Britain had forfeited its right to rule over the colonies.

Beyond military action, Parliament's Prohibitory Act of December 1775 served as Britain's formal declaration of economic and political warfare against the colonies. The act cut off trade with America, seized colonial ships, and encouraged suppression by force, further demonstrating Britain's withdrawal of protection. By hiring Hessian mercenaries and encouraging Native American attacks on frontier settlements, the British escalated hostilities, treating the colonists not as subjects, but as enemies.

The colonists interpreted these actions as an abdication of government—if the king declared them rebels, refused to protect them, and waged war against them, he had effectively dissolved the social contract that bound them to Britain. This Grievance provided one of the strongest justifications for independence, as it framed the revolution not as treason but as self-preservation in the absence of legitimate governance.[84]

Modern Interpretation

Today, this Grievance underscores the importance of stable governance and the federal government's duty to protect its citizens and states. It highlights the need for accountable and responsive leadership, which is fundamental to the functioning of a democratic society.

Summary

Grievance 23 reflects the colonists' rejection of King George III's abandonment of the colonies. The US Constitution and its principles of federalism and a strong executive branch address these concerns by providing a framework for continuous and effective governance and protecting states and citizens.

Constitutional Safeguards for Grievance 23

The U.S. Constitution addresses the need for consistent and effective governance, as well as the protection of the states:

- **Article II:** Establishes the presidency, ensuring continuous federal executive leadership and preventing any abdication of responsibility.
- **Article IV, Section 4:** Guarantees every state protection against invasion and domestic violence, fulfilling the protective role abdicated by the British crown.

The concept of federalism embedded in the Constitution ensures a balance of power between the states and the federal government, providing a structure where neither can unilaterally abdicate its governance responsibilities.

Grievance 24

He Plundered, Ravaged, Burnt & Destroyed

"He has plundered our seas, ravaged our coasts, burnt our towns & destroyed the lives of our people."

NOTE: When British forces attacked American towns, they didn't just target soldiers—they targeted everyone. Homes, ships, and even churches were burned, leaving families with nothing. The King's armies brought war into civilian streets, proving that Britain's goal was not peace or order, but punishment. These fires turned loyal subjects into determined patriots.

From Jefferson's July 1775 draft of *The Declaration of the Causes and Necessity of Taking Up Arms*:

"General Gage, by proclamation bearing date the 12th day of June, after reciting the grossest falsehoods and calumnies against the good people of these colonies, proceeds to declare them all, either by name or description, to be rebels & traitors… burning the town of Charlestown, attacking & killing great numbers of the people residing or assembled therein; and is now going on in an avowed course of murder & devastation, taking every occasion to destroy the lives & properties of the inhabitants."

From Benson J. Lossing's, *Our Country*

When naval commanders were clothed with the powers of custom-house officers, they seized many American vessels; and after the affair at Lexington and Bunker Hill, British ships of war "plundered our seas" wherever an American vessel could be found. They also "ravaged our coasts and burnt our towns." Charlestown, Falmouth (now Portland, in Maine), and Norfolk were burnt, and Dunmore and others "ravaged our coasts." and "destroyed the lives of our people." And at the very time when this Declaration was being read to the assembled Congress, the shattered fleet of Sir Peter Parker was sailing northward, after an attack upon Charleston, South Carolina.

Historical Background

This Grievance reveals the brutal toll of war on American civilians as British forces carried out harsh campaigns of destruction. Incidents such as the burning of Falmouth (now Portland, Maine), the bombardment of Charlestown, Massachusetts, and the devastation of Norfolk, Virginia, showed that the Crown's strategy had turned from discipline to punishment. These assaults were not just military actions—they were acts of retribution meant to break the spirit of rebellion. Homes, businesses, and whole communities were left in ashes, deepening colonial resolve for independence.

Looking at the map, you will notice these attacks occurred well before the signing of *The Declaration of Independence*. British forces seized ships, destroyed harbors, and burned entire settlements—some during the dead of winter, or just before—sending a clear message that colonial resistance would be met with widespread destruction. In Virginia, Lord Dunmore's raids devastated coastal plantations and towns, while in the Carolinas and Georgia, British forces targeted key ports and supply routes. These actions galvanized support for independence, as colonists recognized that Britain was not merely seeking to suppress a rebellion but was waging war on civilians. The scale and intensity of these attacks left an indelible mark on the revolutionary movement, reinforcing the urgent need for self-defense and independence.[85]

Modern Interpretation

Civilian control over the military—and strict limits on its use—remains a cornerstone of American government. This principle ensures that armed power always serves lawful authority, not the other way around. It reminds us that military strength must be guided by clear rules, respect for civilian life, and the protection of property.

Summary

Grievance 24 reflects deep colonial resentment against the brutal tactics used by the British military. The Constitution's provisions for civilian control of the military, the Third and Fourth Amendments, and the decentralized nature of military power in the US serve as direct responses to these concerns.

Additional Considerations

The actions of Virginia's Royal Governor, Lord Dunmore, and other British officials during this period, such as the seizure of merchant vessels, impressment of sailors, and assaults on colonial towns, underscore the need for legal and ethical guidelines in military conduct. These events influenced the founders' decision to ensure strong civilian oversight of the military and the protection of individual rights in the Constitution and the Bill of Rights.

Constitutional Safeguards for Grievance 24

The U.S. Constitution addresses the need for the protection of citizens and their property:

- **The Third Amendment:** Addresses the issue of quartering soldiers, ensuring that in peacetime, no soldier can be housed in any private residence without the owner's consent. This amendment reflects the colonies' experiences of military intrusion into civilian life.
- **Fourth Amendment:** Protects citizens from unreasonable searches and seizures, safeguarding personal property and privacy against arbitrary government actions.

Article I, Section 8: Grants Congress the power to declare war, raise and support armies, and provide for a navy. This decentralizes military power, placing it under civilian control and ensuring that military actions are accountable to elected representatives.

Grievance 25

Foreign Mercenaries Terrorize Our People

"He is at this time transporting large armies of foreign mercenaries to complete the works of death, desolation & tyranny, already begun with circumstances of cruelty & perfidy unworthy the head of a civilized nation."

NOTE: When Britain ran out of loyal soldiers, it hired strangers to fight its own people. Thousands of German troops were sent to crush the colonists' rebellion. These men—called Hessians—were paid to kill, not to protect. To Americans, this showed that the King's war had lost all honor. He was now waging war against his own children with the swords of foreigners.

From Jefferson's 1774 *Summary View of the Rights of British America*

When in the course of the late war it became expedient that a body of Hanoverian troops should be brought over for the defense of Great Britain, his majesty's grandfather, our late sovereign, did not pretend to introduce them under any authority he possessed. Such a measure would have given just alarm to his subjects in Great Britain, whose liberties would not be safe if armed men of another country, and of another spirit, might be brought into the realm at any time without the consent of their legislature.

From *Our Country, A Household History*, Volume 3, by Benson J. Lossing, 1877

This charge refers to the infamous employment of German troops, known here as Hessians.* Their presence in the colonies was regarded as the final outrage—a refinement of cruelty in which a Christian king made war upon his own people with the swords of strangers.

* One of the committee members, most likely Benjamin Franklin, made an entry on Jefferson's Rough Draft, listing Scottish soldiers as being foreign mercenaries

Historical Background

This grievance marks one of Jefferson's fiercest condemnations of British policy: the employment of foreign soldiers to subdue the King's own subjects.

When King George III turned to German auxiliaries—chiefly Hessians from Hesse-Cassel and Brunswick—he crossed a moral boundary that inflamed colonial outrage. To the Americans, the hiring of foreign mercenaries was more than a military escalation; it was a betrayal of kinship and a confession of tyranny. It revealed a monarch willing to purchase blood rather than reconcile with his own people.

In one of Jefferson's early drafts, he wrote that the King had brought over "foreign mercenaries and Scots," an expression of his resentment toward the Highland regiments Britain often used to enforce colonial order. Several delegates, however, objected—fearing the phrase might insult loyal Scots in America or alienate allies abroad. The word was struck, leaving "foreign mercenaries" to stand alone. The edit demonstrates Jefferson's discipline: passion yielding to prudence, ensuring the moral indictment remained universal rather than ethnic.

The deployment of roughly 30,000 German troops hardened American resistance. These soldiers fought in some of the war's bloodiest engagements—Trenton, Princeton, Brandywine—earning reputations for ferocity and plunder. Reports of Hessian brutality circulated widely in the colonies, serving as powerful propaganda for the patriot cause. As Benson Lossing later wrote, it was "infamy bought at the price of honor," the act of a king who could no longer command loyalty and therefore purchased terror.[86]

Modern Interpretation

Jefferson's grievance endures as a timeless warning: that rulers who outsource justice for force, or domestic authority for foreign arms, forfeit the moral legitimacy of their cause. The hiring of mercenaries symbolized the collapse of Britain's own covenant between king and people.

Today, as nations increasingly rely on private military contractors, the same ethical questions arise—about loyalty, accountability, and the price of power when the sword is wielded without conscience or consent.

Summary

Grievance 25 captures the moment when the struggle for independence became irreversible. When George III sent foreign armies against the colonies, he ceased to be a father to his people and became a buyer of blood. Jefferson's words transformed that act into a moral verdict: that liberty cannot be suppressed by hirelings, nor restored by fear.

Constitutional Safeguards for Grievance 25

- **Article I, Section 8**—Grants Congress the sole power to raise and support armies, ensuring that no executive authority may employ foreign forces without legislative consent.
- **The Third Amendment:** Prohibits the quartering of soldiers in private homes without consent, a lasting safeguard of personal sovereignty born from the abuses of hired troops.
- **The Militia Clauses (Article I, Section 8, Clauses 15–16):** Empower the people's representatives, not the crown, to call forth and govern militias—affirming that the defense of the Republic shall never rest in foreign hands.

The Logan Act (1799): Later enshrined the principle that foreign powers must not manipulate American policy, extending Jefferson's warning into the age of diplomacy.

Grievance 26
Taken Captive to Bear Arms Against Fellow Citizens

"He has constrained our fellow Citizens taken Captive on the high Seas to bear Arms against their Country, to become the executioners of their friends and Brethren, or to fall themselves by their Hands."

NOTE: When British ships captured American sailors, many were forced into the Royal Navy against their will. These men—called "impressed" sailors—were beaten, chained, and made to fight against their own friends. Some were killed in battle; others took their own lives rather than serve their captors. To Jefferson, this was one of the most shocking crimes of all: enslaving men's bodies and their consciences.

Jefferson's Perspective

Forced impressment was not a new or theoretical abuse for Jefferson. This very issue had ignited colonial outrage decades earlier. In November 1747, press-gangs in Boston under Commodore Charles Knowles seized nearly fifty men from docks and vessels, sparking a three-day uprising against forced service in the British navy. Men continued to be pressed into British crews in 1775 and '76—chained, abused, and compelled to fight against their own countrymen. This led Jefferson to accuse the Crown of forcing "our fellow Citizens… to become the executioners of their friends and Brethren."[87]

From *Our Country, A Household History*, Volume 3, by Benson J. Lossing, 1877

An act of Parliament passed toward the close of December, 1775, authorized the capture of all American vessels, and also directed the treatment of the crews of armed vessels to be as slaves and not as prisoners of war. They were to be enrolled for "the service of his majesty," and were thus compelled to fight for the crown, even against their own friends and countrymen. This act was loudly condemned on the floor of Parliament as unworthy of a Christian people, and "a refinement of cruelty unknown among savage nations."

Historical Background:

This grievance strikes at the heart of moral outrage: the forced impressment of American sailors into the service of their oppressor.

For years before the Revolution, British press gangs had seized colonial sailors, merchants, and fishermen—compelling them to serve aboard Royal Navy ships without consent. Many were captured while in port or at sea, torn from their families, and forced to serve under harsh conditions for the very empire they opposed.

By the 1770s, these acts had become a symbol of British contempt for colonial rights. Jefferson, echoing the cry of the seaports, condemned this barbaric practice as the act of a nation that had abandoned all sense of justice.

In June 1776, as reports reached Philadelphia describing the imprisonment and harsh treatment of American sailors, Jefferson transformed outrage into indictment. His words expose a monarchy that not only enslaved men's bodies but sought to enslave their consciences—commanding them to spill the blood of their own brethren or perish at their hands.

Modern Interpretation

This grievance remains hauntingly relevant. The act of coercing individuals to fight against their homeland or conscience violates every principle of moral law and human dignity.

In modern terms, it speaks to the ethical limits of obedience and the sanctity of personal conscience in the face of unjust command. The Founders understood that freedom of conscience was inseparable from freedom of action—and that to force a man to kill for a cause he rejects is to enslave his soul.

In this light, Jefferson's words transcend the eighteenth century. They remind every generation that the test of a nation's justice lies not in its power to command, but in its restraint—in its refusal to demand that citizens commit wrong for reasons of state.

Summary

Grievance 26 transforms the moral agony of captivity into a universal truth: liberty cannot coexist with force.

Jefferson's indictment stands as both historical record and ethical warning—that governments which compel obedience at the expense of conscience destroy the very foundation of lawful rule.

By exposing this cruelty, Jefferson gave voice to the voiceless—the sailors torn from their ships, their families, and home. His words elevate their suffering into testimony, declaring before all nations that true freedom cannot be seized by force, nor maintained by fear.

Constitutional Safeguards for Grievance 26

- **Article I, Section 8:** Grants Congress exclusive authority to define and punish piracy and felonies on the high seas. This ensures that the law of nations—not the whim of monarchs—governs maritime justice and protects individuals from coerced service.

- **The Eighth Amendment:** Prohibits "cruel and unusual punishments," standing as a constitutional rebuke to the brutal coercion and dehumanization condemned in this grievance.

- **The Thirteenth Amendment:** Abolishes involuntary servitude in all forms, enshrining in law the principle that no citizen can be compelled to labor or fight against conscience under threat or force.

The Uniform Code of Military Justice (Article 92): In the modern era, affirms that soldiers and sailors are bound by lawful orders only—a living reflection of Jefferson's doctrine that obedience to dark and unjust causes ends in the light of conscience.

Grievance 27

Inciting Insurrections & Unleashing Merciless Forces

"He has excited domestic insurrections amongst us, and has endeavored to bring on the inhabitants of our frontiers, the merciless Indian Savages whose known rule of warfare, is an undistinguished destruction of all ages, sexes, and conditions."

NOTE: When the British king could no longer win by battle, he tried to turn Americans against each other. He urged uprisings among the enslaved and invited Native nations to attack frontier towns. These acts shocked the colonies. Jefferson saw them not as strategy but as desperation—proof that Britain had lost its conscience and was willing to use fear and bloodshed to hold power.

From Jefferson's Preamble to the Virginia Constitution (Written in Philadelphia just a week or so before):

"by prompting our negroes to rise in arms among us; those very negroes whom he hath from time to time by an inhuman use of his negative he hath refused permission to exclude by law; by endeavouring to bring on the inhabitants of our Frontiers the merciless Indian savages, whose known rule of Warfare is an undistinguished Destruction of all Ages, Sexes, and Conditions of Existance;"

From *Our Country, A Household History*, Volume 3, by Benson J. Lossing, 1877

This was done in several instances, [Royal Governor of Virginia] Dunmore, was charged with a design to employ the Indians against the Virginians as early as 1774; and while ravaging the Virginia coast in 1775 and 1776, he endeavored to excite the slaves against their masters. He was also concerned with Governor Gage* and others, under instructions from the British ministry, in exciting the Shawnoese, and other savages of the Ohio country, against the white people. Emissaries were also sent among the Cherokees and Creeks for the same purpose; and all of the tribes of the Six Nations, except the Oneidas, were found in arms with the British when war began. Thus excited, dreadful massacres occurred on the borders of the several colonies.

Historical Background

This final grievance brings Jefferson's indictment of George III to its darkest moral ground: the charge that he had turned subjects and allies into weapons.

By encouraging enslaved Africans to revolt and Native nations to attack frontier settlements, the King crossed the last boundary of decency in war. It was no longer policy—it was punishment.

Jefferson's outrage reflects more than fear of violence; it is a philosophical condemnation of rulers who corrupt justice itself by turning humanity into an instrument of control. To provoke insurrection within a people's own borders—to unleash "merciless" warfare on civilians—was, in his view, the ultimate confession of tyranny.

In context, Jefferson was also responding to concrete events. Lord Dunmore's 1775 proclamation in Virginia promised freedom to enslaved people who took up arms for the Crown. At the same time, British agents sought to inflame conflict along the frontier, enlisting tribes long manipulated by imperial trade. The resulting terror united even hesitant colonies behind independence. For Jefferson, this grievance was not racial invective but moral indictment: that the British ministry had degraded all peoples—enslaved, Indigenous, and colonial—by using them as pawns in its effort to preserve power.

Modern Interpretation

This grievance resonates wherever governments sow division or incite violence to maintain control. Jefferson's words are a warning that power which survives by fear will perish by it. A free republic cannot sanction policies that pit one group of citizens against another, nor manipulate outside forces to destabilize its own people.

Today, it speaks to the moral responsibility of leadership—to protect life, not exploit it; to heal divisions rather than weaponize them. The Founders' experience reminds us that unity is not mere agreement but shared accountability under just laws. The health of a republic depends on whether it governs through persuasion or coercion.

Jefferson's condemnation of "merciless" tactics thus stands as a timeless rebuke of cruelty in all forms—political, military, or ideological—and a call to resist any power that would sacrifice human dignity for political gain.

Summary

Grievance 27 exposes the moral nadir of monarchy: a ruler willing to burn his own dominion to maintain dominion. The colonies, once petitioners for justice, had now become targets of vengeance.

Jefferson's accusation transformed outrage into moral clarity—that liberty cannot coexist with rulers who unleash chaos upon their own subjects.

This final grievance completes the indictment of George III not merely as a failed sovereign, but as a destroyer of order itself. Having armed fear against freedom, he made independence not rebellion, but survival.

Constitutional Safeguards

- **The Preamble:** Commits the Republic to "insure domestic Tranquility," ensuring that no government may again turn Americans against one another for political advantage.
- **Article I, Section 8:** Grants Congress the authority to regulate commerce and relations with Native nations, ensuring peace and mutual respect where monarchs once sowed conflict.
- **Article II, Section 2:** Vests the power to make treaties in the people's representatives, binding the use of diplomacy and war to the consent of the governed.
- **The Fourteenth Amendment:** Ensures equal protection under the law, repudiating forever the divisions of race, birth, or allegiance that tyranny once exploited.

Jefferson's Lost Clause
The Slavery Clause

NOTE: In his initial draft of *The Declaration of Independence*, Jefferson blamed Britain's King George III for his role in perpetuating and profiting on the transatlantic slave trade—which he described, in so many words, as a crime against humanity.

JEFFERSON'S GRIEVANCE DELETED BY CONGRESS:

"He has waged cruel war against human nature itself, violating its most sacred rights of life & liberty in the persons of a distant people who never offended him, captivating & carrying them into slavery in another hemisphere, or to incur miserable death in their transportation thither. this piratical warfare, the opprobrium of infidel powers, is the warfare of the Christian king of Great Britain. **determined to keep open a market where MEN should be bought & sold**, he has prostituted his negative for suppressing every legislative attempt to prohibit or to restrain this execrable commerce: and that this assemblage of horrors might want no fact of distinguished die, he is now exciting those very people to rise in arms among us, and to purchase that liberty of which he has deprived them, & murdering the people upon whom he also obtruded them; thus paying off former crimes committed against the liberties of one people, with crimes which he urges them to commit against the lives of another."

From Jefferson's 1774 *Summary View of the Rights of British America*

The abolition of domestic slavery is the great object of desire in those colonies, where it was unhappily introduced in their infant state. But previous to the enfranchisement of the slaves we have, it is necessary to exclude all further importations from Africa; yet our repeated attempts to affect this by prohibitions, and by imposing duties which might amount to a prohibition, have been hitherto defeated by his majesty's negative: Thus, preferring the immediate advantages of a few African corsairs to the lasting interests of the American states, and to the rights of human nature, deeply wounded by this infamous practice. Nay, the single interposition of an interested individual against a law was scarcely ever known to fail of success, though in the opposite scale were placed the interests of a whole country. That this is so shameful an abuse of a power trusted with his majesty for other purposes, as if not reformed, would call for some legal restrictions.

Analysis of the Lost Clause

Including the Slavery Clause in the Declaration would have been a brave stand against the slave trade. But slavery was part of the Southern way of life, so ending it would not have been easy. If it had stayed in, America might have solved the issues of slavery much sooner.

So what did Jefferson mean when he wrote… "**We hold these truths to be self-evident, that all men are created equal**, that they are endowed by their Creator with certain unalienable Rights, that among these are Life, Liberty and the pursuit of Happiness," whom did he mean?

Many people today think he meant only White men, because the Declaration doesn't mention slaves, women, or Native Americans. But Jefferson's first draft did include a section condemning slavery. That part was taken out when South Carolina and Georgia refused to sign. **Jefferson's lost words clearly called enslaved people "MEN," written big and bold!**[88]

In 1783 Jefferson Tried Again

Jefferson's Draft To Revise Virginia's Constitution, May–June 1783

After serving as governor under Virginia's 1776 Constitution, Jefferson believed changes were needed and drafted an updated version. One of his most radical proposals dealt with slavery:

> …*"nor to permit the introduction of any more slaves to reside in this state, or the continuance of slavery beyond the generation which shall be living on the 31st. day of December 1800; all persons born after that day being hereby declared free."*[89]

In his initial draft of the Declaration of Independence, Jefferson blamed Britain's King George III for his role in creating and perpetuating the Transatlantic Slave Trade — which he describes, in so many words as essentially, a crime against humanity

Jefferson's Lost Words Against Slavery

Jefferson's first draft of the Declaration spoke out boldly against slavery. He called it a cruel war against human nature itself. If Congress had kept his words, it would have been the longest Grievance in the Declaration—a clear stand that slavery was wrong. But slavery was deeply rooted in the Southern economy, and some colonies refused to sign if this section stayed in. To keep unity, Congress removed it.

When Jefferson wrote that "all men are created equal," he meant everyone—men, women, and children of every race and background. In the rough draft, his "Slavery Clause" even used the word MEN in large letters to show that enslaved people were included. His lost words prove that the promise of equality was meant for all humanity.

A Nation Divided Over Conscience

Removing the Slavery Clause exposed the painful divide among the colonies. Some wanted to end slavery; others feared losing wealth and power if it disappeared. Many hoped the issue would fade on its own, but Jefferson knew it couldn't. How could a nation built on "life, liberty, and the pursuit of happiness" allow people to be bought and sold?

Even though Jefferson himself owned slaves, his writings show a man torn between his world and his conscience. He believed slavery was wrong and that the new nation's freedom would be incomplete until every person could share in it.

Jefferson's Fight Didn't End Here

Jefferson never gave up on trying to stop the slave trade. As governor of Virginia, he worked to limit the importation of enslaved people. On December 2, 1806, he encouraged Congress to ban America's participation in the trade entirely, using much of the same language he had written in his deleted clause from 1776. Congress did so, passing the legislation on March 2, 1807—three weeks before England passed their first such legislation.

He Tried Again to End Slavery

In later years, Jefferson pushed to end slavery in new territories and proposed that no child born after 1800 should remain enslaved. The plan failed by just one vote in Congress, but it showed that Jefferson was still fighting for the freedom he had declared was every person's natural right.

Proof of the King's Role

Jefferson and other leaders accused Britain's King George III of blocking every attempt to limit the slave trade. British merchants made huge profits from selling enslaved Africans, and the King used his power to protect that system. Colonial leaders even passed resolutions urging an end to the trade, but the King vetoed them all—choosing greed over justice:

> "Resolved that it is the Opinion of this Meeting, that during our present Difficulties and Distress, no Slaves ought to be imported into any of the British Colonies on this Continent, and We take this Opportunity of declaring our most earnest Wishes to see an entire Stop for ever put to such a wicked cruel and unnatural Trade."[90]

The King's Own Actions Are Further Exposed

Evidence later showed that British officials encouraged uprisings among enslaved people and promised them freedom if they fought for the Crown. In Virginia, Royal Governor Lord Dunmore issued a "Proclamation of Emancipation," calling the enslaved to rise against their American masters. Jefferson saw this not as mercy, but as proof that Britain would use human lives as weapons to hold power:

> This is further illustrated by events in Virginia in the fall of 1775. The Royal Governor, Lord Dunmore, who had retreated to a British frigate off the Virginia coast, issued a Proclamation of Emancipation on Nov. 7, 1775 in order to call the enslaved to arms against their masters. The governor's proclamation and reaction to it were published in Dixon & Hunter's Gazette on November 25, 1775, page three.

The King *"Prostituted His Negative"*

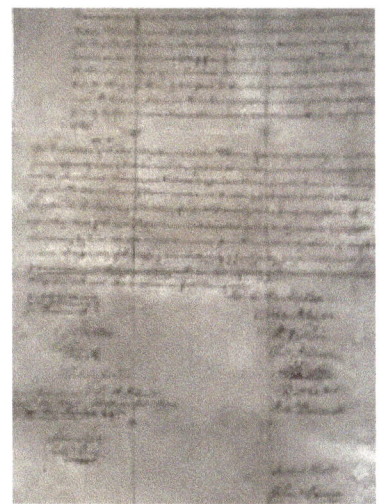

Patrick Michael McFadden of Bucks County, Pennsylvania, is a historical document collector and author of *An American Tale of Freedom's Promise*. Recently, he acquired a rare document revealing how King George III bound the right to collect duties on liquor and enslaved people in Virginia for £100,000 (equivalent to approximately $25 million today). This transaction paints the king as a profiteer, perhaps even "prostituting himself," as Thomas Jefferson suggested in the slavery clause of his rough draft of *The Declaration of Independence*. This performance bond provides direct evidence of the king's personal involvement in the slave trade.

Notably, the document bears the signature of George Wythe—Jefferson's close friend and legal mentor from 1762–67.[91] Wythe witnessed the bond on behalf of the lieutenant governor. A portion of the bond reads:

> Know all men by these Presents that we, Robert Carter Nicholas, John Blair, William Nelson, Thomas Nelson, … Esquires are held & firmly bound to our Sovereign Lord King George the third in the Sum of one hundred thousand pounds to be paid to our said Lord the King, his heirs & successors … Sealed with our Seals and dated this Tenth–day of April–1767.…Robert Carter Nicholas is appointed treasurer of the Revenues arriving from the Duties on Liquors & Slaves imported into this Colony & all other publich Monies payable into the Treasury.

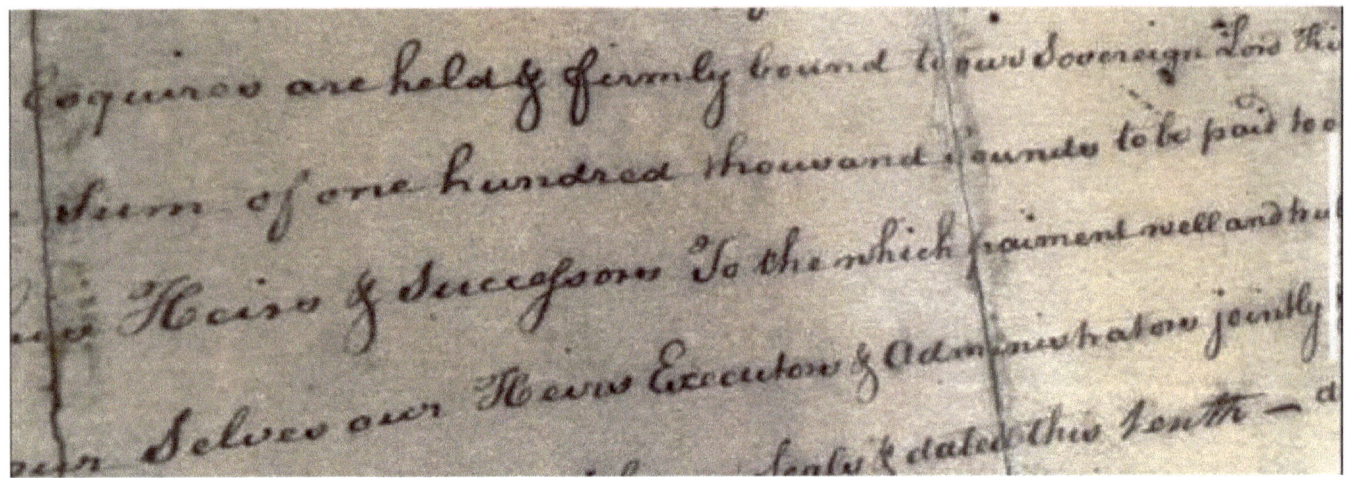

This passage shows that Robert Carter Nicholas and a group of prominent Virginians—including future signers of *The Declaration of Independence*—agreed to be bound to pay £100,000 to the king and his heirs in exchange for the right to collect duties on imported liquor and enslaved people. Such arrangements likely influenced Jefferson's later critique of George III in the Slavery Clause, where he condemned the king for "prostituting his negative" to block colonial efforts to restrict the "execrable commerce" of slavery.

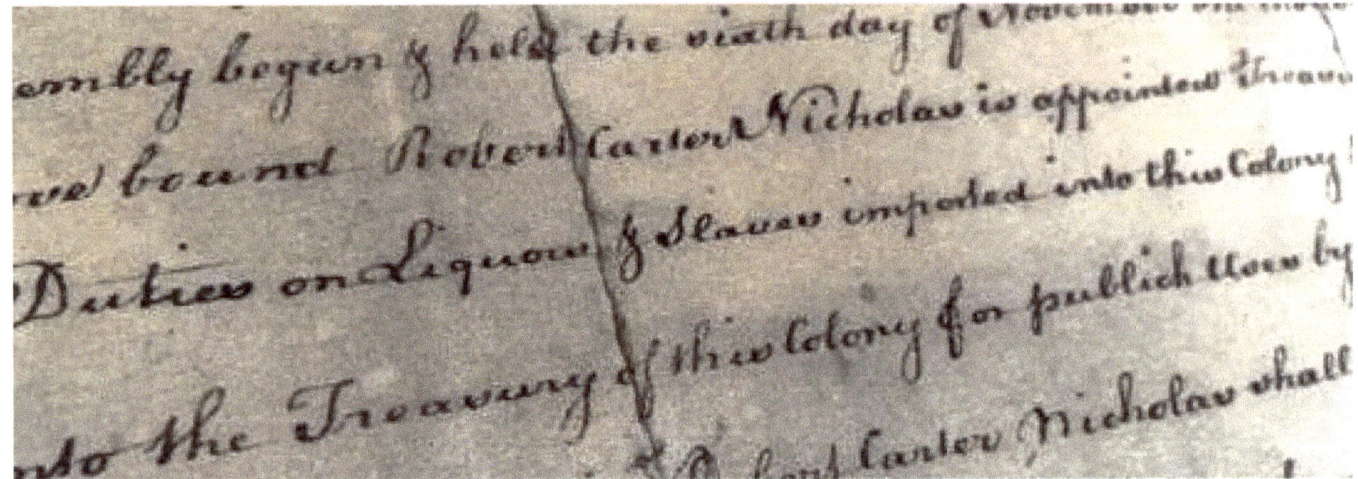

Historical Background
The King Forced Slavery on the Colonies and Blocked Efforts to Stop It
Imagine if a principal forced your school to keep an unfair rule even though the students and teachers wanted to change it, just because certain kids were making money from it. That wouldn't be right, would it?

> That's akin to what happened to the American colonists with slavery. Many of them wanted to stop bringing enslaved people from Africa into the colonies. They tried passing laws to end the slave trade, but King George III blocked every single attempt because he and British merchants were making money from it. Worse, he made sure there was always a market where people could be bought and sold like objects. Thomas Jefferson called this "piratical warfare"—meaning the King was treating human beings like stolen goods.

Jefferson originally included a strong statement against slavery in *The Declaration of Independence*, calling it an "assemblage of horrors" and blaming King George III for keeping the cruel practice alive. But this passage—the longest Grievance in his original draft—was removed because South Carolina and Georgia refused to support independence unless it was taken out.

How Did This Shape America?

The removal of Jefferson's Slavery Clause was one of the biggest compromises of the American Revolution. If it had stayed in *The Declaration of Independence*, slavery might have ended much sooner. Instead, the fight against slavery would take almost 90 more years—and it would take a Civil War to finally abolish it.

Although his words were cut from the Declaration, Jefferson didn't stop fighting against slavery. As governor of Virginia, he spearheaded efforts to ban the importation of enslaved people—one of the first laws of its kind. Later, as president, he convinced Congress to pass a law banning U.S. participation in the transatlantic slave trade in 1807, using some of the same words from his original draft of the Declaration.

Ending the slave trade was not the same as ending slavery itself—and the numbers proved it. According to the 1790 census, 694,207 people remained in bondage. That number would grow to 4 million by 1860. While the Constitution laid a foundation for justice, African Americans and Native American tribes endured stolen land, denied rights, and generations of oppression. This history left deep scars on America and serves as a reminder that achieving justice requires action—not just words.

> **Ben Franklin,** who had previously owned house slaves, began to champion the cause of abolition. His 1790 petition to the House of Representatives and Senate called for decisive action to abolish slavery and the transatlantic slave trade. The petition urged Congress to "devise means for removing this inconsistency from the character of the American people" and **to "promote mercy and justice toward this distressed race."**
>
> Two decades earlier, writing under the pseudonym *"An American,"* Franklin had already expressed his criticism of British policy in his 1770 article, *"A Conversation Between an Englishman, a Scotchman, and an American."* In it, the American observes, **"Several laws heretofore made in our Colonies to discourage the importation of slaves, by laying a heavy duty… have been disapproved and repealed by your Government."**[92]

Summary

"The Rough Draft of *The Declaration of Independence* included a powerful statement against slavery, but it was removed to keep all 13 colonies united to fight against Britain. This decision delayed justice, but it did not end the fight. Over time, Americans fought—and still fight—to fulfill the promise that "all men are created equal."

Modern Interpretation

Jefferson's lost words remind us that freedom and equality don't always come easily. It takes courage to stand up for what is right, even when others try to silence the truth. By learning from history, we can continue striving for a future where liberty and justice are a reality for everyone.

Constitutional Safeguards

- **The 13th Amendment (1865)**: Abolished slavery and involuntary servitude in the United States.
- **The 14th Amendment (1868):** Granted citizenship to all persons born or naturalized in the United States and guaranteed equal protection under the law. It also clarified apportionment by allowing Congress to exclude those engaged in rebellion or other crimes.

The 15th Amendment (1870): Prohibited the denial of the right to vote on account of race, color, or previous condition of servitude.

Indictment

The King is Disqualified by His Tyranny

"In every stage of these Oppressions We have Petitioned for Redress in the most humble terms: Our repeated Petitions have been answered only by repeated injury. A Prince whose character is thus marked by every act which may define a Tyrant, is unfit to be the ruler of a free people."

NOTE: After listing all the wrongs committed by the King, Jefferson ended the Declaration with a powerful verdict. The colonies had begged for peace and fairness, but every request was ignored. In the end, they realized that a ruler who refuses to listen to his people cannot be trusted to lead them. This final part of the Declaration explains why the King had lost his right to rule—and why America had no choice but to stand as a free nation.

From Jefferson's *Declaration of the Causes and Necessity of Taking Up Arms* (1775)

"We have supplicated our king at various times in terms almost disgraceful to freedom; we have reasoned, we have remonstrated with parliament in the most mild & decent language; we have even proceeded to break off our commercial intercourse with them altogether…as the last peaceable admonition that our attachment to no nation on earth should supplant our attachment to liberty: and here we had well hoped was the ultimate step of the controversy. but subsequent events have shewn how vain was even this last remain of confidence in the moderation of the British ministry."

Our Country: A Household History For All Readers. Volume 1, Lossing, 1878

Thus closed that immortal instrument—an arraignment of a monarch unparalleled in the world's history. With calm logic and moral strength the representatives of the people declared that the king had forfeited every claim to their allegiance. He was no longer their sovereign; he was a tyrant, and, as such, unfit to be the ruler of a free people. It was not rebellion but revolution—an act of justice long delayed.[93]

Historical Background

This grievance sits at the heart of the Declaration's indictment against monarchy. Jefferson's charge was not impulsive rebellion—it was a verdict rendered after years of restraint. From petitions and remonstrances to trade boycotts and humble appeals, the colonies had pursued every lawful remedy within the framework of the British constitution. Each attempt was met not with reconciliation but reproach.

By 1776, the colonies were not merely contending with poor governance but with the moral collapse of kingship itself. George III had transformed a covenant of mutual duty into one of domination. Jefferson's words—"unfit to be the ruler of a free people"—strike as much at the idea of divine right as at the person of the king. He was asserting that rulers hold legitimacy only by consent, that power divorced from justice forfeits its claim to obedience. This was a radical statement of civic theology: sovereignty resides not in the crown, but in the will of the people.

The colonists thus stood at the threshold between subjects and citizens. To declare their king unfit was to declare themselves fit to rule—morally, intellectually, and politically. It was a transformation not only of government, but of identity.

Modern Interpretation

Modern democracies, too, must guard against the slow erosion of self-rule. A people who cease to question authority soon become the subjects of it. The Founders understood that liberty's survival depends upon an active and informed citizenry, and upon institutions willing to restrain themselves. Jefferson's words remind us that tyranny does not begin with cruelty—it begins with complacency.

In this light, the Declaration is not an artifact of independence, but a manual of vigilance. It teaches that governments exist only by the ongoing consent of a free and discerning people, and that this consent must never be taken for granted.

Summary

This grievance embodies the moral verdict of a people who had exhausted every peaceful path and found their appeals answered with injury. When all lawful avenues failed, they concluded that loyalty to liberty outweighed loyalty to a king. Jefferson's words sealed that conclusion with logic and dignity: the British crown had abdicated its right to rule, and the colonies had inherited the right to govern themselves.

It was not a rebellion born of passion but a revolution born of principle. The Declaration's closing indictment declared to the world that tyranny, wherever it appears, is incompatible with freedom—and that to depose it is not treason, but justice.

Constitutional Safeguards

- **First Amendment:** Ensures the right of every citizen to speak, assemble, publish, and worship freely—so that truth may challenge power, as Jefferson's pen once challenged the throne.
- **Fifth Amendment:** Protects individuals from unjust accusation and punishment, reaffirming that no authority may deprive a person of liberty without due process.
- **Ninth Amendment:** Guards the unenumerated rights of the people, affirming that freedom is not a gift of government but a condition of humanity itself.

Tenth Amendment: Restrains federal power, reserving undelegated authority to the states and the people—a living safeguard against the consolidation of tyranny Jefferson denounced.

Enemies in War, in Peace Friends

"Nor have we been wanting in attentions to our British brethren. **We have warned them**, from time to time, of attempts by their legislature to extend an unwarrantable jurisdiction over us. We have reminded them of the circumstances of our emigration and settlement here. We have appealed to their native justice and magnanimity, and we have conjured them by the ties of our common kindred to disavow these usurpations, which would inevitably interrupt our connections and correspondence. **They, too, have been deaf to the voice of justice** and of consanguinity. We must, therefore, acquiesce in the necessity, which denounces our separation, and **hold them, as we hold the rest of mankind, enemies in war, in peace friends**."

NOTE: After listing every wrong done by the King, Jefferson ended the Declaration with compassion, not hatred. The colonists had pleaded for peace again and again, but their "British brethren" refused to listen. Jefferson's closing words were not meant to punish but to show that America would fight only when forced—and would still seek friendship when peace returned.

From Jefferson's *Declaration of the Causes and Necessity of Taking Up Arms* (1775)

"But that this declaration may not disquiet the minds of our Friends & fellow subjects in any part of the empire, we do further assure them that we mean not in any wise to affect that union with them in which we have so long & so happily lived, and which we wish so much to see again restored."

From Jefferson's 1774 *Summary View of the Rights of British America*

We shall endeavor to cultivate peace and friendship with all mankind. Let those flatter who fear: it is not an American art. To give up principles, to compromise with wrong, is not in our creed.

Historical Background

This passage represents the final appeal to kinship before the irrevocable step of separation. Jefferson's words are not merely political—they are deeply personal. The colonists did not see themselves as rebels, but as estranged family pleading for reconciliation. Their "British brethren" were bound to them by blood, law, and faith. The colonists had warned Parliament and petitioned the king, but they had also reached out to the British people themselves, appealing to their sense of justice, fairness, and shared history.

Yet these pleas met silence. The British public, distracted or indifferent, remained unmoved by the colonists' appeals to natural justice and common heritage. This failure of empathy—what Jefferson called **being "deaf to the voice of justice and of consanguinity"** *(meaning "shared blood or common ancestry")* —was among the deepest wounds. It forced Americans to acknowledge that reconciliation was no longer possible without the loss of liberty.

The phrase **"Enemies in War, in Peace Friends"** is therefore not an act of defiance but of moral restraint. Jefferson was declaring that the colonists would defend themselves with honor, not hatred—that they would fight for freedom, but not for vengeance. It is, in essence, a declaration of war governed by conscience.

Modern Interpretation

Jefferson's message remains a moral compass for nations and individuals alike: conflict must never extinguish the pursuit of peace. The colonists' decision to separate from Britain was driven not by hatred, but by necessity—by the conviction that liberty cannot survive under submission. Even in declaring war, Jefferson left the door open for reconciliation.

This same spirit defines the best of American diplomacy. The willingness to forgive, to seek friendship after struggle, and to restore peace without surrendering principle reflects the moral architecture of the Republic itself. Jefferson's closing phrase reminds us that strength and mercy are not opposites—they are twin pillars of justice.

In an age of division, his words call America back to the higher standard of its founding: to resist tyranny without hatred, and to seek peace without weakness.

Summary

This grievance completes the emotional journey of the Declaration. The colonists had pleaded as subjects, reasoned as statesmen, and appealed as brethren. Only when every bond had been severed did they accept separation—not as vengeance, but as duty. Jefferson's closing assurance, that they would hold the British as "enemies in war, in peace friends," transformed revolution into redemption.

It was both farewell and benediction—a message to the world that liberty, though won through war, would always seek friendship fostered by peace.

Constitutional Safeguards

- **First Amendment:** Protects the right to speak, publish, and assemble peaceably, ensuring that grievances may be heard and answered without resort to rebellion.
- **Treaty Clause (Article II, Section 2):** Empowers the President, with the Senate, to make peace and alliances, carrying forward the Declaration's spirit of reconciliation among nations.

Foreign Relations Powers: Entrusts Congress and the Executive to prevent unnecessary wars and to secure peace through justice and diplomacy, reaffirming Jefferson's vision of "peace and friendship with all mankind."

They Pledged Their Lives

"We, therefore, the Representatives of the United States of America, in General Congress assembled, appealing to the Supreme Judge of the world for the rectitude of our intentions, do, in the name, and by the authority of the good people of these Colonies, solemnly publish and declare, that these United Colonies are, and of right ought to be, free and independent States; that they are absolved from all allegiance to the British crown, and that all political connection between them and the State of Great Britain is, and ought to be, totally dissolved; and that as free and independent States, they have full power to levy war, conclude peace, contract alliances, establish commerce, and to do all other acts and things which independent States may of right do. And for the support of this declaration, **with a firm reliance on the protection of Divine Providence, we mutually pledge to each other our lives, our fortunes, and our sacred honour.**"

NOTE: Jefferson's final words gave the Declaration its soul. After listing every wrong, the colonies ended not with anger but with unity and faith. These closing lines turned protest into promise. The signers knew they were risking their homes, their families, and their lives—but they believed freedom was worth any cost. In pledging their "lives, fortunes, and sacred honor," they sealed the birth of a nation with courage and trust in God.

From Jefferson's *Declaration of the Causes and Necessity of Taking Up Arms* (1775)

We do then most solemnly, before god and the world declare, that, regardless of every consequence, at the risk of every distress, the arms we have been compelled to assume we will use with perseverance, exerting to the utmost energies all those powers which our creator hath given us, to preserve that liberty which he committed to us in sacred deposit, & to protect from every hostile hand our lives & our properties.

Historical Background

Jefferson's final paragraph unites divine appeal, legal severance, and human sacrifice. By 1776, petitions had failed, appeals had been scorned, and punishment had been promised. The colonies no longer stood as subjects seeking redress—they stood as a people asserting sovereignty. The King had branded them rebels; Jefferson transformed that insult into moral justification.

The signers knew the cost. To affix one's name to the Declaration was to sign one's death warrant should the cause fail. Treason carried the penalty of hanging, confiscation, and disgrace to one's family. Yet they pledged not just property or position, but **"our lives, our fortunes, and our sacred honor."** In that pledge, America was born—not by conquest, but by covenant.

It was the culmination of a moral evolution that began with Jefferson's 1775 appeal to "the Creator" and matured into a firm **"reliance on the protection of Divine Providence."** Where earlier writings sought justification, this final invocation expressed faith. The Founders were not merely appealing to heaven—they were entrusting the fate of liberty to it.

Modern Interpretation

This closing passage speaks across centuries. It is not a call to war, but to accountability before God and conscience. The Founders' courage was rooted not in anger, but in moral clarity—a belief that liberty was a sacred trust to be defended, not merely enjoyed.

In modern terms, Jefferson's phrase **"sacred honor" transcends personal pride. It represents integrity that cannot be bought, bartered, or politically compromised.** The pledge was not transactional—it was spiritual. Each signer placed his honor in the balance of history, believing that moral fidelity would outlast mortal life.

Today, this spirit challenges every generation: **Are we worthy heirs to their pledge? The price of liberty is not just vigilance—it is virtue.** Jefferson's closing line reminds us that **freedom's endurance depends on the moral courage of those entrusted to defend it.**

Summary

This passage is not an ending but an oath. Where the grievances condemn tyranny, **this conclusion consecrates liberty**. Jefferson fuses divine appeal with human resolve—transforming rebellion into responsibility.

Their signatures were not symbols of defiance, but of devotion—a collective vow that liberty, once declared, would be preserved through unity, sacrifice, and faith.

It remains the founding moment of America's moral identity: a nation built not on conquest or crown, but on the conscience of **free men who pledged everything to the cause of human freedom.**

Constitutional Safeguards

- **First Amendment:** Ensures the right to speak, publish, and worship freely, preserving the same liberty of conscience that the Founders appealed to as they signed their names beneath Jefferson's words.
- **The Right to Petition**: Empowers citizens to seek redress before resorting to resistance—the very principle the colonies exhausted before pledging their lives to independence.
- **The Oath of Office Clause (Article II, Section 1):** Requires every president to swear before God to preserve, protect, and defend the Constitution—a living echo of the Founders' sacred pledge.
- **The Treaty Clause (Article II, Section 2):** Grants power to make peace and alliances, ensuring that the Republic born in war would seek its permanence in peace.

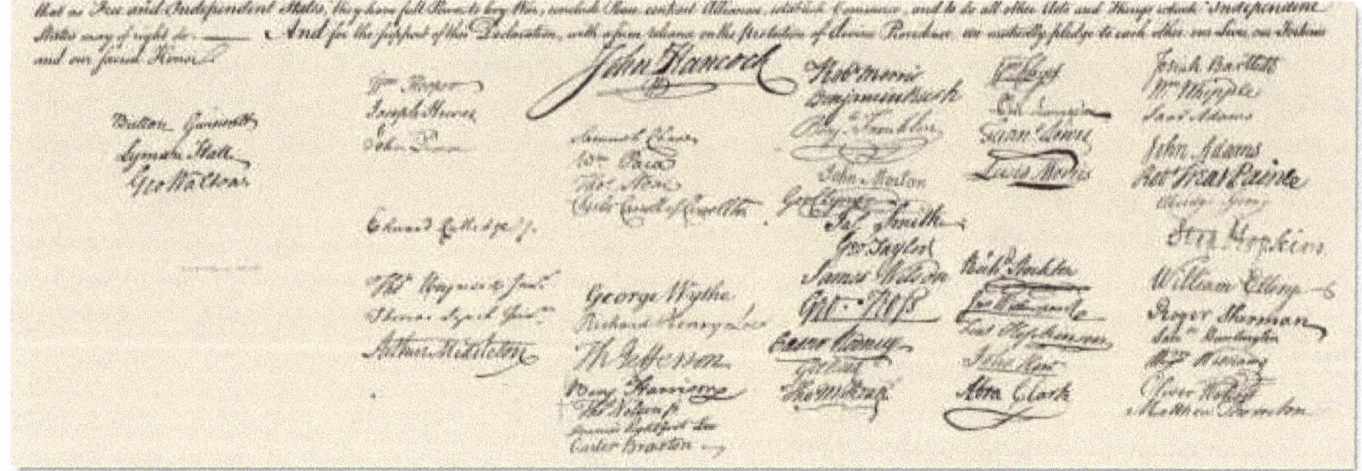

Signing the Declaration

On August 2, 1776, in Philadelphia, fifty-six delegates of the Second Continental Congress took a bold and dangerous step—they signed *The Declaration of Independence*. This happened a month after the Congress had approved the Declaration on July 2, 1776, when they voted to officially break away from Great Britain.

A group of five men—John Adams, Roger Sherman, Robert Livingston, Benjamin Franklin, and Thomas Jefferson—made up the committee to draft of the Declaration. It was written by Jefferson. Adams and Franklin suggested minor edits. Then, after much debate and a few changes, Congress approved a final version.

Once it was finished, a printer named John Dunlap was given the job of making the first copies, called the Dunlap Broadside. About 200 copies were printed, but only 26 survive today. On July 8, 1776, Colonel John Nixon stood in front of a crowd in Philadelphia's Independence Square and read the Declaration out loud for the first time.

The official copy of the Declaration—the engrossed version—was ready for signatures on August 2, 1776. Delegates signed on behalf of their states, beginning with New Hampshire and ending with Georgia. John Hancock, the President of Congress, signed first. His signature was so large and bold that it became famous—people today still say **"Put your John Hancock"** when they mean **"Sign your name!"**

Not everyone signed on August 2. Some signed later, including Henry Lee, George Wythe, Elbridge Gerry, Oliver Wolcott, Lewis Morris, Thomas McKean, and Matthew Thornton. Seven men who had been in Congress on July 2nd never signed at all.[94]

Keeping It a Secret

At first, the names of the signers were kept secret. Britain saw them as traitors, and if the colonies lost, they faced grave danger. In early 1777, Mary Katherine Goddard printed a new version revealing all their names.

Five signers of the Declaration were captured and brutally tortured. Nine fought in the war and died from wounds or hardship. Two lost sons in battle, while two others had sons taken captive. At least a dozen saw their homes pillaged and burned.[95]

A Dangerous Decision

Signing the Declaration was an act of incredible bravery. These men weren't just writing their names on a piece of paper—they were risking everything. By putting their names on this document, they were openly defying King George III and the British government. If they lost the war, they could be arrested, imprisoned, or even executed for treason. John Hancock said at the signing on August 2nd, "There must be no pulling different ways," he declared. **"We must all hang together."** Franklin replied, **"Yes, we must, indeed, all hang together, or most assuredly we shall all hang separately."**[96]

> "All that I have, and all that I am, and all that I hope, in this life, I am now ready here to stake upon it; and I leave off as I begun, that live or die, survive or perish, I am for the Declaration. It is my living sentiment, and by the blessing of God it shall be my dying sentiment, Independence now, and Independence forever."
> —John Adams[97]

Who Signed the Declaration?

The 56 signers came from all 13 colonies. Here's the order in which they signed:[98]

1. **Delaware**: George Read, Caesar Rodney, Thomas McKean
2. **Pennsylvania**: George Clymer, Benjamin Franklin, Robert Morris, John Morton, Benjamin Rush, George Ross, James Smith, James Wilson, George Taylor
3. **New Jersey**: Abraham Clark, John Hart, Francis Hopkinson, Richard Stockton, John Witherspoon
4. **Georgia**: Button Gwinnett, Lyman Hall, George Walton
5. **Connecticut**: Samuel Huntington, Roger Sherman, William Williams, Oliver Wolcott
6. **Massachusetts**: John Adams, Samuel Adams, John Hancock, Robert Treat Paine
7. **Maryland**: Charles Carroll, Samuel Chase, William Paca, Thomas Stone
8. **South Carolina**: Thomas Heyward, Thomas Lynch, Arthur Middleton, Edward Rutledge
9. **New Hampshire**: Josiah Bartlett, William Whipple, Matthew Thornton
10. **Virginia**: Carter Braxton, Benjamin Harrison, Thomas Jefferson, Richard Henry Lee, Francis Lightfoot Lee, Thomas Nelson Jr., George Wythe
11. **New York**: William Floyd, Francis Lewis, Philip Livingston, Lewis Morris
12. **North Carolina**: Joseph Hewes, William Hooper, John Penn
13. **Rhode Island**: Stephen Hopkins, William Ellery

Summary

The men who signed *The Declaration of Independence* knew the risks—but they signed anyway. They believed so strongly in freedom that they pledged their lives, their fortunes, and their sacred honor to the cause. Their courage helped create a new nation, and their signatures became a powerful symbol of the fight for liberty.[99]

The Price They Paid

Have you ever wondered what happened to the men who signed *The Declaration of Independence?*

Five signers were captured by the British and held as prisoners. Twelve had their homes ransacked and burned. Two lost sons in the war; another had two sons captured. Nine fought in the Revolution and died from wounds or war-related hardships.

What kind of men were they?
- Twenty-four were lawyers and jurists.
- Eleven were merchants,
- Nine were farmers and plantation owners—men of means and education.

Yet they signed the Declaration knowing that if caught, they could be executed for treason. They pledged their lives, their fortunes, and their sacred honor.

Their Sacrifices
- **Carter Braxton (VA),** a wealthy planter and trader, lost his shipping fleet to the British navy. He sold his properties to pay debts and died in financial ruin.
- **Thomas McKean (DE**) was pursued by the British, forcing his family into hiding. He served in Congress without pay and lost much of his fortune.
- **Thomas Nelson Jr. (VA)** saw the British take over his home in Yorktown. He urged Washington to fire on it. The home was destroyed, and he died bankrupt.
- **Francis Lewis (NY)** had his home and properties destroyed. His wife was captured and later died from mistreatment.
- **John Hart (NJ)** fled his home while his wife was dying. His children scattered, his land was ruined, and he spent a year in hiding. He returned to find his wife dead and died soon after.
- **Richard Stockton (NJ)** was imprisoned for his role in the Revolution. He never fully recovered from mistreatment.
- **Edward Rutledge, Arthur Middleton, and Thomas Heyward Jr. (SC)** were captured at the Siege of Charleston and held prisoner for over a year.

The Truth Behind the Legends
While no signer was executed, their sacrifices were real. Some suffered financially, others endured imprisonment or the loss of loved ones. They were not reckless rebels but principled men willing to risk everything for liberty.[100]

As they pledged in 1776: *"For the support of this Declaration, with a firm reliance on the protection of Divine Providence, we mutually pledge to each other our lives, our fortunes, and our sacred honor."*

These men gave us an independent America. Can we keep it?

Comparing the Grievances

Thomas Jefferson's grievances in *The Declaration of Independence* is a slight expansion to the grievances proclaimed in the Preamble to the Virginia Constitution, which he wrote during mid-May to early June 1776.

Each charge against King George III appears in both documents, often with identical wording. Jefferson was not merely influenced by the Virginia grievances—but was their sole author. The complaints outlined in his Virginia draft were not confined to the concerns of a single colony; they served as a sweeping indictment of British rule, articulating frustrations shared throughout all thirteen colonies.

When tasked with drafting the Declaration, Jefferson did not need to construct a new case for independence—he had already done so for Virginia. Instead, he refined and expanded his well-established arguments, elevating them from a regional protest to a unifying call to the colonies. Striking similarities between the two documents confirm the ideological foundation for American independence was firmly in place before the Second Continental Congress acted. This was not merely a precursor—it was the foundation of America's call for independence.

From *"A Summary View"* to the Grievances

These grievances did not emerge in isolation; they distilled the essence of Jefferson's complaints first laid out in *A Summary View of the Rights of British America*, written two years earlier in July 1774. That document, delivered to Virginia delegates in session at Williamsburg, was Jefferson's bold attempt to define the American colonies' rights and to condemn British oppression.

His 1776 grievances generally follow the same sequence as those in his *Summary View*, beginning with the king's obstruction of colonial laws, his refusal to approve necessary reforms, and his interference with representative government. Jefferson denounced the king's dissolving of colonial legislatures, his failure to call new assemblies, and his restrictions on westward expansion—issues that also appear at the forefront of both the Virginia grievances and his Rough Draft of the Declaration. Condemning standing armies, foreign mercenaries, controlling our trade, and taxation without representation all appeared in his 1774 arguments.

By the time he wrote the Virginia grievances and the Declaration, Jefferson was not merely reacting to recent events—he was reinforcing a well-established case for independence that he had been refining for years.

Final Edits to the Grievances in The Declaration of Independence

As Jefferson copied the grievances from his Virginia document into the Rough Draft of *The Declaration of Independence*, he made very few changes. All the complaints stayed, with small tweaks to make them stronger. Some were expanded, like the King sending soldiers, and trifling with courts. Later, the clause blaming King George for promoting slavery was cut because southern colonies refused to sign if it remained. Other parts were reworked, showing how difficult it was for delegates to unanimously agree on content and phrasing. Referring to edits and deleting the Slavery Clause, Jefferson wrote that Congress had mangled it.[101]

The Table of Grievances

Grievances that follow are not the product of passion, but of patience worn thin. Jefferson organized them like a lawyer drafting an indictment—each charge precise, supported by precedent, and escalating in moral force. Together they transform a list of colonial complaints into a sweeping legal and philosophical case for independence. The table that follows traces this evolution, comparing Jefferson's Virginia arguments to his final Declaration text and showing how his earlier logic matured into America's charter of accountability. Grievances highlighted in gray indicate those added in the final Declaration, appearing for the first time after the earlier drafts.

Refining the Grievances

#	Declaration of Independence Official Printed Version June 15+/-– 28, 1776	Declaration of Independence, Rough Draft June 11 – 14+/-, 1776	Jefferson's Preamble to the Virginia Constitution Mid-May – June 10+/-, 1776
1	He has refused his Assent to Laws, the most wholesome and necessary for the public good.	he has refused his assent to laws the most wholesome and necessary for the public good:	by putting his negative on laws the most wholesome & necessary for ye public good;
2	He has forbidden his Governors to pass Laws of immediate and pressing importance unless suspended in their operation till his Assent should be obtained; and when so suspended, he has utterly neglected to attend to them.	he has forbidden his governors to pass laws of immediate & pressing importance, unless suspended in their operation till his assent should be obtained; and when so suspended, he has neglected utterly to attend to them.	by denying to his governors permission to pass laws of immediate and pressing importance, unless suspended in their operations for his assent, and, when so suspended, neglecting to attend to them for many years;
3	He has refused to pass other Laws for the accommodation of large districts of people unless those people would relinquish the right of Representation in the Legislature, a right inestimable to them and formidable to tyrants only.	he has refused to pass other laws for the accomodation of large districts of people unless those people would relinquish the right of representation, a right inestimable to them, formidable to tyrants alone:	by refusing to pass certain other laws, unless the person to be benefited by them would relinquish the inestimable right of representation in the legislature.
4	He has called together legislative bodies at places unusual, uncomfortable, and distant from the depository of their public Records, for the sole purpose of fatiguing them into compliance with his measures.	*Not in the Rough Draft, but comes from the Virginia House of Burgesses Resolution (May 24, 1774) where Jefferson was a delegate:* "This House, being deeply impressed with the deplorable condition of our sister colony of Massachusetts Bay, whose Assembly is now held in a place at a distance from their records and from the body of their constituents."	
5	He has dissolved Representative Houses repeatedly, for opposing with manly firmness his invasions on the rights of the people.	he has dissolved Representative houses repeatedly & continually, for opposing with manly firmness his invasions on the rights of the people:	by dissolving legislative assemblies repeatedly and continually for opposing with manly firmness his invasions on the rights of the people;
6	He has refused for a long time, after such Dissolutions, to cause others to be elected; whereby the Legislative Powers, incapable of Annihilation, have returned to the People at large for their exercise; the State remaining, in the meantime, exposed to all the Dangers of Invasion from without, and convulsions within.	he has refused for a long space of time to cause others to be elected, whereby the legislative powers, incapable of annihilation, have returned to the people at large for their exercise, the state remaining in the mean time exposed to all the dangers of invasion from without, & convulsions within:	when dissolved, by refusing to call others for a long space of time, thereby leaving the political system without any legislative head;

7	He has endeavored to prevent the population of these States; for that purpose obstructing the Laws for Naturalization of Foreigners; refusing to pass others to encourage their migrations hither, and raising the conditions of new Appropriations of Lands.	he has endeavored to prevent the population of these states; for that purpose obstructing the laws for naturalization of foreigners; refusing to pass others to encourage their migrations hither; & raising the conditions of new appropriations of lands:	by endeavoring to prevent the population of our country, & for that purpose obstructing the laws for the naturalization of foreigners & raising the condition lacking appropriations of lands;
8	He has obstructed the Administration of Justice, by refusing his Assent to Laws for establishing Judiciary powers.	Albemarle County Resolves: Jefferson, July 26, 1774: "We will ever maintain the legal and constitutional power of our own courts of justice, and protest against any attempt by the King or Parliament of Great Britain to suspend their operation or prevent the due course of justice within this colony."	
9	He has made Judges dependent on his Will alone, for the tenure of their offices, and the amount and payment of their salaries.	While no direct precedent appears in Jefferson's earlier writings, this grievance evolved naturally from colonial outrage over one of the Intolerable Acts, the 1774 Massachusetts Government Act, which made judges dependent upon royal will and salaries—widely condemned as the destruction of judicial independence.	
10	He has erected a multitude of New Offices, and sent hither swarms of Officers to harrass our people, and eat out their substance.	he has erected a multitude of new offices by a self-assumed power, & sent hither swarms of officers to harrass our people & eat out their substance:	This is not in the Virginia Preamble, but "Erected swarms of officers" was inserted between lines just above Grievance 11 on the Composition Draft.
11	He has kept among us, in times of peace, Standing Armies without the Consent of our legislatures.	he has kept among us in times of peace standing armies & ships of war:	by keeping among us, in times of peace, standing armies and ships of war;
12	He has affected to render the Military independent of and superior to the Civil Power.	he has affected to render the military, independant of & superior to the civil power:	lacking to render the military independant of & superior to the civil power;
13	He has combined with others to subject us to a jurisdiction foreign to our constitution, and unacknowledged by our laws; giving his Assent to their Acts of pretended Legislation:	he has combined with others to subject us to a jurisdiction foreign to our constitutions and unacknoleged by our laws; giving his assent to their pretended acts of legislation,	by combining with others to subject us to a foreign jurisdiction, giving his assent to their pretended acts of legislation.
14	For quartering large bodies of armed troops among us:	for quartering large bodies of armed troops among us;	for quartering large bodies of troops among us;
15	For protecting them, by a mock Trial, from punishment for any Murders which they should commit on the Inhabitants of these States:	The Administration of Justice Act allowed any Crown official accused of murder or other capital crimes in Massachusetts to be removed from the colony and tried elsewhere—often in England—by courts sympathetic to the Crown. In practice, it placed royal officers above colonial law, ensuring that even the gravest abuses could escape local justice under the guise of a "lawful" trial.	
16	For cuttingxs off our Trade with all parts of the world	for cutting off our trade with all parts of the world;	for cutting off our trade with all parts of the world;
17	For imposing taxes on us without our consent:	for imposing taxes on us without our consent;	for imposing taxes on us without our consent;
18	For depriving us in many cases, of the benefits of Trial by Jury:	for depriving us of the benefits of trial by jury;	for depriving us of the benefits of trial by jury;

19	For transporting us beyond Seas to be tried for pretended offenses:	for transporting us beyond seas to be tried for pretended offences:	for transporting us beyond seas to be tried for pretended offences;
20	For abolishing the free System of English Laws in a neighbouring Province, establishing therein an Arbitrary government, and enlarging its Boundaries so as to render it at once an example and fit instrument for introducing the same absolute rule into these Colonies:	From: Jefferson's July 1775 draft of: *The Declaration of the Causes and Necessity of Taking Up Arms:* "They have erected in a neighbouring province, acquired by the joint arms of Great Britain and America, a tyranny dangerous to the very existence of all these colonies." He drafted this as a delegate to the Second Continental Congress in Philadelphia. His draft was considered a bit too harsh, so it was modified by John Dickinson to tone down the rhetoric.	
21	For taking away our Charters, abolishing our most valuable Laws, and altering fundamentally the Forms of our Governments:	for taking away our charters, & altering fundamentally the forms of our governments;	This Grievance does not appear in Jefferson's Virginia Preamble. It was added during the drafting of the Rough Draft and also appears in the Composition Draft—evidence of his bidirectional editing process.
22	For suspending our own Legislatures, and declaring themselves invested with power to legislate for us in all cases whatsoever.	for suspending our own legislatures & declaring themselves invested with power to legislate for us in all cases whatsoever:	for suspending our own legislatures & declaring themselves invested with power to legislate for us in all cases whatsoever;
23	He has abdicated Government here, by declaring us out of his Protection and waging War against us.	he has abdicated government here, withdrawing his governors, & declaring us out of his allegiance & protection:	and finally, by abandoning the Helm of Government, and declaring us out of his Allegiance and Protection;
24	He has plundered our seas, ravaged our coasts, burnt our towns, and destroyed the lives of our people.	he has plundered our seas, ravaged our coasts, burnt our towns & destroyed the lives of our people:	by plundering our seas, ravaging our coasts, burning our towns and destroying the lives of our people;
25	He is at this time transporting large Armies of foreign Mercenaries to complete the works of death, desolation, and tyranny, already begun with circumstances of Cruelty & Perfidy scarcely paralleled in the most barbarous ages, and unworthy the Head of a civilized nation.	he is at this time transporting large armies of foreign mercenaries to compleat the works of death, desolation & tyranny, already begun with circumstances of cruelty & perfidy unworthy the head of a civilized nation:	by transporting at this time a large army of foreign mercenaries to compleat the works of death, desolation & tyranny already begun with circumstances of cruelty & perfidy so unworthy the head of a civilized nation;
26	He has constrained our fellow **Citizens** taken Captive on the high Seas to bear Arms against their Country, to become the executioners of their friends and Brethren, or to fall themselves by their Hands.	On June 5, 1776, The Philadelphia Gazette reported that American sailors had been captured or impressed into British service—men forced to man the very guns turned against their countrymen. Between June 8 and 10, Congress received additional dispatches describing the abuse of American prisoners aboard British ships. Jefferson, seething at these reports, transformed outrage to ink by adding this to the Fair Copy of *The Declaration of Independence* after he had completed the Rough Draft.	

27	He has excited domestic insurrections amongst us, and has endeavored to bring on the inhabitants of our frontiers, the merciless Indian Savages whose known rule of warfare, is an undistinguished destruction of all ages, sexes, and conditions. *(Later umbering on the Composition Draft shows Jefferson's instructions to move the second grievance in the Rough Draft up, which resulted in him appending it at the beginning, making these a single Grievance)*	he has endeavored to bring on the inhabitants of our frontiers the merciless Indian savages, whose known rule of warfare is an undistinguished destruction of all ages, sexes, & conditions of existence: *(The text below was moved in the Rough Draft, as per a notation made in the Composition Draft)* he has incited treasonable insurrections in our fellow-~~subjects~~ **citizens**, with the allurements of forfeiture & confiscation of our property:	*(This is two clauses higher in Virginia Constitution's Preamble)* by inciting insurrections of our fellow **subjects**, with the allurements of forfeiture and confiscation; *(These are two separate grievances in the Virginia Preamble)* by endeavouring to bring on the inhabitants of our Frontiers the merciless Indian savages, whose known rule of Warfare is an undistinguished Destruction of all Ages, Sexes, and Conditions of Existance;

Jefferson's Lost Clause—The "Slavery Clause"

Final Declaration of Independence	Rough Draft of the Declaration of Independence	Preamble to the Virginia Constitution
The Slavery Clause in Jefferson's Rough Draft was removed at the insistence of representatives from Georgia and South Carolina. Those delegates refused to sign the Declaration if this clause remained. Eleven states were in favor of this clause. It was imperative that all of the colonies were united in this effort or it was doomed to fail. Jefferson blamed not only Southern interests for its removal, but also Northern slave merchants, "for tho' their people have very few slaves themselves yet they had been pretty considerable carriers of them to others." [102] In the end, Jefferson was dejected, feeling Congress had "mangled it."	he has waged cruel war against human nature itself, violating its most sacred rights of life & liberty in the persons of a distant people who never offended him, captivating & carrying them into slavery in another hemisphere, or to incur miserable death in their transportation thither. this piratical warfare, the opprobrium of infidel powers, is the warfare of the <u>CHRISTIAN</u> king of Great Britain. determined to keep open a market where **MEN** should be bought & sold, he has prostituted his negative for suppressing every legislative attempt to prohibit or to restrain this execrable commerce: and that this assemblage of horrors might want no fact of distinguished die, he is now exciting those very people to rise in arms among us, and to purchase that liberty of which he has deprived them, & murdering the people upon whom he also obtruded them; thus paying off former crimes committed against the liberties of one people, with crimes which he urges them to commit against the lives of another.	by prompting our negroes to rise in arms among us; those very negroes whom he hath from time to time by an inhuman use of his negative he hath refused permission to exclude by law;

Indicting King George III

In every stage of these Oppressions We have Petitioned for Redress in the most humble terms: Our repeated Petitions have been answered **only** by repeated injury.	in every stage of these oppressions we have petitioned for redress in the most humble terms; our repeated petitions have been answered by repeated injury.	by answering our repeated petitions for redress with a repetition of injuries;
A Prince whose character is thus marked by every act which may define a Tyrant, is unfit to be the ruler of a free people.	**a prince whose character is thus marked by every act which may define a tyrant, is unfit to be the ruler of a people** who mean to be free. future ages will scarce believe that the hardiness of one man, adventured within the short compass of 12 years only, on so many acts of tyranny without a mask, over a people fostered & fixed in principles of liberty.	Jefferson's First Draft of his Proposed Virginia Constitution: "From all which premises it appears that the sd. George Guelp, not only for his criminal abuses of the high duties of the kingly office, but also by his own free & voluntary act of abandoning & putting us from his allegiance subjection & dominion, may now lawfully, rightfully, & by consent of both parties be divested of the kingly powers:"[103]

Jefferson's introduction to the Virgina grievances was introduced in the Virginia Constitution with these words:

> "Whereas George Guelf king of Great Britain and Ireland and Elector of Hanover, heretofore entrusted with the exercise of the kingly office in this government hath endeavored to pervert the same into a detestable and insupportable tyranny;"[104]

The Welf family—also spelled Guelf in old English—is one of the oldest noble families in Europe. The family originated in what is now southern Germany, and were part of the House of Hanover, a German royal dynasty.[105]

When Jefferson called King George III "George Guelf," he was invoking the king's German ancestry. The name served as a subtle but pointed reminder that George was not truly British. Not only was he a tyrant, but, as Jefferson implied, "he's not even—really—one of us." The word Guelf is derived from the Old High German word Welf, which literally means "whelp" or "wolf."

Jefferson's indictment of King George III was not an act of rebellion but the culmination of two years of reason and composition. It began with his May-June 1774 *Albemarle County Resolves*, written in defense of Boston's suffering under tyrannical edicts, where he first linked local injustice to universal rights. It continued with his *Summary View of the Rights of British America* in June-July 1774—a sweeping argument that the colonies were independent by nature, joined to Britain only by mutual consent. The following year, in the *Declaration of the Causes and Necessity of Taking Up Arms*, Jefferson transformed protest into principle, asserting that liberty justified resistance. By May 1776, his Preamble to the Virginia Constitution refined these ideas into a compact series of grievances—becoming, in essence, the pre–Rough Draft of *The Declaration of Independence*.

Thus, the Grievances of 1776 were not spontaneous outrage but the polished result of years spent reasoning through tyranny and contradiction. Each stage of Jefferson's writing was both rehearsal and revelation, bringing clarity to America's moral purpose. The final Declaration did more than indict a king—it completed a philosophical journey that began in Albemarle and ended in Philadelphia. Liberty was declared. Principle became law. Jefferson's words captured the voice and conscience of a nation.

Grievances Added After the Rough Draft

After Jefferson shared his Rough Draft with Adams and Franklin and incorporated their suggestions, he prepared a new "Fair Copy." In it, he refined the wording of several Grievances and added six more—not simply at the end, but placed deliberately within the document's structure. The full extent of Jefferson's revisions before presenting this copy to Congress is unknown, but the language and placement of these added Grievances reflect his distinctive style. The Fair Copy itself, along with any edits made by Congress, was lost after being sent to the printer.

#	Added After the Rough Draft	Source Text
4	He has called together legislative bodies at places unusual, uncomfortable, and distant from the depository of their public Records, for the sole purpose of fatiguing them into compliance with his measures.	Virginia House of Burgesses Resolution (May 24, 1774): Jefferson, present as a delegate, described Massachusetts' Assembly as removed to a distant place—separated from its records and constituents to force compliance.
8	He has obstructed the Administration of Justice, by refusing his Assent to Laws for establishing Judiciary powers.	Drawn from Jefferson's Albemarle County Resolves (July 26, 1774), which condemned parliamentary interference with "our internal polity and administration of justice." Jefferson later charged that the King obstructed justice by refusing assent to judicial laws.
9	He has made Judges dependent on his Will alone, for the tenure of their offices, and the amount and payment of their salaries.	No direct precedent appears in Jefferson's earlier writings. The Grievance reflects colonial outrage over the Massachusetts Government Act (1774), which made judges dependent on royal will and salaries—undermining judicial independence. Jefferson expanded this into a broader indictment of executive control over justice.
15	For protecting them, by a mock Trial, from punishment for any Murders which they should commit on the Inhabitants of these States.	The Administration of Justice Act (May 20, 1774) allowed royal officials accused of capital crimes to be tried outside the colony—often in Great Britain—shielding them from local accountability.
20	For abolishing the free System of English Laws in a neighbouring Province, establishing therein an Arbitrary government, and enlarging its Boundaries so as to render it at once an example and fit instrument for introducing the same absolute rule into these Colonies.	Source: Jefferson's June 1775 draft of *The Declaration of the Causes and Necessity of Taking Up Arms*. He warned that Britain had established arbitrary rule in a neighboring province—dangerous to the liberties of all the colonies.
26	He has constrained our fellow Citizens taken Captive on the high Seas to bear Arms against their Country, to become the executioners of their friends and Brethren, or to fall themselves by their Hands.	Reports in June 1776 described American sailors captured and impressed into British service—forced to fight against their own country. Jefferson transformed these accounts into this Grievance. Here, he also employs the term "citizens," reflecting his shift from subjects of the Crown to members of a political community.

Working Composition Draft

Thomas Jefferson, Draft of the Virginia Constitution, 1776. Manuscript. Library of Congress, Manuscript Division.

Above: Jefferson inserted a 16 above number 10 as an instruction to move it to where he bracketed a grievance further along. Over number 11, he inserted a 14, and moved it there in the Rough Draft. The 13 was added later to append it to the first part of 13 instead of a separate number 14. This shows why numbers 11 and 13 in the Virginia Preamble are combined in the final *Declaration*.

Below: He inserted "citizens" above "subjects" after wiping out the wet ink above "subject" in the Rough Draft of the *Declaration* and writing "citizens" over the ink smudge. Below it shows how Jefferson noted the change made in the *Declaration* text.

The Working Composition Draft

Evidence suggests that Jefferson drafted the grievances of the *Declaration of Independence* with his earlier Working Composition Draft physically at hand. This Composition Draft is the first page of his proposed constitution for Virginia, which he composed in that very same room over the preceding weeks.

Numbered insertions, bracketed rearrangements, and directional notations visible here are not casual edits; they are instructions for reordering and combining grievances to compose the Rough Draft. The grievances did not emerge from improvisation, but were synthesized from his earlier writings with deliberate care.

The Working Composition Draft functioned as a reference map—guiding structure, sequence, and meaning—while the Declaration refined language and force. Jefferson was not inventing grievances in June 1776; he'd already written them.

A Repeated Method from 1775

Jefferson had used this same drafting method the year before while composing the *Declaration of the Causes and Necessity of Taking Up Arms*. As the work evolved from rough draft to fair copy, Jefferson returned to the earlier manuscript and interlineated it—writing between the lines to note changes that had already been incorporated into the later version. The rough draft thus became a working reference document, annotated after the fact to reflect structural and conceptual decisions made to its successor.

This pattern mirrors what appears in the Working Composition Draft used during the drafting of *The Declaration of Independence*. In both cases, Jefferson was not revising ideas as he went, but reconciling documents—directing changes and bringing earlier drafts into alignment with a more refined composition. The manuscripts record a writer managing continuity across texts, not searching for arguments anew.

Changes reflect rearrangement, not reconsideration. Jefferson moved grievances forward or merged them where logic required compression, not revision. This same process explains his correction from "subjects" to "citizens." After copying "subjects" into the Declaration, Jefferson visibly noted—and corrected—the conceptual shift already made in the Declaration itself. The smudged ink and overwritten word record an epiphany already resolved in principle: no longer subjects of a crown, but citizens of a new nation asserting natural rights—a new social contract.

Jefferson's Epiphany
No longer Subjects, but Citizens

In his Rough Draft of *The Declaration of Independence*, Thomas Jefferson wrote, **"he has incited treasonable insurrections in our fellow-citizens."** But before he had written "citizens," he had written **"subjects,"** copying it from his Preamble to the Virginia Constitution. "Subjects" had defined people's relationship to a king for centuries. Right then, **Jefferson had an epiphany—** *We are no longer subjects to a king!* **He wiped out the word "subjects" while the wet ink was still wet, and wrote "citizens."**

With this one simple change, Jefferson transformed not just a sentence, but the entire future of America. By choosing citizens over subjects, he made it clear: the people of the new United States were not just members of a country—they were co-owners of it. In that moment, we became not just a new nation, but a new people—with a new social contract where we were **no longer "Subjects," but "Citizens."**

A Hidden Change, Discovered Centuries Later

For years, historians suspected that Jefferson had changed his mind when writing this part of the Declaration. But the proof didn't come until 2010, when scientists at the Library of Congress used a special imaging technology called hyperspectral imaging to examine Jefferson's draft.[106]

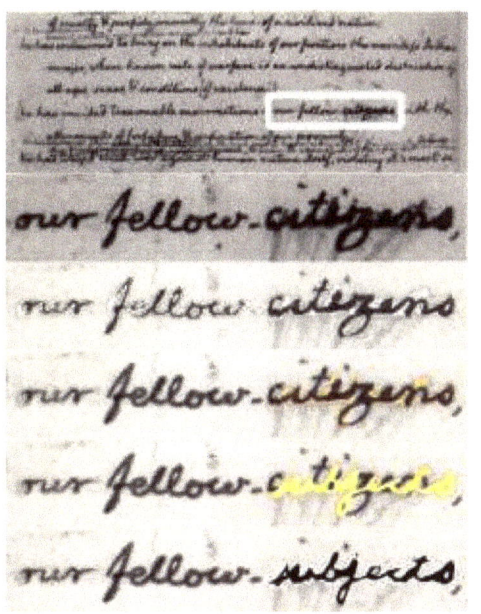

Hyperspectral imaging takes pictures using different parts of the light spectrum—including ones invisible to the human eye. This helped scientists see through the ink smudge and reveal the hidden word underneath.

Dr. Fenella France, one of the scientists, described the moment she realized what she had found:

"It had been a spine-tingling moment when I was processing data late at night and realized there was a word underneath citizens."

She carefully examined the images and confirmed what no one had been able to see for over 230 years—Jefferson had originally written "subjects" and then deliberately changed it to "citizens."

This discovery was huge. It revealed an important moment in Jefferson's thinking. The people of the colonies weren't subjects anymore. They were free citizens of a new republic.

Was This the First Time Jefferson Used "Citizens"?

After learning about this moment, this author wondered: Had Jefferson ever used the word "citizens" before? Or was this truly his epiphany—the moment when he realized what the American people had become?

Digging deep into historical record, may be found:

- **John Locke's Treatises on Government** – Locke used "subjects" and "people" hundreds of times, but never "citizens."
- **Jefferson's *Summary View of the Rights of British America*** – No sign of the word "citizens."

    Jefferson's Preamble to the Virginia Constitution – No mention of "citizens."

Before the Declaration

By the summer of 1776, Americans were ready to break from Britain. But how would they govern themselves? The Declaration would explain that separation—but it did not begin it.

The Exhaustion of Reconciliation

For more than a year, the colonies sought reconciliation through formal appeals, including the Olive Branch Petition and the Declaration of the *Causes and Necessity of Taking Up Arms*. These documents affirmed loyalty while protesting injustice. No meaningful response came. Instead, the King declared the colonies in rebellion and expanded military force. By early 1776, reconciliation was no longer a political option.

Give Me Liberty or Give Me Death

March 23, 1775: Before the battles at Lexington and Concord, Patrick Henry lit a flame with the concluding lines of his speech to the Second Virginia Convention. In the crowd were George Washington, Thomas Jefferson, and Richard Henry Lee.

"Gentlemen may cry, Peace, Peace—but there is no peace. The war is actually begun!... Is life so dear, or peace so sweet, as to be purchased at the price of chains and slavery? Forbid it, Almighty God! I know not what course others may take; but as for me, give me liberty or give me death!"[107]

April 1776: Adams's Thoughts on Government

By April, the crisis was no longer just talk—it required action. Royal authority had collapsed, and new governments had to be built. In *Thoughts on Government*, John Adams explained how Americans could govern themselves. He outlined key ideas for new state constitutions, including:[108]

1. Government exists to serve the people
2. Separation of powers
3. A two-part legislature
4. An executive with veto power

May 10, 1776: Permission to Govern

Congress recommended that each colony form its own government, based on the authority of the people. It did not yet declare independence—but it made self-government official.

May 15, 1776: Authority Transferred

Congress declared that royal authority had failed and must be suppressed. All powers of government were to be exercised under the authority of the people. The resolution was sent to the colonial legislatures, urging them to form governments grounded in the authority of the people.

May 15th Virginia Proposes Independence

On the same day in Williamsburg, the Fifth Virginia Convention declared its former government dissolved and instructed its delegates in Congress to propose independence—what became known as the Lee Resolution.

June 7-11: The Lee Resolution

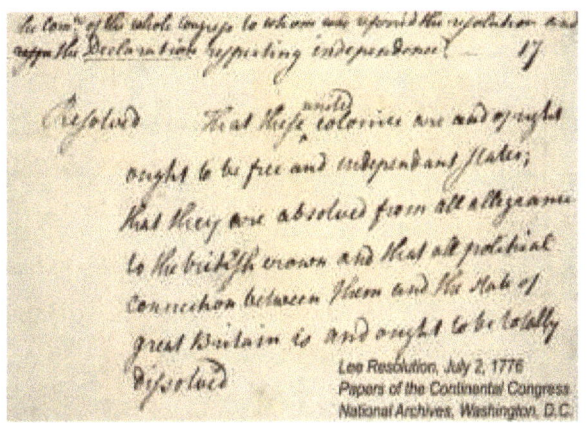

Lee Resolution, July 2, 1776
Papers of the Continental Congress
National Archives, Washington, D.C.

On June 7, Richard Henry Lee introduced a resolution **"that these United Colonies are and of right ought to be free and independent States..."** Congress delayed the final vote and, on June 11, appointed three committees:

1. To draft a declaration of independence, including Jefferson, Adams, Franklin, Sherman, and Livingston
2. To prepare foreign alliances, which included Adams and Franklin, among others
3. To draft a plan of confederation, with representatives from each state, including Sherman and Livingston

Congress did not proceed immediately to a vote on these resolutions. Under the leadership of Benjamin Harrison of Virginia, presiding as chairman of the Committee of the Whole, and with the urging of John Adams, final debate on independence was postponed until July 1. The delay was deliberate. Several colonies had not yet authorized their delegates to support independence, and time was needed to secure unity.

The same care shaped the presentation of the Declaration itself. Though drafted in mid-June, it was not submitted until June 28, just days before the final debate— ensuring that once independence was approved, its explanation would be ready without delay—and without prolonged time for revision before the July 2nd vote. This was not just timing—it was risk management. John Dickinson and Robert Morris—who thought alliances and confederation should precede independence—could fracture the moment if mishandled. With deliberation imminent, Congress would now have the opportunity to review the document, decide, and then declare.

Liberty and Order

By the end of May 1776, independence was already in operation. Congress was deliberating, Washington was commanding the Continental Army, new governments were forming, and royal power was collapsing. The Declaration did not initiate this change—it explained it, justified it, and presented it to the world.

The work of independence required more than agreement—it required preparation. John Adams focused on structure, pressing for constitutions, governments, and institutions in each state to sustain independence once royal authority was removed. Thomas Jefferson gave voice to the cause, articulating principles that moved the people toward separation. Jefferson lit the fuse that inspired action; Adams provided foresight and structure— ensuring that liberty would bring order, not chaos.

Why This Matters

Understanding these April, May, and early June actions clarifies the function of the Declaration of Independence itself. When Congress appointed a committee to draft it on June 11, it had not yet officially voted on whether to separate from Great Britain; that decision had been postponed until July 1. Congress was preparing for the moment it might—determining how that separation would be explained and justified to foreign powers and to history, in accordance with the principles of natural and constitutional law.

The Declaration did not initiate independence. It gave formal voice to it. It explained what Americans would soon declare, and why they believed they were justified in doing so. A new nation was declared with those words.

Journey to Philadelphia

For nearly a year before the Declaration, Thomas Jefferson had been serving almost continuously in the Second Continental Congress.

Since the previous May, he had worked on a string of committees, drafting reports, resolutions, and replies—quietly enlarging his reputation for precision with the pen. In late March 1776, family and estate obligations, drew him home to Virginia.

Jefferson requested a six-week leave to tend to his mother, Jane Randolph Jefferson, who was gravely ill, and personal affairs that demanded attention.

On May 7, Jefferson departed Monticello, bound once more for the Continental Congress. His journey north covered approximately 300 miles, traced through Northern Virginia's court towns.

Jefferson's Journal recorded his journey. The mileage between stops is estimated:[109]

- May 7 – Monticello to Orange Court House (30 mi)
- May 8 – Orange Court House to Culpeper Court House (15 mi)
- May 9 – Culpeper Court House to Fairfax Court House (55 mi)
- May 10 – Fairfax Court House to Leesburg and Potomac crossing (20 mi)
- May 11 – Potomac crossing to Frederick Town and Taneytown (55 mi)
- May 12 – Taneytown to Wright's Ferry on the Susquehanna (40 mi)
- May 13 – Wright's Ferry to Lancaster (15 mi)
- May 14 – Lancaster to central Philadelphia (60 mi)

On May 14, 1776, his carriage rolled into it final destination—seven days after leaving home. The man who had gone home to bury his mother returned to the Congress of the colonies, travel-worn but resolute, ready to lend his pen to the cause of independence.

Upon arriving, Jefferson would learn that Adams was ready to send instructions for each colony to draft a constitution. He may have preferred to return to Williamsburg to assist in writing the commonwealth's constitution, but he wrote that he was committed in Philadelphia:

> "I had been elected a delegate to the Convention of Virginia, but was detained in Congress by the duty of preparing a Declaration of Independence. I prepared a Constitution for my native State, and sent it to the Convention."[110]

June 7-11: The Lee Resolution

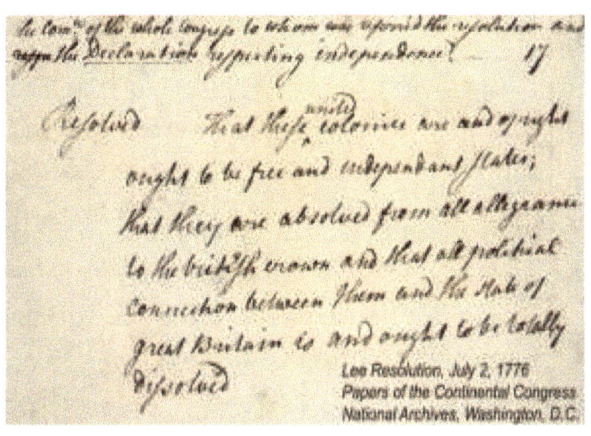

Lee Resolution, July 2, 1776
Papers of the Continental Congress
National Archives, Washington, D.C.

On June 7, Richard Henry Lee introduced a resolution **"that these United Colonies are and of right ought to be free and independent States…"** Congress delayed the final vote and, on June 11, appointed three committees:

1. To draft a declaration of independence, including Jefferson, Adams, Franklin, Sherman, and Livingston
2. To prepare foreign alliances, which included Adams and Franklin, among others
3. To draft a plan of confederation, with representatives from each state, including Sherman and Livingston

Congress did not proceed immediately to a vote on these resolutions. Under the leadership of Benjamin Harrison of Virginia, presiding as chairman of the Committee of the Whole, and with the urging of John Adams, final debate on independence was postponed until July 1. The delay was deliberate. Several colonies had not yet authorized their delegates to support independence, and time was needed to secure unity.

The same care shaped the presentation of the Declaration itself. Though drafted in mid-June, it was not submitted until June 28, just days before the final debate— ensuring that once independence was approved, its explanation would be ready without delay—and without prolonged time for revision before the July 2nd vote. This was not just timing—it was risk management. John Dickinson and Robert Morris—who thought alliances and confederation should precede independence—could fracture the moment if mishandled. With deliberation imminent, Congress would now have the opportunity to review the document, decide, and then declare.

Liberty and Order

By the end of May 1776, independence was already in operation. Congress was deliberating, Washington was commanding the Continental Army, new governments were forming, and royal power was collapsing. The Declaration did not initiate this change—it explained it, justified it, and presented it to the world.

The work of independence required more than agreement—it required preparation. John Adams focused on structure, pressing for constitutions, governments, and institutions in each state to sustain independence once royal authority was removed. Thomas Jefferson gave voice to the cause, articulating principles that moved the people toward separation. Jefferson lit the fuse that inspired action; Adams provided foresight and structure—ensuring that liberty would bring order, not chaos.

Why This Matters

Understanding these April, May, and early June actions clarifies the function of the Declaration of Independence itself. When Congress appointed a committee to draft it on June 11, it had not yet officially voted on whether to separate from Great Britain; that decision had been postponed until July 1. Congress was preparing for the moment it might—determining how that separation would be explained and justified to foreign powers and to history, in accordance with the principles of natural and constitutional law.

The Declaration did not initiate independence. It gave formal voice to it. It explained what Americans would soon declare, and why they believed they were justified in doing so. A new nation was declared with those words.

Journey to Philadelphia

For nearly a year before the Declaration, Thomas Jefferson had been serving almost continuously in the Second Continental Congress.

Since the previous May, he had worked on a string of committees, drafting reports, resolutions, and replies—quietly enlarging his reputation for precision with the pen. In late March 1776, family and estate obligations, drew him home to Virginia.

Jefferson requested a six-week leave to tend to his mother, Jane Randolph Jefferson, who was gravely ill, and personal affairs that demanded attention.

On May 7, Jefferson departed Monticello, bound once more for the Continental Congress. His journey north covered approximately 300 miles, traced through Northern Virginia's court towns.

Jefferson's Journal recorded his journey. The mileage between stops is estimated:[109]

- May 7 – Monticello to Orange Court House (30 mi)
- May 8 – Orange Court House to Culpeper Court House (15 mi)
- May 9 – Culpeper Court House to Fairfax Court House (55 mi)
- May 10 – Fairfax Court House to Leesburg and Potomac crossing (20 mi)
- May 11 – Potomac crossing to Frederick Town and Taneytown (55 mi)
- May 12 – Taneytown to Wright's Ferry on the Susquehanna (40 mi)
- May 13 – Wright's Ferry to Lancaster (15 mi)
- May 14 – Lancaster to central Philadelphia (60 mi)

On May 14, 1776, his carriage rolled into it final destination—seven days after leaving home. The man who had gone home to bury his mother returned to the Congress of the colonies, travel-worn but resolute, ready to lend his pen to the cause of independence.

Upon arriving, Jefferson would learn that Adams was ready to send instructions for each colony to draft a constitution. He may have preferred to return to Williamsburg to assist in writing the commonwealth's constitution, but he wrote that he was committed in Philadelphia:

> "I had been elected a delegate to the Convention of Virginia, but was detained in Congress by the duty of preparing a Declaration of Independence. I prepared a Constitution for my native State, and sent it to the Convention."[110]

Refining the Language of Liberty

Jefferson is often portrayed as young and inexperienced, but good with a pen. But for nearly two years, he had been rehearsing and writing the Declaration's logic, law, and conscience. He was preparing for his moment. Together, these documents formed the arc of Jefferson's political thought, like movements in a symphony.

A Succession of Jefferson's Revolutionary Documents

1. July 1774: *Albermarle County Resolves*   705 Words

Written in response to the Boston Port Act, which closed the harbor and punished an entire town for the actions of a few, Jefferson framed the closure of the harbor as collective punishment, not lawful governance. A year later, In Taking Up Arms, he warned that such measures reduce free people to submission by force. An attack on one colony, he argued, was an attack on all. Resistance, therefore, became a shared duty.

> "We will ever be ready to join with our fellow subjects... in exerting all those rightful powers, which God has given us, for the re-establishing and guaranteeing such their constitutional rights, when, where, and by whomsoever invaded."[111]

Leading Virginians recognized the power in Jefferson's words and urged him to expand upon his ideas.

2. August 1774: *A Summary View of the Rights of British America*   7,017 words

His Summary View established thirty-one-year-old Thomas Jefferson among the leading minds of the American political class. John Adams noted that Jefferson had **"the reputation of a masterly pen … in consequence of a very handsome public paper which he had written for the House of Burgesses, which had given him the character of a fine writer."**

In its argumentative structure, listing of grievances, and direct reproach of King George III, A Summary View of the Rights of British America is Jefferson's striking precursor to the Declaration of Independence.

Friends of Jefferson engaged Mrs. Clementina Rind, editor of the Williamsburg Virginia Gazette, to publish the Summary View as a twenty-nine-page pamphlet. It was also published by firms in Philadelphia and London and distributed throughout the colonies and England, establishing Jefferson as a leading defender of colonial rights.[112]

Thomas Jefferson, A Summary View of the Rights of British America 1774. Library of Congress

3. June 1775: *Declaration of the Causes and Necessity for Taking Up Arms*   2,390 words

Jefferson drafted *The Declaration of the Causes* and *Necessity of Taking Up Arms*. It was the sister document to the Olive Branch Petition—the final pair of appeals issued by Congress, one to the King for peace, the other to the world for understanding. Jefferson's Declaration was not an argument for separation, but for moral legitimacy—a statement that armed resistance was an act of conscience when every appeal to justice had been denied.[113]

Congress ultimately replaced Jefferson's version with a more conciliatory version, edited by John Dickinson. Yet Jefferson's original draft burned with the same fire that guided his *Summary View*: that liberty was sacred, reason was divine, and submission to tyranny was a sin against both. It was written not to the King, but to mankind—a justification of the colonial imperative to claim their rights before God and the world. He didn't leave those words behind; he carried them forward, refining their form and preserving their fire.

4. May & Early June 1776: *Jefferson's Proposed Virginia Constitution* 1,250+/- words

When Jefferson arrived, Congress was already moving toward independence. John Adams had urged each colony to draft its own constitution—prompting Jefferson to complete his proposed constitution for Virginia.

Writing in rented rooms on High Street—now Market Street, later known as the "Declaration House"—Jefferson spent several weeks drafting a proposed Virginia constitution.[114]

Grievances as a Constitutional Preamble

Declaring that King George III had reduced his government to a **"detestable & insupportable tyranny,"** Jefferson set down a list of grievances that became the preamble to the 1776 Virginia Constitution. Each of those grievances was carried forward into the Declaration's initial draft.

His proposed constitution was comprehensive—providing for separation of powers, a bicameral legislature, an executive with veto power, and more—including:

- **Prohibition of Slavery**
  "**No person hereafter coming into this country shall be held in slavery under any pretext whatever.**"
  No one entering Virginia in the future could be enslaved for any reason.

- **Equality in Inheritance**
  "**Descents shall go according to the laws of Gavelkind, save only that females shall have equal rights with males.**"
  Women and men could have equal rights to inherit property.

- **Freedom of Religion**
  "**All persons shall have full and free liberty of religious opinion; nor shall any be compelled to frequent or maintain any religious institution.**"
  People could believe and worship freely, without being forced to follow any church.

- **Protection Against Quartering of Troops**
  "**No soldier shall be quartered in any house in time of peace without consent of the owner.**"
  Soldiers could not live in private homes without the owner's permission.

- **Fair Purchase of Indian Lands**
  "**No lands shall be appropriated until purchased of the Indian native proprietors; nor shall any purchases be made of them but on behalf of the public, by authority of acts of the General Assembly.**"
  Native lands had to be bought lawfully—no one could simply take them.

- **Right to Bear Arms**
  "**No freeman shall ever be debarred the use of arms.**"
  Citizens could have the right to own weapons for protection.

These were not abstract ideals, but a moral architecture drawn from life and experience—reflecting Jefferson's belief that God-given rights exist before governments, and that governments endure only by the will of the people.

Drafting the Declaration

1,337 words

When Congress turned to independence, Jefferson gave final form to ideas he had been developing for years.

As a member of the Committee of Five, he was tasked with drafting the Declaration. What he produced was not a first draft of thought, but a final expression of it.

> ### Adams's note to Timothy Pickering (1822)
> "He shewed it to Dr. Franklin and me. I was delighted with its composition. I made no correction of consequence. Dr. Franklin made a few verbal amendments."[115]
>
> **Adams later recalled that Jefferson was chosen to draft the Declaration not by chance, but by preparation. In his autobiography, Adams wrote:** "Mr. Jefferson had the reputation of a masterly pen… I had a great opinion of the elegance of his pen and none at all of my own."[116]

Working in his rented rooms at the Graff House on High Street—today's Market Street—Jefferson drafted what would become *The Declaration of Independence*. He wrote quickly, but not impulsively. The structure was already formed: a preamble grounded in natural law, a list of grievances drawn from lived experience, and a conclusion asserting the right of a people to separate and govern themselves.

He drew directly from his earlier writings. The principles of natural rights had been clearly stated in *A Summary View of the Rights of British America*. The moral case for resistance had been sharpened in *The Declaration of the Causes and Necessity of Taking Up Arms*. And the structure of grievances—carefully ordered and forcefully expressed—had already taken shape in his proposed Virginia Constitution. These were not separate efforts, but parts of a single, developing argument.

Jefferson's initial draft reflected this preparation. The preamble established universal principles—rights not granted by governments, but inherent in man. The grievances followed, not as scattered complaints, but as evidence—each one supporting the charge that the King had violated those principles. The conclusion did not create independence; it declared what had already become necessary.

After completing the draft, Jefferson shared it with John Adams and Benjamin Franklin. Their revisions were few but meaningful—Franklin's change from "sacred and undeniable" to "self-evident" refined the tone, while Adams offered suggestions that strengthened clarity and force.

Jefferson prepared a Fair Copy with edits and additions, which was presented to Congress on June 28th.

The "Fair Copy"

The document that Jefferson and the Committee of Five presented to Congress was edited—Jefferson said Congress mangled it—and sent to be printed on July 4th. That copy was lost or discarded after being set to type.

In the days after July 4, however, a distressed Jefferson wrote several "fair copies" of his original submission, as edited by Congress, for five or six friends, including George Wythe and Richard Henry Lee. The New York Public Library holds one of four copies that have survived.[117]

Jefferson's underlining show text deleted by Congress—most notably the Slavery Clause—providing a valuable, near-contemporary record of what the Fair Copy contained, and what was removed by Congress.

June 28–July 2: The Declaration was Tabled as Congress Debated Independence

While Congress debated independence, Jefferson's manuscript lay on the table as the Lee Resolution was taken up once more. Most state delegations were ready, but Delaware's Caesar Rodney—suffering from facial cancer—rode through the night from Dover to Philadelphia, arriving on July 2 to cast the deciding vote for independence.

With the vote for independence secured, Congress turned to the Declaration—not to decide the question, but to explain it. For nearly three days, the Fair Copy had waited. Now it would be read, debated, and revised.

July 2–4: Congress Debates and Edits

Meeting as a Committee of the Whole, Congress worked through Jefferson's text line by line. according to Jefferson, Congress "mangled it," by removing the Slavery Clause. What Jefferson produced was not the end of the process—but the beginning of its final test.

Congress at work—debating, revising, and approving the Declaration before it was sent to the printer.

Evening of July 4: To the Printer

After final approval, the marked-up Fair Copy was delivered to printer John Dunlap. Hancock and Thomson signed it for authentication. Dunlap set the type that night and began printing. The Fair Copy was then lost.

July 5: The Dunlap Broadsides

Some 200 copies were printed overnight and sent by express to General Washington, the state assemblies, and American agents abroad. The word was out. The colonies were now a nation.

July 19–August 2: The Engrossed Parchment

Congress ordered a formal copy to be engrossed on parchment. Timothy Matlack, assistant secretary, penned the elegant version we know today. Fifty-six delegates ultimately signed it, beginning August 2.

January 18, 1777: The Goddard Broadside

When the British threatened Philadelphia, Congress fled to Baltimore. There, Mary Katharine Goddard, postmaster and printer to Congress, was authorized to produce a new edition—the first to include the names of all fifty-six signers. From Jefferson's silver pen to Goddard's press, the Declaration had passed through many hands, but only one voice.

American Scripture

Jefferson later wrote that he was not "striving for originality of principle or sentiment," but for an "expression of the American mind." Within about a week of his appointment, he had completed the Rough Draft—drawing together ideas he'd been developing for years.

Over the next ten days or so, he added several grievances and refined the language, tuning it like the strings of a violin until the words flowed as harmoniously as they were revolutionary—crafted to persuade the mind and move the heart. For 250 years, *The Declaration of Independence* has continued to resonate, stirring the hearts of freedom-loving people everywhere. It has become America's scripture—the *Psalms of Liberty*.

Classical Ear and Architectural Prose

Jefferson wrote not merely as a political thinker, but as a man trained in form. His education in the Greek and Roman classics shaped how he heard language—how sentences balanced, how ideas returned upon themselves, and how prose could carry meaning through structure as much as through words. This classical influence is audible throughout *The Declaration of Independence*, where Jefferson's writing moves with the logic of music and the symmetry of architecture.

Jefferson's prose frequently follows an ABA pattern—a statement, a development or tension, and a return. This structure is common in classical rhetoric and music alike. It allows an idea to advance without losing coherence. In the opening, principles are stated, elaborated, and then reaffirmed with greater force. The effect is cumulative rather than linear: the reader is not pulled forward abruptly, but carried outward and then back to the center.

Jefferson also employed chiasmus, the classical technique in which ideas are presented and then mirrored in reverse order. This creates balance, emphasis, and inevitability. Jefferson does not argue by piling clause upon clause, but by arranging concepts so that they answer one another. Liberty and government, rights and duties, cause and consequence—each is placed in relation, often crossing in structure even when not obvious at first glance. The result is prose that feels right before it is fully analyzed.

This architectural quality reflects a musical ear. His sentences are shaped by cadence and proportion. Clauses lengthen and contract deliberately. Parallel phrases establish rhythm; variation prevents monotony. Even when the subject is grievance, the tone remains measured. The Declaration persuades through harmony, not just passion. Its music is inseparable from its message. His message never changed. His contemporaries, uncertain at first, eventually caught up.

When Jefferson Dined Alone

In April 1962, President John F. Kennedy welcomed a group of Nobel Prize winners to the White House. Looking out at the assembled scientists, writers, and thinkers, he paused and observed:

> "I think this is the most extraordinary collection of talent, of human knowledge, that has ever been gathered together at the White House—with the possible exception of when Thomas Jefferson dined alone."[118]

Kennedy's remark was playful, but its insight was real. Jefferson was not merely a statesman or political theorist; he was a classical scholar, a musician, an architect, and a writer with a trained ear for balance and form.

Three Immortal Composers

Many conflate the missions and writings of Adams, Jefferson, and Mason as separate movements, rather than as composers working in parallel, drawing from the same American mind. Adams pressed for structure—urging states to form governments that would sustain independence. Mason defined rights, his Virginia Declaration shaping many early state constitutions.

Jefferson gave the cause its voice. In the midst of war, he framed the moral and legal argument that united and inspired a nation already in arms. They did not merely declare independence— they made it speak.

Notes on the State of Virginia
Including Observations on Slavery and Africans
Jefferson, 1785

Origin, Structure, and Purpose

Notes on the State of Virginia did not originate as a philosophical treatise, a moral manifesto, or a retrospective defense of American slavery. It began as a response to a formal list of queries posed to François Marbois, secretary to the French legation in Philadelphia. The questions were broad, unevenly organized, and reflective of Enlightenment interests in geography, natural history, population, law, religion, manners, and political economy. Jefferson later reorganized them into a more systematic sequence, but he remained, throughout, a respondent rather than a polemicist.[119]

This structure matters. Jefferson's most troubling passages—as well as his most penetrating moral insights—appear not as digressions, but as direct replies to specific questions. His reflections on slavery's effect on manners answer one query; his examination of race appears in another, framed within the language of natural history common to European science of the period. These answers were written in proximity, by the same hand, for the same audience, and intended as analysis, yet his purported "scientific analysis" of enslaved Africans is troubling.

What follows is not an attempt to rescue Jefferson from his words, nor to isolate those words from their context. We do not lionize Thomas Jefferson. We do not obfuscate his failures. We do not condemn him by modern slogan or selective quotation. We present him—in full—as he wrote, as he reasoned, and as he lived, including the contradictions he never resolved.

Manners, Slavery, and Self-Indictment

In his reply to the query concerning manners, Jefferson offers one of the most severe indictments of slavery written by any American founder. He argues that the master-slave relationship is a school of tyranny, teaching domination to one party and submission to the other, and that children raised within this system inevitably absorb its habits. Slavery, in his telling, does not merely oppress the enslaved; it deforms the moral character of the enslaver and corrodes republican virtue across generations.

He describes a society in which despotism becomes habitual, passions are unchecked, and moral restraint is weakened. He warns that such a system endangers liberty itself and invites divine judgment. This is not a casual observation. It is a diagnosis of social decay—and Jefferson does not exempt himself or his class from its effects. These passages are not incidental. They are Jefferson thinking carefully, soberly, and with evident moral concern about the consequences of slavery for Virginia and for the republic. They also precede and undermine his later attempt to explain perceived differences between races as natural rather than circumstantial. Having already explained how slavery suppresses development, distorts behavior, and rewards submission, Jefferson nevertheless attributes the resulting conditions to nature.

It is important to note that these reflections arise from different questions answered in sequence. Jefferson's condemnation of slavery's effect on manners is offered in direct response to one query. His later examination of race appears in reply to another, framed in the idiom of natural history. Both were intended as descriptive analysis. The difficulty lies not in Jefferson's willingness to answer, but in the fact that his answers do not agree. This internal contradiction is central. Jefferson supplies, within his own work, the strongest argument against his later conclusions—and fails to follow it. Read today, these conclusions are deeply troubling.

Race, Error, and Constraint

In responding to a different query—one framed in the idiom of natural history—Jefferson advances a deeply flawed examination of the African race. He speculates on physical, intellectual, and imaginative differences, relying on anecdote, aesthetic preference, and observation untested by method. These conclusions are wrong. They are methodologically unsound, logically inconsistent, and morally troubling. Yet they do not arise from ignorance of slavery's effects. They arise in tension with what Jefferson already knew.

This tension cannot be understood apart from Jefferson's lived circumstances. By the time Notes was written, Jefferson was entangled in a legal and financial system that treated enslaved people as property and collateral. He had inherited massive debt through his father-in-law's estate. Creditors demanded cash. Under Virginia law, enslaved people were among the most liquid assets available to satisfy debt, and attempts at manumission prior to satisfying creditors could be voided and reversed, resulting in seizure and resale.

Jefferson understood that public auction—the most common method of liquidation—frequently separated families and sent people into harsher forms of plantation slavery. When forced to sell, he sometimes arranged private sales, often to relatives or known planters, occasionally at below-market rates, in an effort—however inadequate—to mitigate harm and preserve family stability. These actions do not redeem the institution. They do, however, demonstrate the cruel arithmetic of a system in which every available option was morally compromised.

Constraint explains Jefferson's behavior. It does not erase responsibility. Moral understanding without moral courage remains Jefferson's failure, even though courage to do right would carry great—even catastrophic—cost.

Banneker, Chronology, and Partial Retreat

In 1791, nearly a decade after the manuscript for Notes on the State of Virginia was drafted and several years after its publication, Benjamin Banneker wrote directly to Thomas Jefferson, enclosing his almanac and appealing to the principles Jefferson himself had articulated in *The Declaration of Independence*. Banneker did not argue in abstraction. He presented evidence—his own work—and asked Jefferson to reconcile principle with practice. *(A section on Benjamin Banneker—mathematician, astronomer, surveyor, clockmaker, and free black—is presented in the Afterward.)*

The letter does not precede Jefferson's racial claims; it follows them. It therefore cannot be dismissed as contradicted by later writing. Instead, it stands as Jefferson's most explicit and cautious reconsideration of his earlier conclusions. In it, Jefferson expresses hope that Banneker's accomplishments demonstrate equal intellectual capacity, acknowledges the distorting effects of enslavement, and adopts a noticeably more tentative tone than in Notes.

This is not a retraction. It is not an apology in the modern sense. It is a crack in certainty. Jefferson did not fully escape his error. But when confronted with a living contradiction to his theory, he listened—partially, cautiously, and incompletely. The republic he helped found would eventually do what he could not: test his assumptions against broader evidence and reject them.

Jefferson's writings on slavery, manners, and race trouble us because they should. They trouble us even more when read together. Presented whole, they reveal not clarity, but strain—a mind wrestling unsuccessfully with moral insight, inherited assumption, and lived constraint.

History requires neither our approval nor our outrage. It requires not merely judgment, but attention and consideration— and the humility to learn from it.

A Wolf by the Ears
Jefferson's Lament

On April 22, 1820, Jefferson wrote, **"We have the wolf by the ears, and we can neither hold him nor safely let him go. Justice is in one scale, and self-preservation in the other."** His solution was preparation—to end the trade, educate the rising generation, and build civic and institutional foundations that could sustain emancipation.[120]

Jefferson stood at the edge of a chasm, liberty shining in the distance, and set himself to build a bridge across it. He could see the promise clearly—but he would not live to cross the span. The work he began—to reconcile freedom's words with liberty for all—was left to others and, in time, to us.

He tried to build the bridge before cutting the chains that held a people in bondage. His tragedy was not hypocrisy, but limitation—a man ahead of his time who was bound by laws of the Commonwealth. Jefferson's wolf was real: a nation's moral peril, snarling in its grasp. He feared that to hold it was ruin, yet to release it prematurely would bring chaos.

In his *Summary View* of 1774, Jefferson charged the king with waging "cruel war against human nature itself," accusing Britain of obstructing every colonial attempt to stop the slave trade—the first step in ending slavery. He wrote that *"the abolition of domestic slavery is the great object of desire in those colonies where it was unhappily introduced,"* but that it must begin by cutting off the traffic from Africa. To free the enslaved while new captives continued to arrive, he warned, would be a futile exercise— one injustice replacing another—justice postponed, not achieved. Thus, he resolved to strangle slave imports before general emancipation.

Jefferson's Efforts to End the Importation of Slaves

In 1778, while serving in the Virginia legislature, Jefferson's long-urged demand was realized: the General Assembly passed the first state law in history to ban the importation of slaves—a principle he had pressed for in letters and bills since his earliest years in public life. Even later, when writing to Washington about the 4 percent annual increase in enslaved labor's market value, Jefferson's words were not boast but indictment—despair at a moral system that rewarded bondage and punished reform.

In 1783, Jefferson proposed amending the Virginia constitution, writing that all persons born after December 31, 1800, would be free. It failed—too much, too soon—but it revealed his method: end the inflow, build an infrastructure, educate the children, then free the slaves. A firm foundation was necessary to avoid chaos.

President Jefferson's Message to Congress

Jefferson wrote to Congress on December 2, 1806. His message was clear: importation of these "unoffending people from Africa" must end. Three months later, on March 2, 1807, Congress acted—and banned the importation of slaves beginning January 1, 1808—three weeks before Britain passed its own legislation.

After thirty years, Jefferson's *"lost clause"* of 1776 had found its been reclaimed. He could finally congratulate a nation for beginning, at least in law, what it had promised in principle thirty years earlier. Yet Jefferson's victory was incomplete, and his conscience unquiet. He had inherited enslaved people from his father and father-in-law—along with their debts. By Virginia law, manumitted slaves could be seized to satisfy creditors or forced to leave the state within a year. To free them was to condemn them to exile or re-enslavement. His bondage was therefore twofold: he was held by law as surely as they were held by chains.

Jefferson and His Slave, Sally Hemings

Sally Hemings, a woman history remembers as both enslaved and intimately connected to Jefferson, was the half-sister of Jefferson's late wife, Martha. Her mother, Elizabeth Hemings, was half white; her father, John Wayles, was was also Martha's father. In a tragic twist of inheritance, Sally and Martha were family by blood, yet divided—one enslaved, one free.

Jefferson's relationship with Sally—whether one calls it love or dominance—defies easy judgment. Was theirs a relationship of mutual affection constrained by custom and law prohibiting interracial marriage? We cannot know.

Under Virginia law, their union could never be sanctified; marriage between races was forbidden. Yet she lived in relative privilege at Monticello, their children were educated and eventually freed, and one—Madison Hemings—later wrote that Jefferson had kept his promise: that his children "should be free."

Jefferson bore the wolf in silence. Condemnation from posterity was certain; yet to act rashly in his time might have undone what progress he had made. He wrote that slavery condemned both master and slave—a moral disease infecting both sides of the whip.

The Missouri Compromise of 1820

The Missouri Compromise of 1820 broke that fragile hope. Jefferson, old and failing, watched in despair as Congress bartered arithmetic for morality—granting Maine's statehood in exchange for Missouri entering the Union as a slave state to balance power in the Senate. The outcry was immediate. Citizens from Maine felt betrayed and used, asking, "How can a nation born in liberty give birth to slavery anew?" Jefferson, horrified, called it "a fire bell in the night," warning that the question of slavery's expansion would tear the Union apart. He was right.

Jefferson tried to build the bridge before cutting the chains. His tragedy was not hypocrisy but foresight without power —vision to see the peril, the will to resist it, but the inability to end it. He stood where Moses stood, seeing the promised land from afar. Lincoln crossed the river; King dreamed upon its banks. The bridge still stands incomplete—its span reaching toward us.

Five Centuries of African Slavery in America

Two hundred and fifty years before the Declaration, Lucas Vázquez de Ayllón brought enslaved Africans to the coast of what is now South Carolina. Another 250 years have passed.[121] We now stand upon that bridge. Liberty has not yet finished her crossing. The wolf still prowls; the chains still rattle with millions in bondage even today. Jefferson's dream—that reason and conscience might one day reconcile—remains within our sight. It is ours now to finish what he began.

Afterword

⚠ Teacher & Family Advisory

The following pages explore some of the most difficult truths surrounding the settlement of the New World—slavery and human exploitation. These passages are not meant to shock, but to help readers understand what can happen when freedom is denied. Adults may wish to read and discuss these pages with younger readers, offering context, reassurance, and hope.

Facing history with honesty deepens our appreciation for liberty and strengthens our empathy for those who endured injustice. Yet alongside these painful stories stand uplifting accounts of courage and compassion—little-known heroes who helped shape a better world. As we commemorate 250 years of America's journey, there is much to remember, rediscover, and celebrate.

Jefferson's Struggle with Slavery and the Slave Trade

Thomas Jefferson, a man both celebrated and criticized, embodied the contradictions of America's founding. In 1776, as he wrote *The Declaration of Independence*, he boldly stated that all men are created equal and have unalienable rights to life, liberty, and the pursuit of happiness. Yet, at the same time, he was a slave owner.

Jefferson originally included a powerful statement condemning the transatlantic slave trade in his first draft of the Declaration. However, delegates from Southern states demanded its removal, as they depended on slavery for their economies. Even so, Jefferson continued to push for change.

As governor of Virginia in 1778, he signed a law banning the importation of enslaved people into the state. Later, as president, he urged Congress to outlaw American participation in the transatlantic slave trade. In 1807, Congress passed a law banning the importation of slaves, taking effect on January 1, 1808—the earliest date allowed by the Constitution. The United States was only the second country to pass such a law, following Denmark's 1792 ban, which took effect in 1803.[122]

Although Great Britain passed a similar law in 1807, it did not fully enforce the ban in its Caribbean colonies for decades. In fact, British ships transported more than 25,000 enslaved Africans to the West Indies even after the trade was technically outlawed. Denmark and Great Britain did not abolish slavery in their colonies until 1848 and 1833, respectively.[123]

Indentured Servitude and Its Brutality

Even after slavery was abolished in British territories, many former slaves were placed into indentured servitude. Indentured laborers were typically bound by contracts that required them to work for four to eleven years in exchange for passage to a new land. In theory, they would be free after their contracts ended, but in reality, they were often trapped in brutal conditions.

Indentured servitude was especially common after Britain ended slavery in its Caribbean colonies in 1833. To replace enslaved labor, plantation owners brought millions of workers from India, China, and Africa to work in sugar plantations and mines across the British, French, Dutch, and Danish empires. Between 1834 and 1917, over 1.3 million Indian laborers were sent to distant colonies, creating large Indian diaspora communities in places like Jamaica, Trinidad, Mauritius, and Fiji.[124]

Although indentured servitude was not the same as chattel slavery—where enslaved people were considered property for life—many indentured laborers suffered terrible mistreatment. Some were tricked or kidnapped into signing contracts they could not read. Others faced extreme punishment for trying to escape. Their struggle is an important but often overlooked part of history.[125]

The "Duty Boys" of 1619

The story of slavery in North America did not begin with the arrival of Africans in Jamestown. It began in England with the **Project of 1619**—the transporting of **White, adolescent indentured servants to Jamestown**.

Duty Boys

In the spring of 1619, two English ships, the *Jonathan* and the *Duty*, arrived in Jamestown carrying 140 children who had been taken from the streets of England. Many of these **"Duty Boys"** had been held in London's Bridewell Prison, generally for vagrancy, since 1617

These children were **sent to the colonies to "learn a trade."** The Duty Boys were from eight to sixteen years of age, and forty percent were young girls. None of these children was of age to sign legal contracts of indenture. **Of the first 300 children brought to Jamestown, 12 remained alive after three years.** [126]

The planters had these servants for a finite period of time and tended to get as much out of them as they could. These servants often worked between twelve to sixteen hours a day. In 1619 John Rolfe, the man responsible for the tobacco industry wrote that there was a wanton "buying of men and boys." The historian Edmund Morgan wrote this was "a system of labor that treated men as things."[127]

The White Lion

A few months after the Duty Boys arrived, another ship landed near Jamestown in August of 1619—the **White Lion. This British ship traded "twenty and some odd" Africans for food**. This was recorded by John Rolph, whose wife was Pocahontas. John Rolph wrote that the Africans were traded for "victuals."

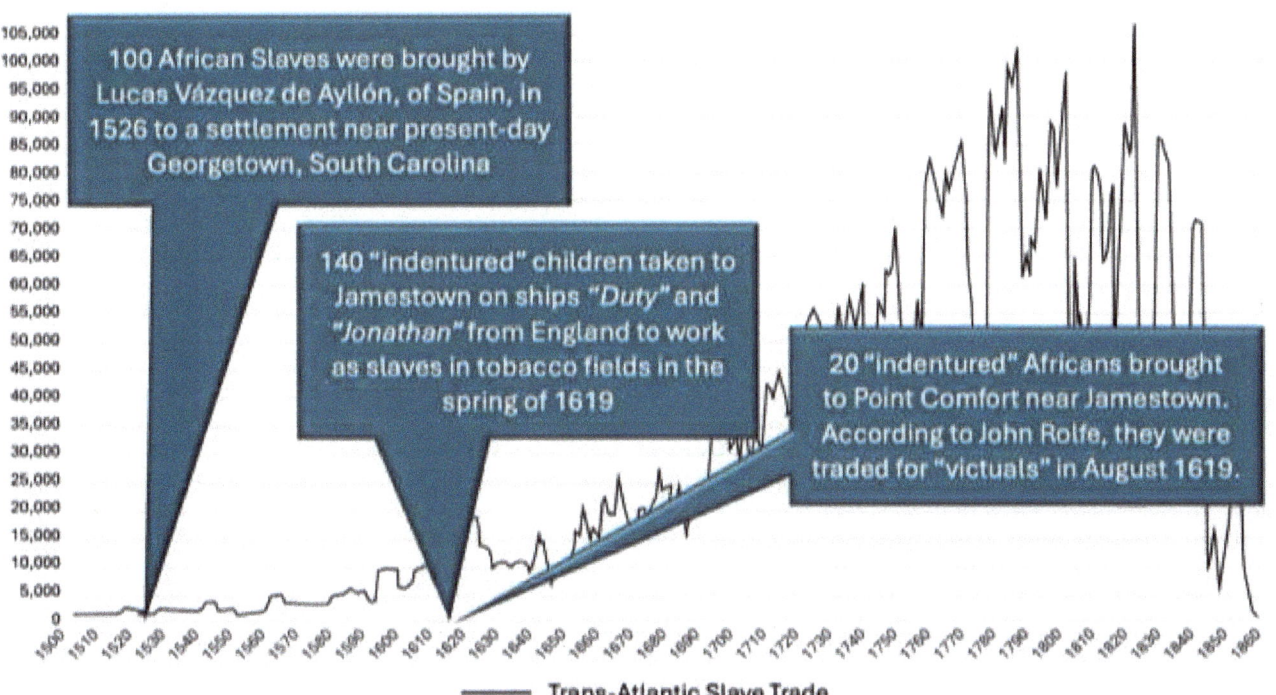

First Recorded African Slaves in Mainland North America
Presented over a graph representing the entire 364 years of the Trans-Atlantic Slave Trade

100 African Slaves were brought by Lucas Vázquez de Ayllón, of Spain, in 1526 to a settlement near present-day Georgetown, South Carolina

140 "indentured" children taken to Jamestown on ships *"Duty"* and *"Jonathan"* from England to work as slaves in tobacco fields in the spring of 1619

20 "indentured" Africans brought to Point Comfort near Jamestown. According to John Rolfe, they were traded for "victuals" in August 1619.

—— Trans-Atlantic Slave Trade

The Origins of Slavery in America

The Project of 1619 wasn't the beginning of slavery in the Americas. More than a century earlier, Portugal and Spain had already transported thousands of African slaves to South and Central America. By the time the English established Jamestown in 1607, slavery was already firmly entrenched in the Spanish and Portuguese colonies.

The First African Slaves in Mainland North America

The idea that African slavery in America began in 1619 is not accurate. Nearly a century earlier, in 1526, Spanish explorer Lucas Vázquez de Ayllón brought 100 enslaved Africans to a settlement called San Miguel de Gualdape, likely near present-day Georgetown, South Carolina. When Ayllón died, a mutiny broke out among the Spanish settlers. In a twist of fate, the African slaves helped suppress the rebellion. Soon after, the struggling colony collapsed. The Spanish survivors fled back to Hispaniola, but the Africans reportedly remained, integrating with local Indigenous tribes—perhaps the first free Black community in what would become the United States.[128]

Indentured Servants: The Forgotten Majority

Before the American Revolution, over two-thirds of European immigrants arrived in the colonies as indentured servants, working off the cost of their passage. Between the 16th and 18th centuries, around 320,000 indentured servants—primarily from England, Scotland, and Ireland—crossed the Atlantic to labor under harsh contracts. Many endured grueling conditions, but they were promised freedom, and often land, once their service ended.[129]

Transported Convicts: Criminals or the Desperate Poor?

Not all indentured servants came voluntarily. British authorities emptied jails, sending convicts—many guilty of minor offenses like stealing bread or failing to pay debts—to the colonies. Though treated as slaves and outcasts during their term of indenture, they still retained the hope of eventual freedom.[130]

A Stark Contrast: Indentured Servitude vs. Slavery

Of 500,000 European immigrants to America prior to the Revolution, around 320,000 were indentured servants, compared to about 269,300 enslaved Africans imported during the same period. Yet, their experiences were vastly different. While indentured servants faced brutality, they had a contractual path to freedom. African slaves, by contrast, were trapped in a system that condemned them—and their descendants—to lifelong bondage under laws that denied them even the faintest hope of liberty.

The Project of 1619 tells a more complex story than the simplified narrative of slavery's origins. It reveals that forced labor in America took many forms, but only one group—enslaved Africans—was permanently stripped of their humanity and future.[131]

How Slavery Became the Law

While both indentured servitude and slavery existed in early America, the defining difference became law. In the mid-1600s, colonial legislatures began passing statutes that codified lifelong slavery. In 1662, Virginia declared that children inherited the status of their mother, ensuring that slavery became hereditary. By the end of the 17th century, race-based chattel slavery had fully replaced indentured servitude as the dominant labor system in the American colonies.[132]

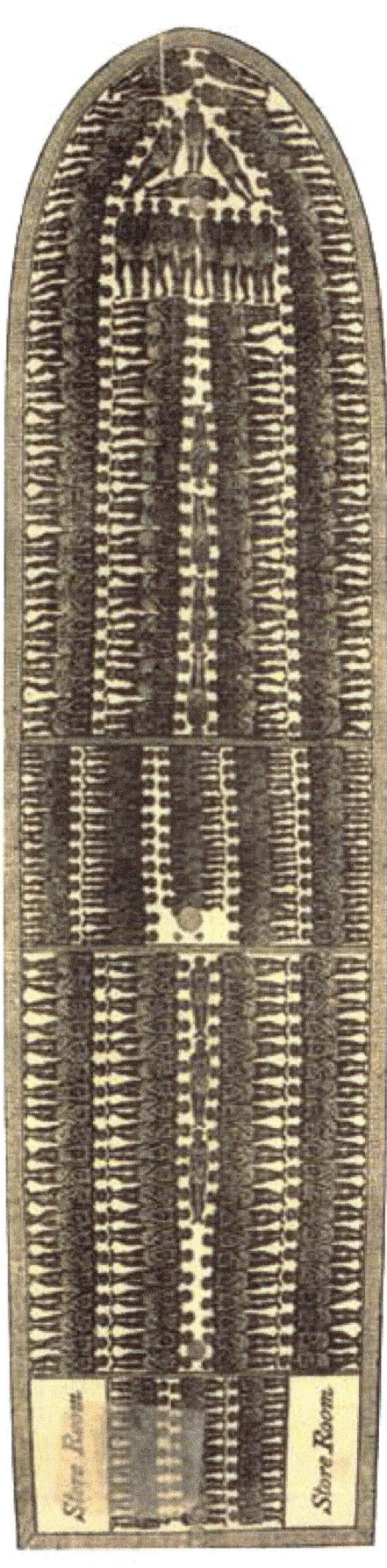

Slave Ship Brookes

The image on this page is one of the most famous drawings ever made about slavery. It shows how enslaved people were packed tightly into the British slave ship Brookes in 1788. The ship was designed to carry cargo, not people, but enslaved Africans were crammed in like supplies—stacked in rows with almost no space to move. This drawing was created by abolitionists (people who wanted to end slavery) in England to show the world the cruelty and inhumanity that defined the transatlantic slave trade.[133]

Britain was responsible for transporting about 2.5 million enslaved Africans to the New World—including over 300,000 to the British colonies in North America. These ships took people from Africa and forced them to work on plantations, mostly in the Caribbean and the American South. The people on board were treated not as human beings, but as property.

How Cramped Were the Conditions?

The Brookes was not supposed to carry more than 470 people, but slave traders ignored those limits. At one point, it carried 609 enslaved men, women, and children—more than the ship was built to hold.

How much space did each person have?

- **Men** – 6 feet long, 1 foot 4 inches wide (but crammed together, often with only 9 inches of width, forcing them to lay on their sides, or on top of each other).

- **Women** – 5 feet 10 inches by 1 foot 4 inches.

- **Boys** – 5 feet by 1 foot 2 inches.

- **Girls** – 4 feet 6 inches by 1 foot.

The space between decks was only 2 feet 7 inches high, meaning most people could not even sit up. They were forced to lie on top of each other for weeks at a time.

The reality of life below deck was horrifying. People were chained together at the wrists and ankles, packed so tightly that they could barely move. The heat, lack of fresh air, and terrible sanitation caused disease to spread quickly. Twenty-percent died.

A Picture That Changed the World

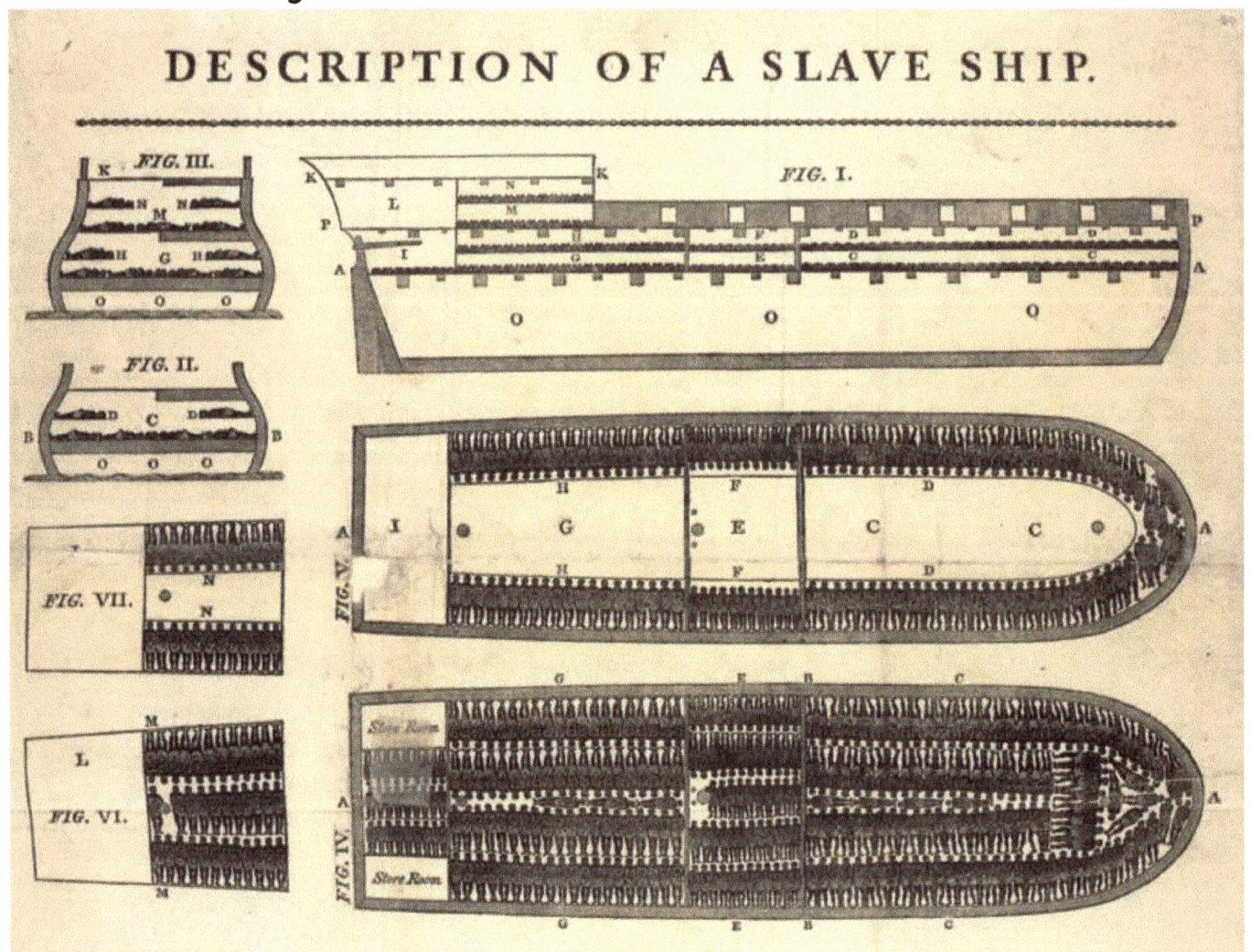

Life Aboard a Slave Ship

A survivor of the slave trade later described the suffering:

> **"The men, instead of lying on their backs, were placed on their sides, or on each other. In the morning, some were found dead."**

Slave traders forced the enslaved to come up on deck for "exercise," which they called "dancing"—but it was really just a way to keep them alive long enough to be sold. If the weather was bad, people stayed below deck for days or weeks, causing sickness to spread even faster.

One witness reported that during a storm:

> **"Fifty slaves perished in that small space of time."**

Even the sailors on board suffered from the stench and disease. Some people claimed the slave trade helped train new sailors, but in reality, many died from the conditions on board.

Ending the Slave Trade

The Brookes drawing became one of the most powerful tools in the fight to end slavery. Abolitionists in Great Britain used it to show how inhumane the slave trade was, helping to convince people that it needed to stop. People who had never seen the inside of a slave ship were shocked.

The movement to end the transatlantic slave trade gained momentum, and in 1807, two major nations took action. **The United States passed a law banning participation in the slave trade on March 2, 1807**, but it couldn't take effect immediately until the 20-year limit ended in 1808. The law was written with a "trigger clause," making it **officially take effect on January 1, 1808**.

William Wilberforce was inspired by revelations of the Slave Ship Brooks and lead the fight against the slave trade in England. Three weeks after the U.S. law was passed, **Britain passed its law on March 25, 1807**.[134] Though these laws stopped the legal importation of enslaved people, both nations remained involved in slavery—Great Britain being primarily involved in the Caribbean. The fight for full abolition was far from over.

The images and descriptions of the Brookes represent one of the darkest aspects of human history. They serve as a stark reminder of the atrocities committed and the suffering endured. Yet, they also reflect the power of truth and exposure to spur social change. The horrors revealed in the Brookes engraving galvanized the abolitionist movement, ultimately challenging the moral conscience of a nation and the world.

DESCRIPTION OF A SLAVE SHIP.

The PLAN and SECTIONS annexed exhibit a slave ship with the slaves stowed.* In order to give a representation of the trade against which no complaint of exaggeration could be brought by those concerned in it, the Brooks is here described, a ship well known in the trade, and the first mentioned in the report delivered to the House of Commons last year by Captain Parrey, who was sent to Liverpool by Government to take the dimensions of the ships employed in the African slave trade from that port. These plans and sections are on a scale of the 8th of an inch to a foot.

DIMENSIONS OF THE SHIP

	Feet	Inches
Length of the Lower Deck, gratings, bulk-heads, included At AA	100	0
Breadth of Beam on the Lower Deck inside, BB	25	4
Depth of Hold, OOO from ceiling to ceiling	10	0
Height between decks from deck to deck	5	8
Length of the Men's Room, CC on the lower deck	46	0
Breadth of the Men's Room, CC on the lower deck	25	4
Length of the Platforms, DD in the men's room	46	0
Breadth of the Platforms in men's rooms on each side	6	0
Length of the Boys Room, EE	13	9
Breadth of the Boys Room	25	0
Breadth of Platforms, FF in boy's room	6	0
Length of the Women's Room, GG	28	6
Breadth of the Women's Room	23	6
Length of the Platforms in women's room	6	0
Breadth of the Platforms in women's room	10	6
Length of the Gun Room, II on the lower deck	10	6
Breadth of the Gun Room on the lower deck	12	0
Length of the Quarter Deck, KK	33	6
Breadth of the Quarter Deck	19	6
Length of the Cabin, LL	14	0
Height of the Cabin	5	2
Length of the Half Deck, MM	16	6
Height of the Half Deck	6	2
Length of the Platforms, NN on the half deck	16	6
Breadth of the Platforms on the half deck	6	0
Upper deck, PP:		
Nominal tonnage	297	
Supposed tonnage by measurement	320	
Number of Seamen	45	

The number of slaves which this vessel actually carried appears from the accounts given to Capt. Parrey by the slave-merchants themselves as follows:

Men	351	
Women	127	Total
Boys	90	609
Girls	41	

The room allowed each description of slaves in the plan is:
- To the Men, 6 feet by 1 foot 4 inches.
- Women, 5 feet 10 in. by 1 foot 4 in.
- Boys, 5 feet by 1 foot 2 in.
- Girls 4 feet 6 in. by 1 foot

* This is the usual manner of placing the slaves, but it varies according to the position of the ship, and the practice of the different commanders.

With this allowance of room, the utmost number that can be stowed in a vessel of the dimension of the Brooks, is as follows, (being the number exhibited in the plan) and is less than 1 1/2 to a ton, viz. †

			On the Plan.	Actually carried.
Men - on the lower deck, at	CC		124	
Ditto on the platform of ditto,	CC	DD	66	
			190	351
Boys - lower deck EE			46	
Ditto - platform FF			24	
			70	90
Women - lower deck, GG			83	
Ditto - platform, HH			40	
Women Half deck, MM			36	
Ditto Platform ditto, NN			24	
			183	127
Girls Gun room, II			27	41
General Total			470	609

The principal difference is in the men. It must be observed, that the men, from whom only insurrections are to be feared, are kept continually in irons, and must be stowed in the room allotted for them, which is of a more secure construction than the rest.

In this ship the number of men actually carried was	351
The number of men stated in the plan at 1 foot 4 inches each	190
Difference	161

As the ship on this plan would stow 42 women, boys and girls in the places here allotted to them more than she did carry, supposing that number of men taken from the men's room, and placed in their stead, this will reduce the number of men to 309 in the men's room; of course the room allowed them, instead of being 16 inches as in the plan, was in reality only 10 inches each; but if the whole number of 351 were stowed in the men's room, they had only 9 inches each to lay in.

The men therefore, instead of lying on their backs, were placed, as is usual, in full ships, on their sides, or on each other. In which last situation they are not unfrequently found dead in the morning.

The longitudinal section, fig. I. shews the manner in which the slaves were placed on all the decks and platforms, which is also further illustrated by the transverse sections, fig. II. & III. By which it appears, that the height between the decks is 5 feet 8 inches, which, allowing 2 inches for the platform and its bearers, makes the height between the decks and the platform 2 feet 9 inches; but then the beams and their knees, with the carlings, taking 4 inches on an average, this space is unequally divided, and above or under the platforms cannot be estimated at more than 2 feet 7 inches; so that the slaves cannot, when placed either on or under the platform, relieve themselves by sitting up; the very short ones excepted, nor can they, except on board the larger vessels. The average of 9 vessels measured by Captain Parrey, being mostly large ships, was only 5 feet 2 inches. The height of the Venus between decks was 4 feet 2 inches; of the Kitty 4 feet 4 inches, both of which had platforms. In these smaller vessels therefore, they have not 2 feet under or upon the platforms.

In fig. I. under the upper deck PP, and the lower deck AA, the beams and intervening carlings are represented by shaded squares. The beams are also introduced on one side of the transverse sections II and III, in order to shew the space which a slave placed under a beam has to lie and breathe in.

† It must be noted, that every possible advantage of stowing is allowed in the plan. There are or ought to be in each apartment one or more poopoo tubs; there are also stanchions to support the platforms and decks; for which no deduction is made; but the deck is supposed clear of every incumbrance whatever.

Transatlantic Slave Trade

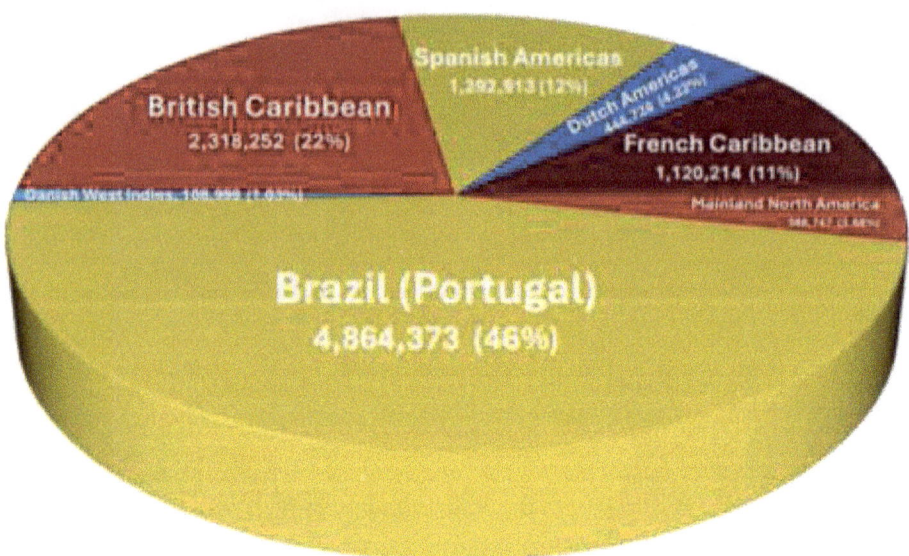

Above: Six civilized European nations were heavily involved in the Trans-Atlantic Slave Trade. Portugal, which had been given permission by the Pope in 1450 to place Africans into perpetual slavery, was by far the greatest offender, with nearly five million. Great Britain was next, with about 2.5 million. The Spanish and French each brought over a million. The Netherlands brought 444 thousand to the Dutch Americas, and Denmark shipped 109,000 slaves to the Danish West Indies.[135]

Breakdown of Mainland North America African Slave Imports

British Flag Merchants	264,912	France	8,876
New England Colonial Merchants under British Rule	37,013	Spain	1,851
Total under British Rule	**301,925**	Denmark/Baltic	1,489
		Netherlands	1,212
U.S.A. (Under 20 year clause, 1789-1808)	63,927	Portugal/Brazil	382
During the Articles of Confederation	5,086		
Illegal Smuggling after constitutional ban until 1860	4,505	**Total North America Slave Imports**	**388,747**

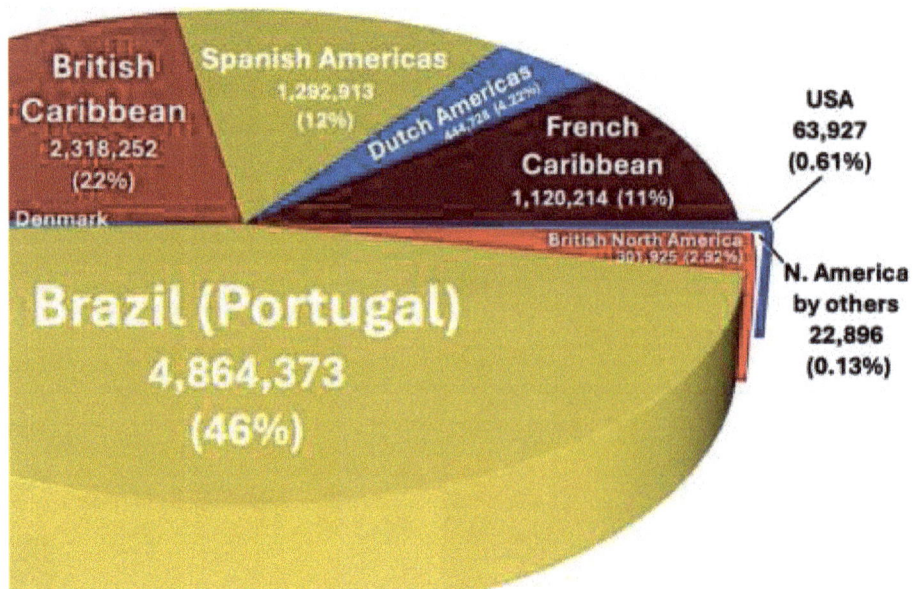

Of the 10.5+ million African Slaves brought to the Americas, 388,747 landed in Mainland North America.

Of those, **301,925 were brought by British and New England ships sailing under the British crown prior to 1776.**

American ships brought 5,086 under the Articles of Confederation and **63,927 that were allowed by the 20 year compromise** in the U.S. Constitution when America could finally regulate the trade.

Other nations and smugglers imported 18,315.

Horrors of Slavery in Africa

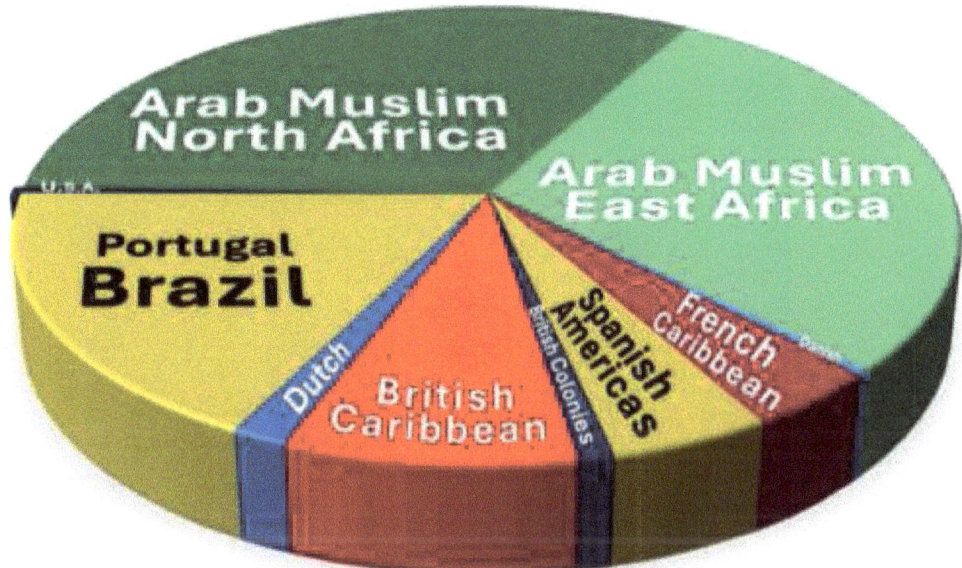

Above: Chart of African slave trade. Representation of the 1,300 year Arab Muslim slave trade is approximate.[136]

The Congo Rubber Terror (1885-1909)

Below: At the Berlin Conference of 1885, Belgian King Leopold was given the Congo Free State in Africa as his personal kingdom. He was going to "civilize and uplift the Congolese population." But the pneumatic tire had been invented by John Dunlap of Scotland. This drove demand for rubber sky high and he enslaved nearly the entire population.[137]

Approximately **35 million were enslaved** and forced by terrible cruelty to meet rubber production quotas. The next decades came to be known as the **"Rubber Terror."** If a village did not produce enough rubber, members of the 18,000 man "Force Publique" cut off the hands of thousands of children to encourage compliance.[138] Slavery and death over that 25 year period exceeded that of the entire 364 years of the Trans-Atlantic Slave Trade and the Arab-Muslim Slave Trade. **Ten to fifteen million slaves died as Leopold became the richest man in the world**. He was worth up to $18 billion in today's dollars. Author Mark Twain's satire ***King Leopold's Soliloquy*** voiced outrage over the enslavement and massacre of the Congolese people. Leopold was forced to cede the Congo to Belgium in 1908. His funeral cortege was booed as it passed through Brussels.[139]

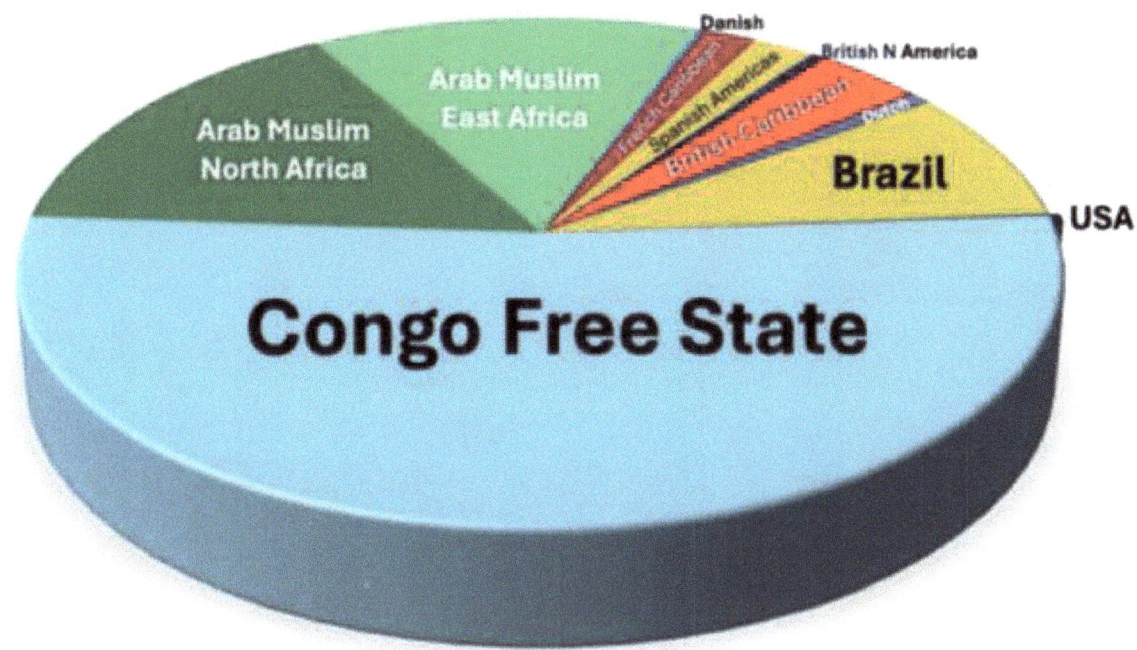

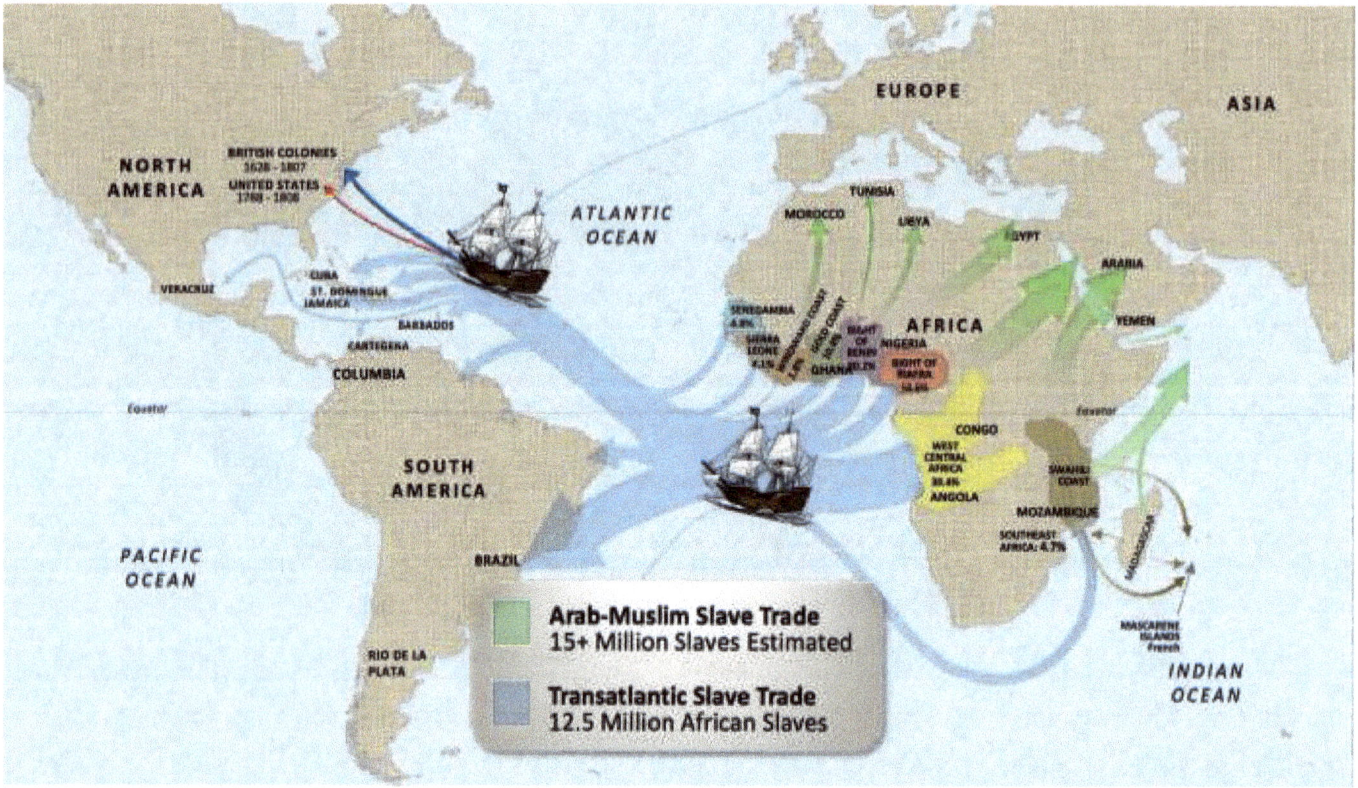

Representations of Trans-Atlantic Slave Trade Transport and Death[140]

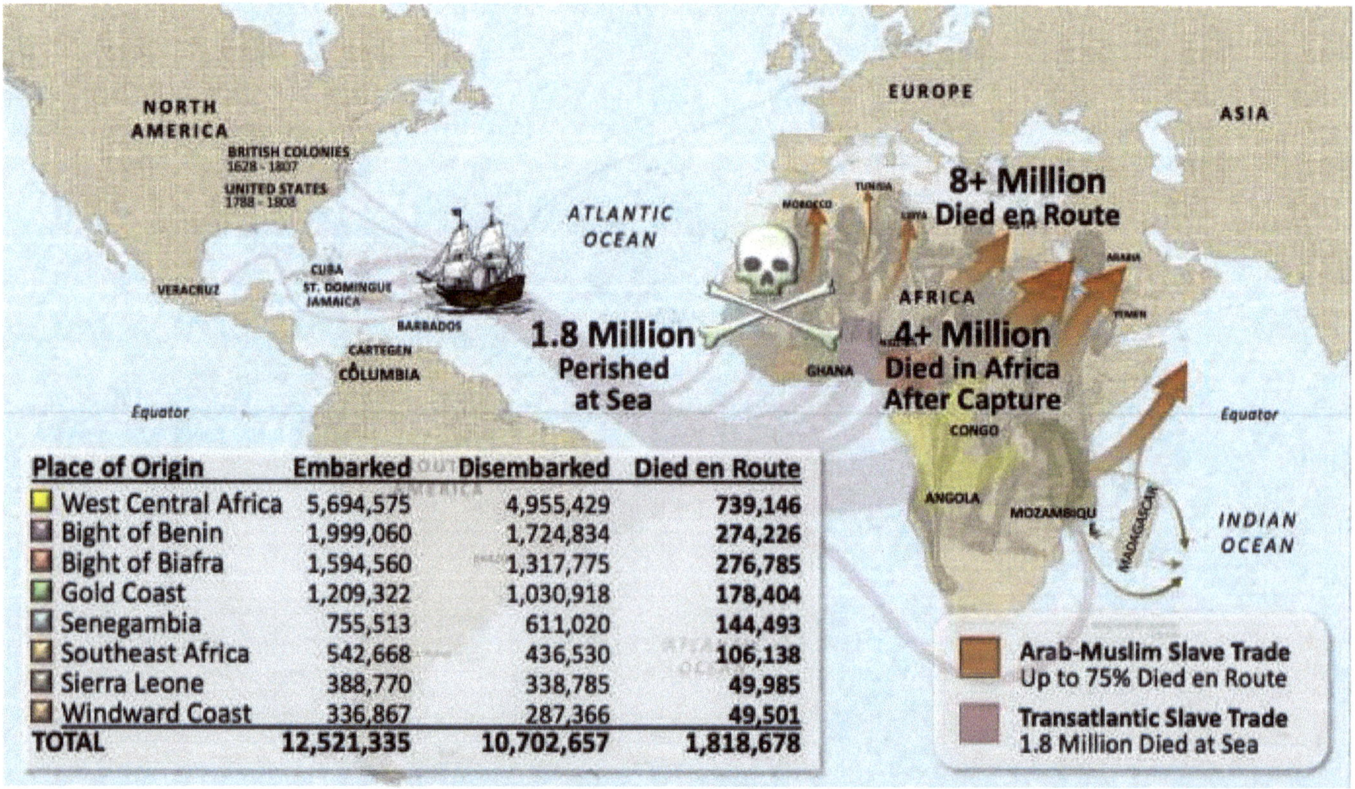

Place of Origin	Embarked	Disembarked	Died en Route
West Central Africa	5,694,575	4,955,429	739,146
Bight of Benin	1,999,060	1,724,834	274,226
Bight of Biafra	1,594,560	1,317,775	276,785
Gold Coast	1,209,322	1,030,918	178,404
Senegambia	755,513	611,020	144,493
Southeast Africa	542,668	436,530	106,138
Sierra Leone	388,770	338,785	49,985
Windward Coast	336,867	287,366	49,501
TOTAL	12,521,335	10,702,657	1,818,678

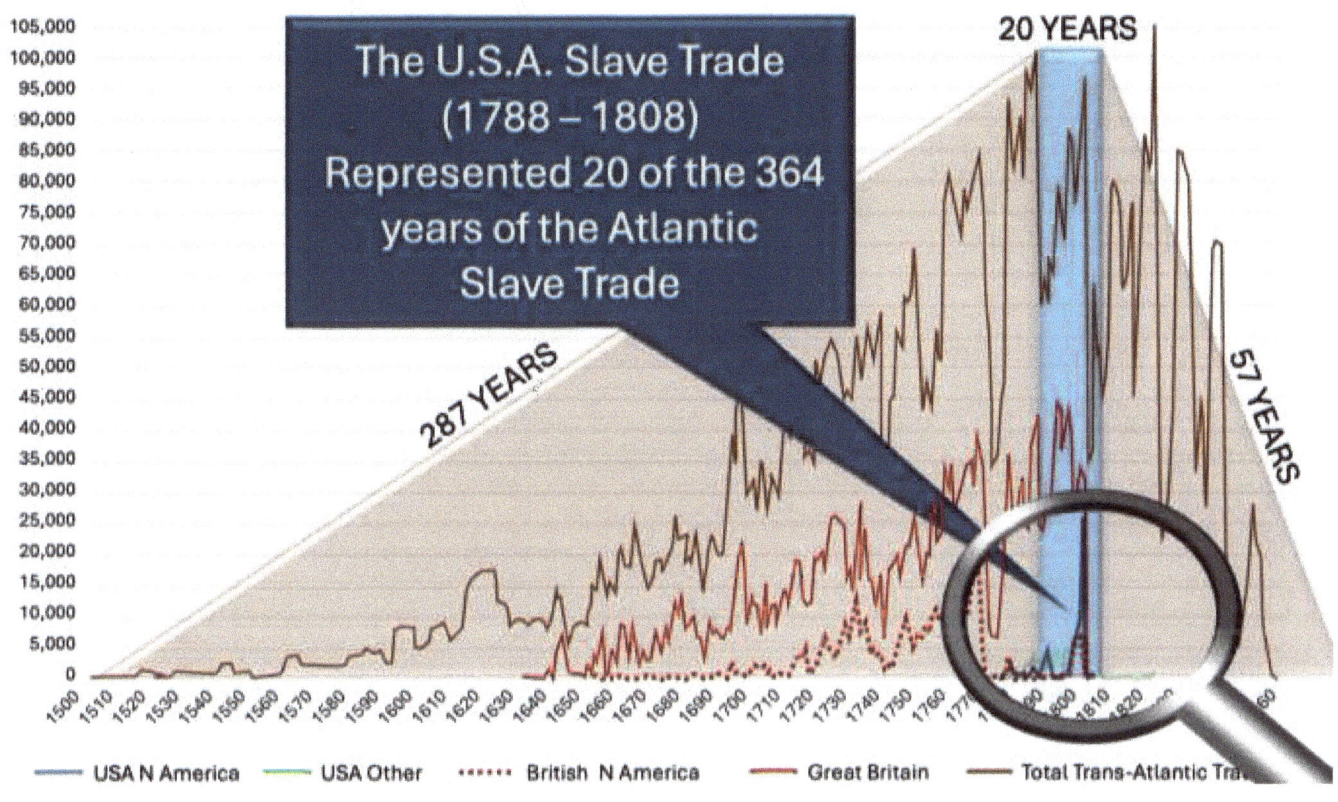

Above: U.S.A., British North America, all British, and total slave trade

Below: Transport and death by slave-trading nation

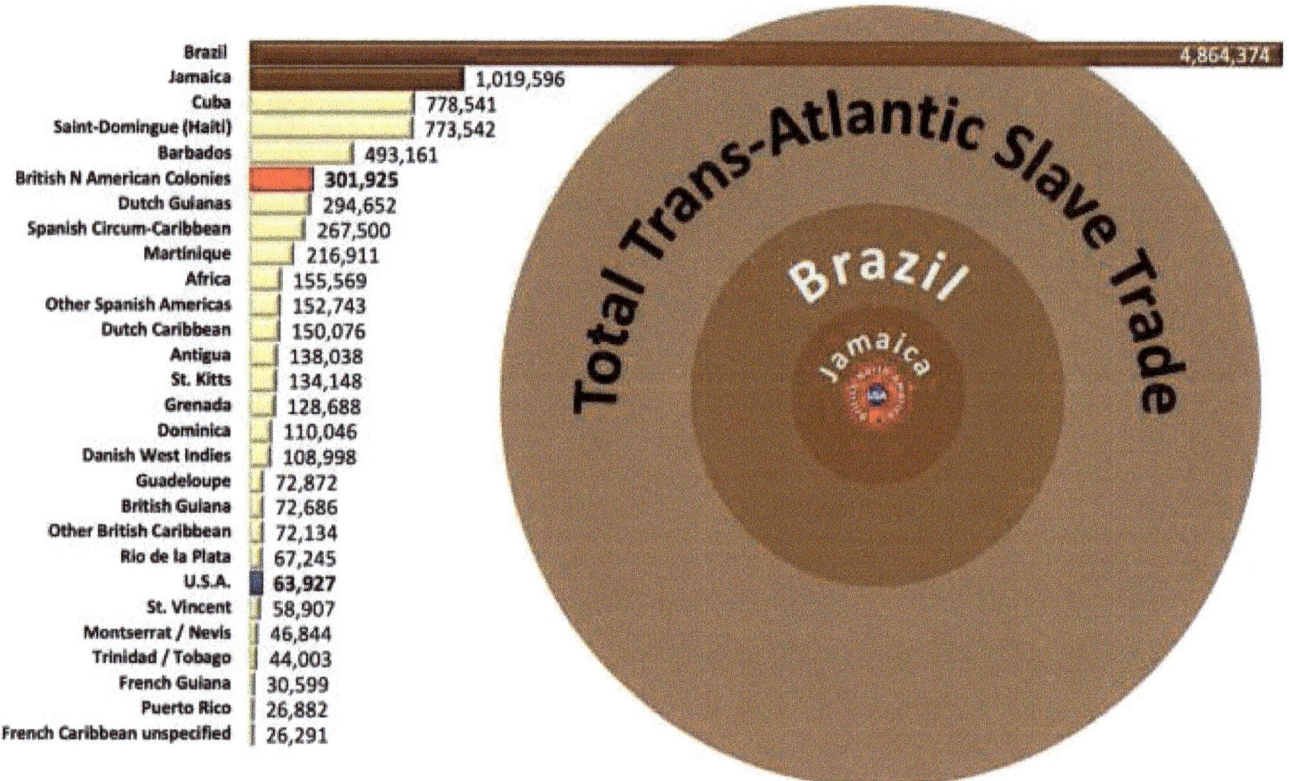

Above: Western hemisphere Trans-Atlantic slave trade destinations.

Below: This screenshot displays SlaveVoyages.org analysis of African Slaves transported under U.S. ships to the United States between 1788 and 1808. It also gives the number of slaves transported by New England slave merchants during that same period. The majority of their destinations outside of the United States were to the Caribbean and West Indies. The data on slides related to the slave trade were extracted from this database, the gold standard in slave trade research. The image below is used with permission from Slave.Voyages.org.

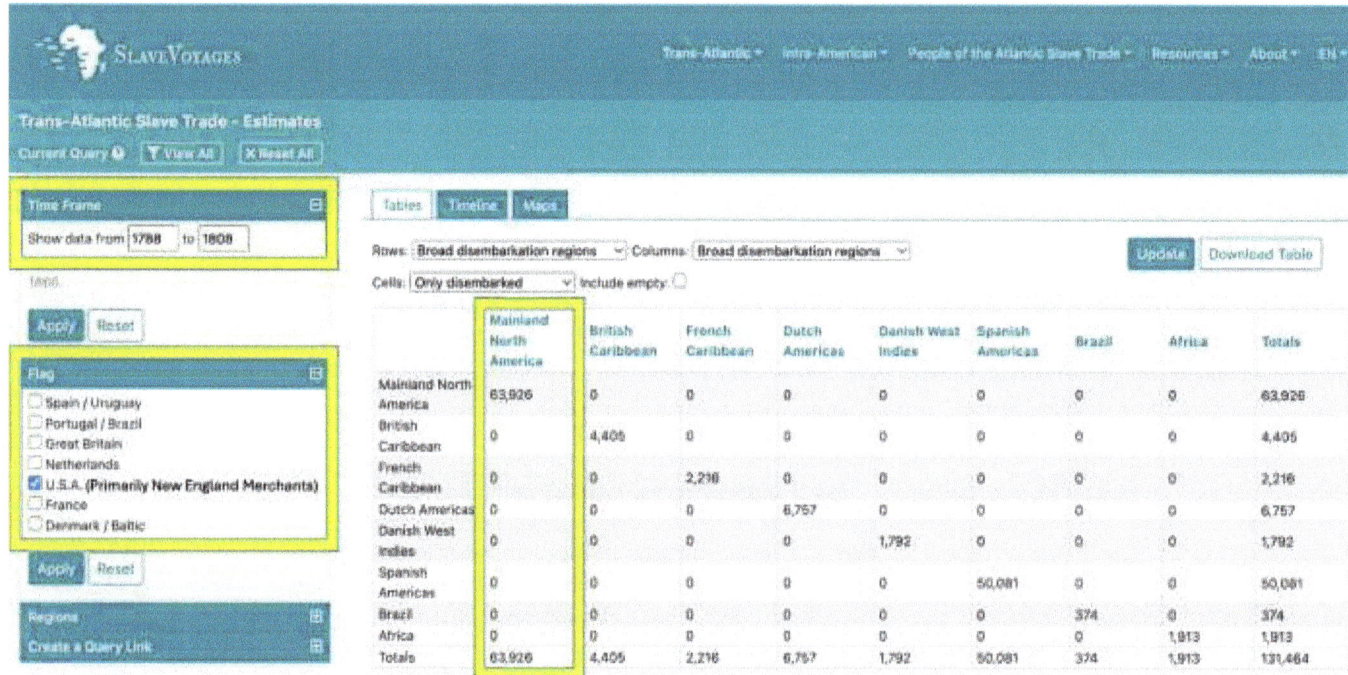

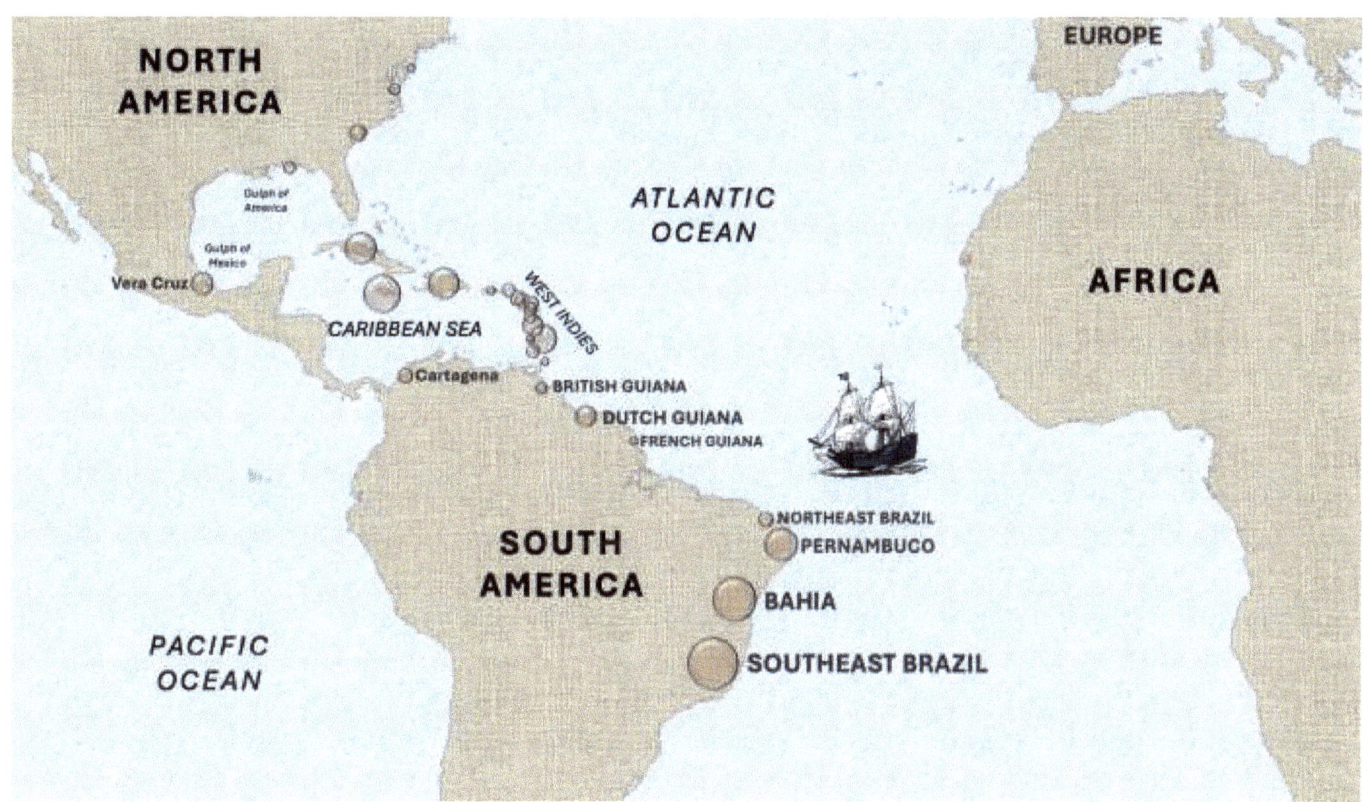

"Bubbles" in the maps above and below represent the relative number of imported slaves.

Above: Five million enslaved Africans arrived in South America, most taken to Brazil by Portuguese traders.

Below: Five million were taken to the Caribbean and West Indies, of which the British were responsible for nearly half.[141]

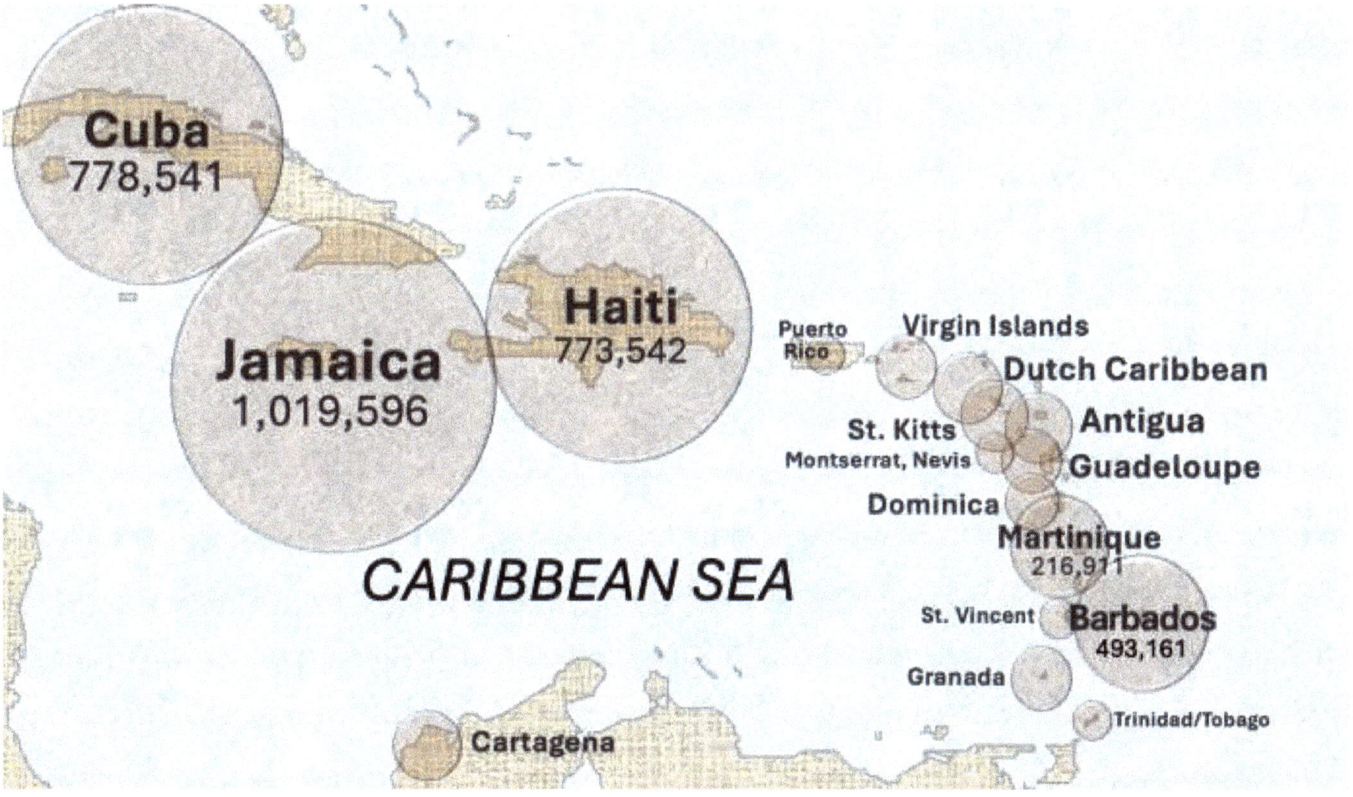

The Three-Fifths Compromise

The Three-Fifths Compromise: A Difficult Decision

The U.S. Constitution decided that each state's population would determine its number of representatives in Congress. But there was a problem—should enslaved people be counted as part of the population?

Some Southern states wanted to count all enslaved people to increase their representation and power in Congress—even though enslaved people had no rights and couldn't vote. But Northern states argued that if enslaved individuals weren't treated as citizens, they shouldn't be counted as part of the voting population.

This led to a fierce debate. If the South got its way, it would have 38 representatives to the North's 36, giving pro-slavery states control of Congress. If the North's plan won, Northern states would have a clear 36 to 25 majority, weakening the South's influence. The South said, "No." Neither side would agree to the other's plan.[142]

Finding a Middle Ground

James Wilson of Pennsylvania proposed a compromise—enslaved people would be counted as three-fifths (60 percent) of a person for both federal taxation and representation. While this 3/5 number seems strange today, it was not about measuring a person's worth. It was a way to manage the South's power in Congress while still keeping them in the Union.

By counting only three-fifths of enslaved people, the North held a slight majority in Congress—35 representatives to the South's 30. This meant pro-slavery states couldn't fully control federal laws. Without this compromise, Southern states might have refused to join the United States at all. Alexander Hamilton later said, "No union could have possibly been formed" without it.

What It Meant for America

The three-fifths compromise weakened the power of slaveholding states, preventing them from having control over national policies. It didn't end slavery, but it made it harder for the South to pass laws that expanded it.

Although the compromise wasn't perfect, it was an important step toward creating a government where all people could eventually be free. Later, after the Civil War, the 13th Amendment abolished slavery entirely, making sure no one could ever be counted as "three-fifths" of a person again.

A Step Toward Change

The three-fifths compromise was not a perfect solution, but it was part of a long struggle to limit the power of slavery in America. Over time, more and more people spoke out against slavery, and new laws were passed to challenge it. The fight for freedom didn't stop with the Constitution—it continued through the Civil War, the 13th Amendment, and beyond.

This debate also showed that compromise was essential in forming the United States. Without it, the Southern states might have refused to join the Union, leaving the country divided before it had even begun. By agreeing to the compromise, the Founders ensured that America could move forward, setting the stage for future generations to continue working toward true equality.

THE CONSTITUTION'S THREE-FIFTHS COMPROMISE & REPRESENTATION

North	Slaves	Total Population	Pct. Slave	Population Minus Slaves	3/5 of Slave Population	Effective for Representation	South Plan	North Plan	Actual 3/5's Plan
Pennsylvania	3,707	443,611	1%	439,904	2,224	442,128	9	9	8
Massachusetts	0	378,566	0%	378,566	0	378,566	7	7	8
New York	21,193	340,241	6%	319,048	12,716	331,764	7	6	6
Connecticut	2,648	237,655	1%	235,007	1,589	236,596	5	5	5
New Jersey	11,423	184,139	6%	172,716	6,854	179,570	4	3	4
New Hampshire	157	141,899	0%	141,742	94	141,836	3	3	3
Rhode Island	958	69,112	1%	68,154	575	68,729	1	1	1
Total	**40,086**	**1,880,564**	**2%**	**1,755,137**	**24,052**	**1,779,189**	**36**	**36**	**35**
South									
Virginia	292,627	747,550	39%	454,923	175,576	630,499	15	9	10
North Carolina	100,783	395,005	26%	294,222	60,470	354,692	8	6	5
Maryland	103,036	319,728	32%	216,692	61,822	278,514	6	4	6
South Carolina	107,094	249,073	43%	141,979	64,256	206,235	5	3	5
Georgia	29,264	82,548	36%	53,284	17,558	70,842	2	1	3
Delaware	8,887	59,096	15%	50,209	5,332	55,541	1	1	1
Total	**654,121**	**1,926,677**	**34%**	**1,211,309**	**385,015**	**1,596,324**	**38**	**25**	**30**

Source: 1790 U.S. Census

© 2024 Charles A Castleberry

THREE-FIFTHS COMPROMISE BY REGION

U.S. House Representatives by State

North	South Plan	North Plan	Three Fifths Compromise
Pennsylvania	9	9	8
Massachusetts	7	7	8
New York	7	6	6
Connecticut	5	5	5
New Jersey	4	3	4
New Hampshire	3	3	3
Rhode Island	1	1	1
Total	**36**	**36**	**35**
South			
Virginia	15	9	10
North Carolina	8	6	5
Maryland	6	4	6
South Carolina	5	3	5
Georgia	2	1	3
Delaware	1	1	1
Total	**38**	**25**	**30**

Source: 1790 U.S. Census

Map labels (State Left/Center/Right = South Plan / North Plan / 3/5 Compromise):
- NH 3/3/3
- New York 7/6/6
- MA 7/7/8
- CT 5/5/5
- Rhode Island 1/1/1
- Pennsylvania 9/9/8
- New Jersey 4/3/4
- Delaware 1/1/1
- Maryland 6/4/6
- Virginia 15/9/10
- North Carolina 8/6/5
- South Carolina 5/3/5
- Georgia 2/1/3

Key: Plan
Left — South Plan
Center — North Plan
Right — 3/5 Compromise

© 2024 Charles A Castleberry

The Three-Fifths and 20-Year Compromises

The Constitution: Racist or Not?

Many today believe that the U.S. Constitution declared Black Americans to be "three-fifths of a person." This misunderstanding has fueled claims that our founding documents were inherently racist. The reality, however, is quite different.

The Three-Fifths Compromise was not a statement of human worth—**it was a strategic constitutional measure to limit the power of slaveholding states**. Southern states wanted enslaved individuals fully counted in the population to gain more congressional representation and more influence in presidential elections. Northern delegates, many of whom opposed slavery, argued that if the South treated enslaved people as property, they should not be counted at all, but taxed as property. The compromise prevented the Southern states from gaining excessive political control and, in doing so, slowed the spread of slavery.

More importantly, **by limiting the political power of the Southern states, the compromise helped lead to enough will in Congress to pass legislation on March 2, 1807, banning U.S. involvement in the international slave trade**, to take effect on January 1, 1808. President Jefferson had encouraged this action in his December 2, 1806, "State of the Union" letter to Congress, where he praised them for being the body that would finally remove the nation from participating in such a barbaric trade.

A Delicate Balancing Act

This compromise also played a key role in shaping the balance of power between North and South, influencing future legislative battles over slavery. While the Southern states sought to maintain and expand slavery, the restriction on their representation prevented them from gaining unchecked influence in the federal government. Over time, as free states grew in population and influence, they were able to push back more effectively against the expansion of slavery. However, it took our nation's deadliest war and a constitutional amendment to end it.

Additionally, the idea that the Constitution was designed to protect slavery ignores the broader historical context. Many of the Founding Fathers were deeply troubled by the institution of slavery, and several took active steps to restrict or abolish it in their respective states. The Northwest Ordinance of 1787, passed under the Articles of Confederation and reaffirmed under the new Constitution, prohibited slavery in new territories north of the Ohio River. This demonstrated that even in the nation's infancy, leaders took steps to curtail the spread of slavery.

Our Founding Fathers were not perfect men, but they laid the foundation for a system that ultimately led to freedom for all. The Constitution, far from being a document that enshrined racism, became the very tool used to abolish slavery and expand liberty through its amendment process. The Three-Fifths Compromise is a reminder that even in difficult circumstances, strategic decisions can bend the arc of history toward justice.

The Twenty-Year Compromise

The Constitution included another important compromise regarding slavery: a twenty-year delay before Congress could ban the importation of enslaved people. This provision, found in Article 1, Section 9, Clause 1, prevented Congress from stopping the transatlantic slave trade until January 1, 1808.

Hamilton later explained to New York's ratifying convention that ***"without this indulgence, no union could have possibly been formed."***[43]

Although this delay allowed the slave trade to continue for two more decades, it didn't stop individual states from taking action. Many Northern states outlawed slavery during this period, but some Southern states—especially South Carolina—ramped up their imports of enslaved people before the deadline.

When the twenty-year period was about to end, Congress acted quickly. **On March 2, 1807, Congress passed the law banning American participation in the transatlantic slave trade, with the ban taking effect on January 1, 1808.** Remarkably, this occurred three weeks before Britain's own abolition of the trade, underscoring America's early—if imperfect—step toward moral leadership. The law had a built-in "trigger" that made it go into effect automatically at the start of 1808. No further votes or legislative actions were required.

However, even after the ban, illegal smuggling continued. Historians estimate that about 5,000 enslaved people were secretly brought into the U.S. after 1808. Still, this number was small compared to the 2.9 million Africans were enslaved and transported to the Americas by Spain and Portugal during the same period.[144]

A Changing Nation

Before the Constitution, **under the *Articles of Confederation*, the federal government had no power to regulate trade**, meaning each state set its own policy on slavery. The new Constitution changed that, but only after the twenty-year waiting period. However, prior to 1808, every state except South Carolina had banned the importation of slaves from Africa.[145]

The compromise also reflected the Founders' attempt to balance immediate union with future justice. They knew that without agreement, the southern states would refuse to join the new Constitution—and the dream of a single republic would collapse before birth. The framers therefore accepted a flawed provision, not to enshrine slavery, but to create the framework through which it could one day be abolished by law rather than entrenched by disunion. In that sense, the Constitution was both a shield and a time-bomb—protecting unity while setting a fuse under the very institution it temporarily tolerated.

This compromise was one of many that held the young nation together. Northern states accepted the delay to keep the Southern states in the Union, and Southern states agreed to the future federal ban on the transatlantic slave trade. While this was not an immediate victory for abolition, it helped limit the expansion of slavery in America.

Jefferson may have lost thirty years earlier when Congress struck his antislavery clause from *The Declaration of Independence*—but he was given a second chance, and this time, it worked:

> "I congratulate you, fellow citizens, on the approach of the period at which you may interpose your authority constitutionally to withdraw the citizens of the United States from all further participation in those violations of human rights."   —Thomas Jefferson, State of the Union Message, Dec. 2, 1806

Summary

The charts on the following pages show how the transatlantic slave trade changed leading up to and after the 1808 ban. Notice how U.S. slave imports averaged just 1,026 per year after the Constitution was signed, but skyrocketed as the twenty-year deadline approached. In 1807 alone, imports surged past 25,000—mostly because South Carolina's slave owners feared Congress might vote to ban the trade as soon as they were allowed to.

At the time, there was no guarantee that Congress would take action—the Constitution only prevented them from banning the trade before 1808. Many feared Northern lawmakers would heed **Jefferson's plea to "withdraw the citizens of the United States from all further participation in those violations of human rights."** They were right. Congress acted at the first lawful opportunity—March 2, 1807—and the ban took effect on January 1, 1808, the earliest date the Constitution allowed.

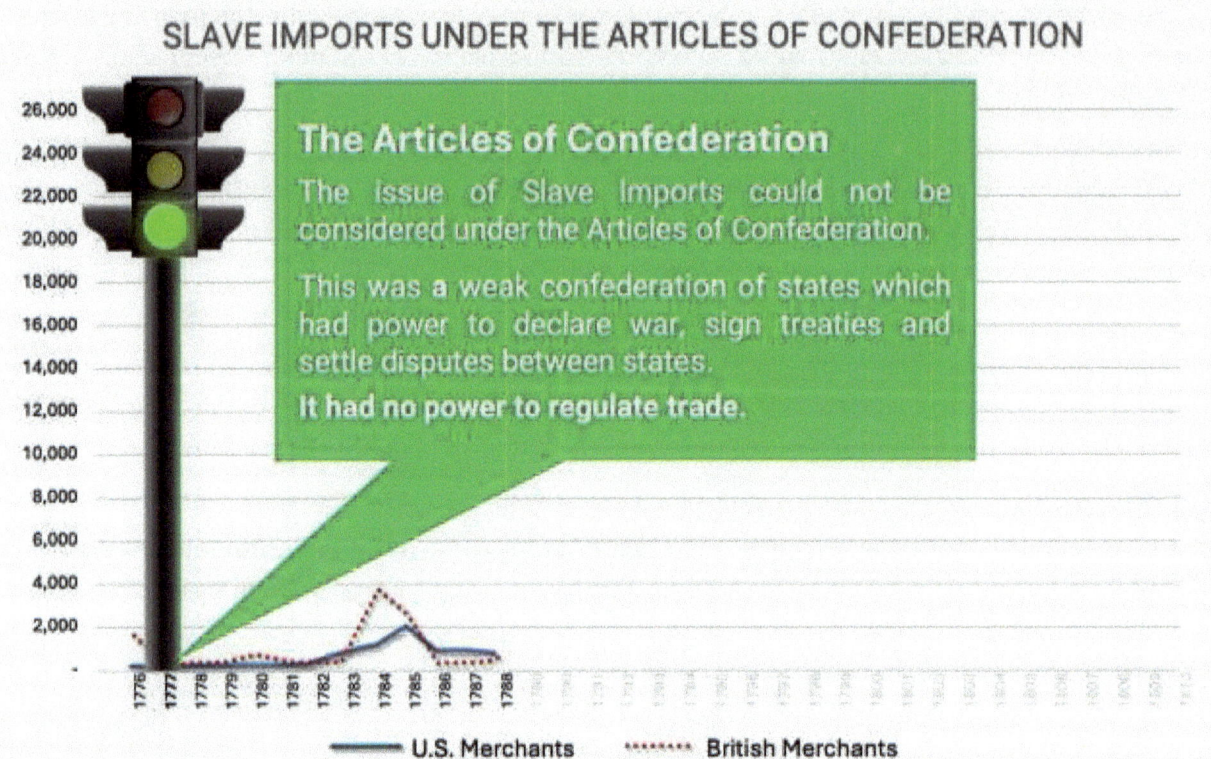

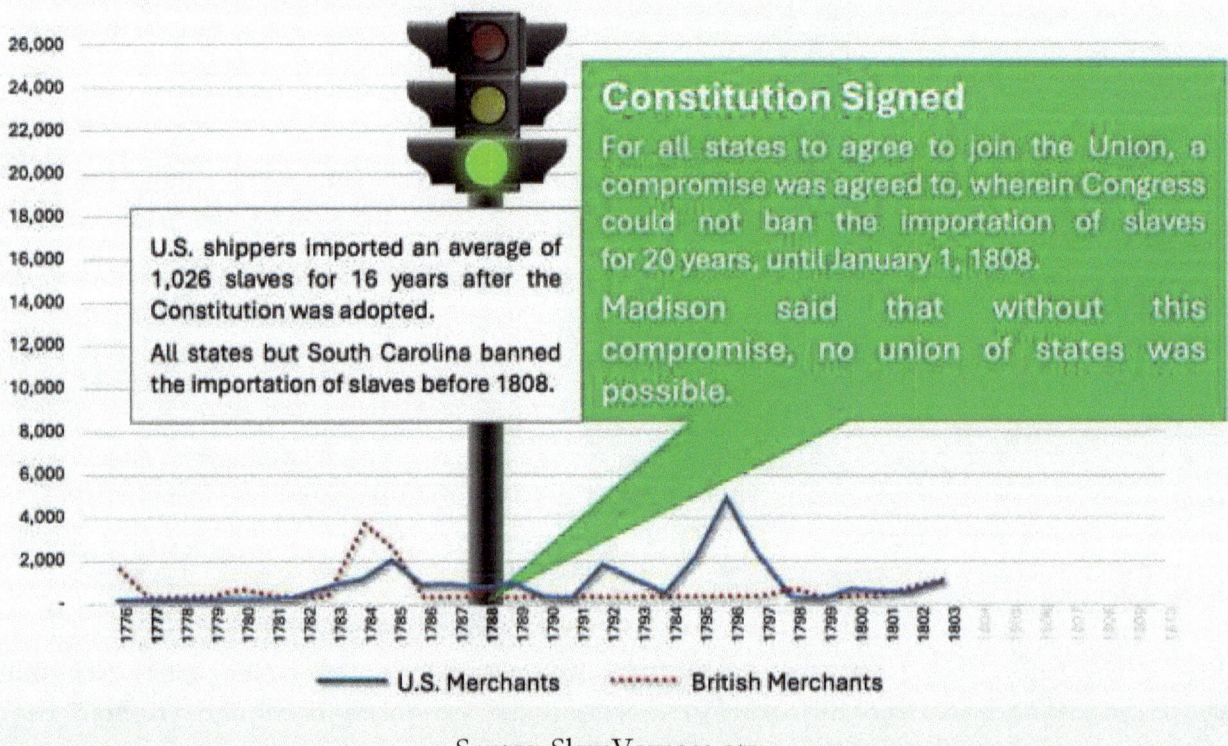

Source: SlaveVoyages.org

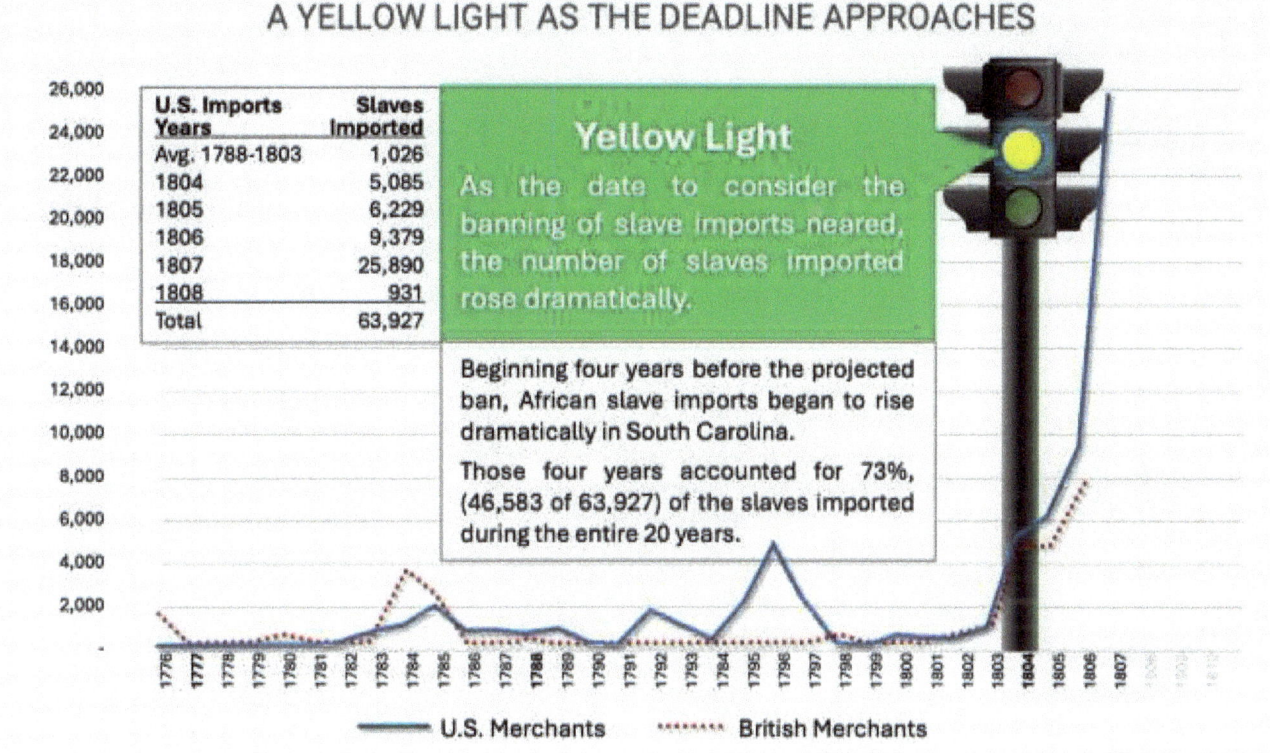

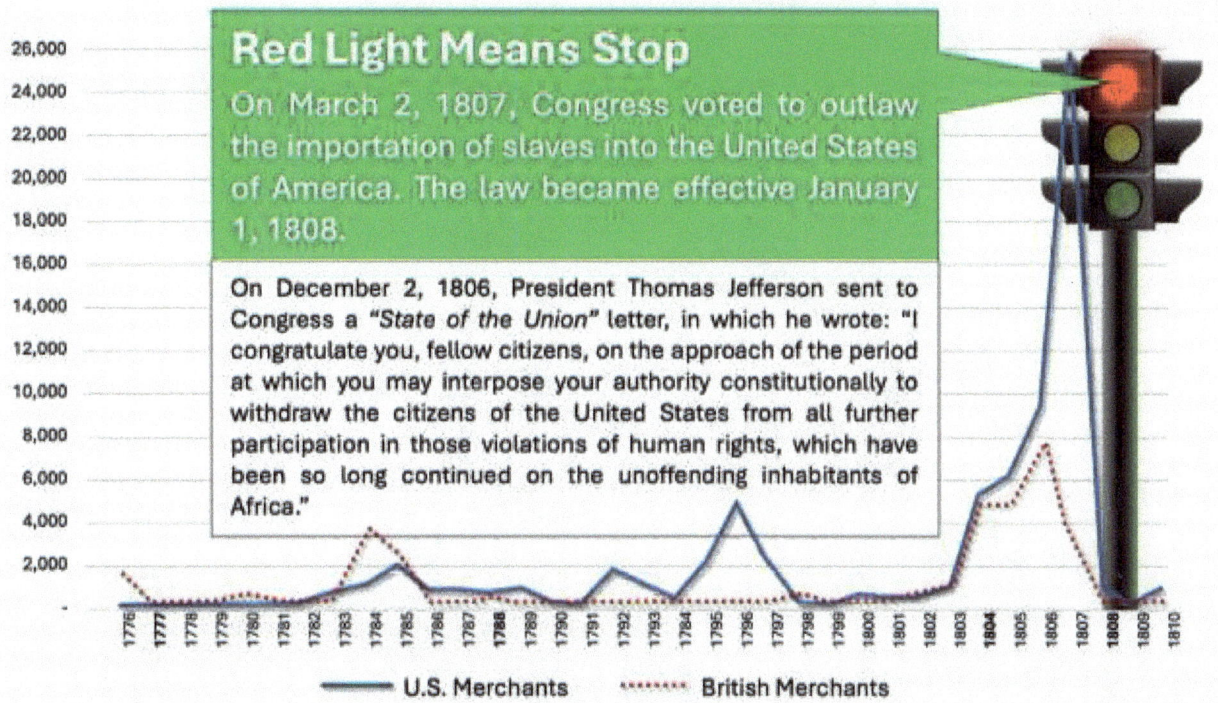

Source: SlaveVoyages.org

American Slave Merchants

New England Triangular Trade

Newport, Bristol, and Providence merchants engaged in commerce with West Africa, the West Indies, the Caribbean, and North American port cities:

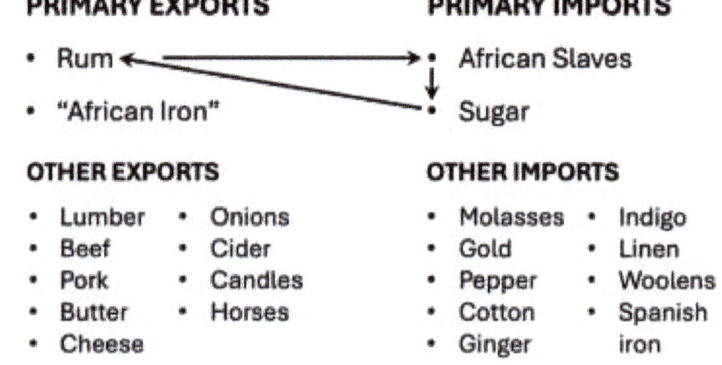

Above: Eleven million gallons of rum were exchanged by Rhode Island slave merchants for over 100,000 slaves in Africa between 1709 and 1809. Exchange was often; 130 gallons for a males, women for 110 gallons, 80 for a child. Major universities were founded on profits from this illicit trade, such as Yale and Brown (named for a major slave trading family).[146]

Below: An illustration of a sample Rhode Island slave trading voyage. This is what came to be called the New England Triangular Trade. It paled in comparison to the British Triangular Trade which resulted in the transport of more than 2.5 million slaves, primarily to the British Caribbean.

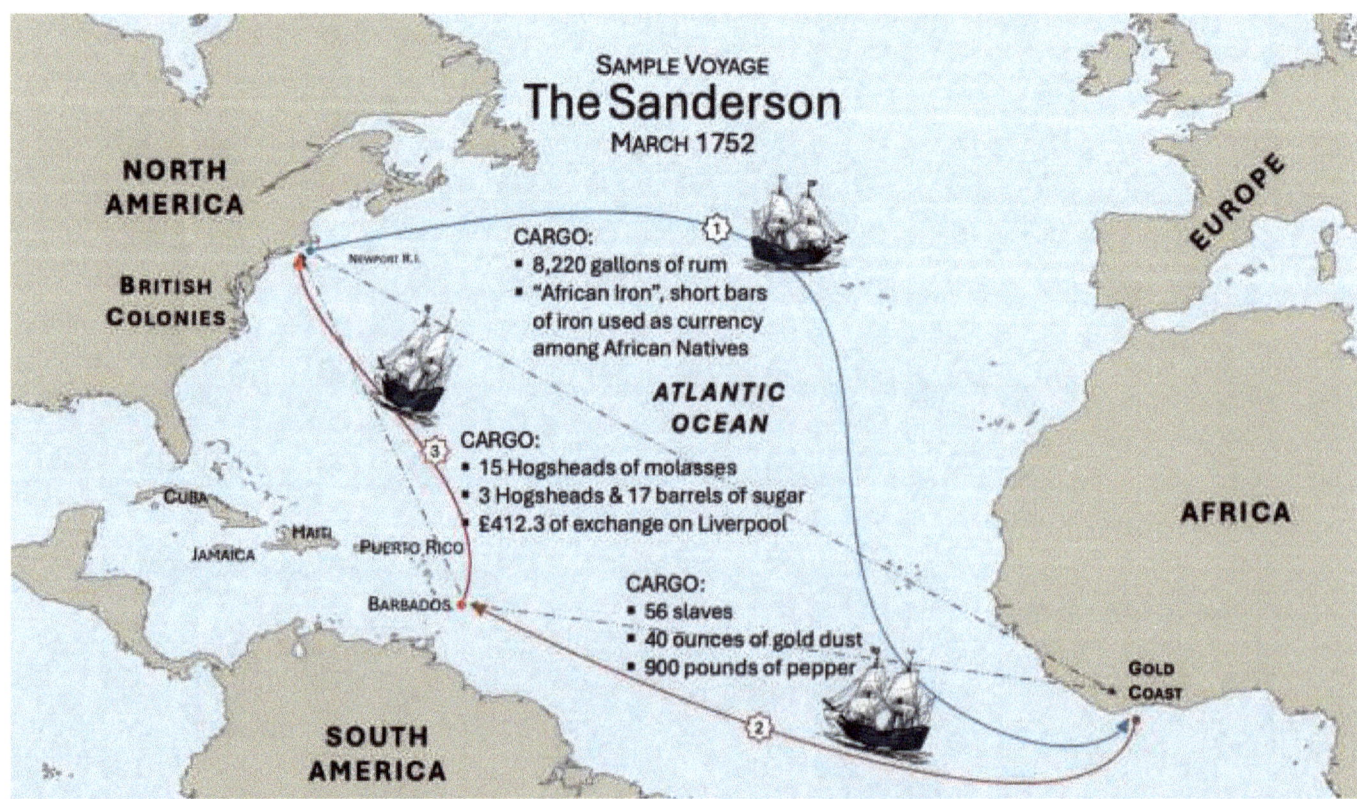

The Distorted Legacy of Jeremiah Dixon

In June of 1761, British astronomer, Charles Mason, and a surveyor, Jeremiah Dixon, were sent by the Royal Society of London to Sumatra to measure the transit of Venus across the sun. They never made it. They were attacked by French ships of war and sailed back to England with cannonballs in the ship's hull. Their trip resumed, but they only made it as far as Cape Town, South Africa, in time to take their measurements. Their findings were later triangulated with teams who had taken readings at distant locations to determine the size of the sun and its distance from the Earth, with similar results regarding Venus.

Amid these groundbreaking contributions to science, Mason and Dixon were called upon to settle a colonial dispute that would ultimately define their legacy.

A Royal Dispute

King Charles I awarded Maryland's charter in 1632, setting its northern boundary at the 40th parallel. Problems soon arose because the king's mapmakers did not know America very well and didn't know where the 40th parallel actually was. Later, in 1681, King Charles II paid off debts he had owed to William Penn's father with a grant of the Province of Pennsylvania. Conflicting interpretations of the boundaries fueled disputes that lasted for 80 years, even leading to Cresap's War in the mid-1730s. 147

The Mason-Dixon Line

By 1763, after decades of disputes, Mason and Dixon were contracted to establish the boundary once and for all.

Mason and Dixon began their work by confirming the line between the Lower Counties of Pennsylvania (now Delaware) and Maryland. They then started the east-west boundary between Maryland and Pennsylvania, which began at a point 15 miles south of the southernmost house in Philadelphia and extended west from the Delaware River. First, they had to survey a 12-mile radius around New Castle, Delaware. Then, they moved westward into the wilderness, taking bearings from the sun and stars as they traversed the rugged terrain.

Within about 20 miles of their intended endpoint, Mason and Dixon's Native guides refused to go further. Some historians speculate that they had crossed into lands reserved for Native nations under the 1763 Proclamation Line, reinforcing the reality that British surveyors had little control over these contested territories. With no way to proceed safely, Mason and Dixon turned back, completing their portion of the line in 1767.

A Tainted Legacy

When Mason and Dixon completed their survey in 1767, slavery existed in every colony, North and South. Yet in 1820, during the debate over Missouri's admission as a slave state, the term "Mason-Dixon Line" was invoked for the first time as a symbolic dividing line between free and slave states. Over time, Jeremiah Dixon's name—"Dixie"—became tangled in the rhetoric of division. Rather than being honored for their precision and problem-solving which healed division, Mason and Dixon's legacy has been distorted into a symbol of division and strife.

The First Slavery Protest
The 1688 Germantown Petition Against Slavery

When most people think about the fight against slavery, they picture events from the 1800s—like the Underground Railroad or the Civil War. But nearly a century before America became a country, a small group of settlers near Philadelphia took a stand against slavery.

In 1683, a group of German immigrants arrived in Pennsylvania searching for religious freedom. They settled in an area that became Germantown, just outside of Philadelphia. Their first winter was brutal—many had to live in caves along the Delaware River to survive. But through hardship, they held onto their strong belief in justice and equality.

One of their leaders, Francis Daniel Pastorius, saw something happening in the colony that deeply troubled him—people were being bought and sold as slaves. The Quakers, the religious group these settlers belonged to, believed in peace and equality—but surprisingly, more than half of British Quakers owned slaves.

Pastorius and three other settlers refused to stay silent. In 1688, they wrote a bold protest called the 1688 Germantown Petition Against Slavery—the first formal document against slavery in American history.[148]

A Bold Stand for Freedom
The petition was simple but powerful. It asked an important question:

> "How can we say we believe in equality while keeping others in chains?"

The petition argued that slavery was wrong because it violated basic human rights. The men presented their petition to their local Quaker Meeting—the group that made decisions for their religious community.

But instead of taking action, Quaker leaders hesitated. They agreed slavery was a serious issue, but they weren't ready to take a stand. The petition was passed from one Quaker meeting to another, eventually reaching Philadelphia and then the Yearly Meeting in Burlington, New Jersey. The official response? "It is too weighty a matter."

Hoping for more support, the men sent their petition to England, believing that Quaker leaders—or even the king—might take notice. But it arrived at a terrible time. England was in the middle of the Glorious Revolution, a major political crisis. The petition was likely lost in the chaos.[149]

For years, the petition was forgotten. But its words did not disappear. Over time, more and more Quakers came to believe that slavery was wrong. By 1776—the year of *The Declaration of Independence*—the Quakers had officially banned slavery in their communities, becoming the first religious group in America to take such a stand.

What Did the Petition Say?

Even though the petition was written in 1688, its ideas still make sense today. If we put its arguments into modern words, it might sound like this:

- **Would you want to be enslaved?** (If not, how can we do it to others?)
- **Pennsylvania was built on freedom,** but slavery **took away people's freedom.**
- **People in Europe wouldn't want to move to a place where people were treated like animals.**
- **Just because someone has darker skin doesn't mean they should be enslaved.**
- **Slaveholders broke families apart, forcing men and women into adultery against their will.**
- **Slavery was stealing**—if Quakers believed stealing was wrong, how could they allow people to be stolen from Africa? And if they purchased slaves they were buying stolen goods!
- **If enslaved people fought back for their freedom, wouldn't they have the right to do so?**

The 1688 Germantown Petition was rejected at first, but its ideas were ahead of their time. It was **the first religious protest in American history to demand the end of slavery**, and it **helped lay the foundation for the abolitionist movement**—the people who fought to end slavery.[150]

Why This Matters

It took almost 90 more years before Pennsylvania officially abolished slavery. It was another 177 years before slavery ended nationwide. But the petition shows that from the very beginning, **there were people in America who believed in freedom for all**.

This document reminds us that standing up for what's right isn't always easy—but it can change history. Today, the petition is recognized as an incredible first step toward ending slavery in America.

The original document is carefully stored in a safe in Lutnick Library at Haverford College near Philadelphia. The author of this book had the rare opportunity to hold that historic petition in his hands—and his immigrant great-grandmother, Catherine, was among those who attended that first protest.

A House Divided Against Itself Cannot Stand
The Fight to End Slavery

On June 16, 1858, Abraham Lincoln gave a speech in Springfield Illinois. This speech was given to over 1,000 delegates at the Illinois State Republican Convention, when he and Stephen A. Douglas were candidates for the U.S. Senate. Many believe the Civil War was not about ending slavery and freeing four million enslaved persons. They claim it was about "States Rights." Sure, the right to own slaves!

This speech led to Lincoln's defeat in his 1858 bid for the Senate but set him up for the 1860 Presidential Election.

> We are now far into the fifth year, since a policy was initiated (The Kansas-Nebraska Act), with the avowed object, and confident promise, of putting an end to slavery agitation. Under the operation of that policy, that agitation has not only, not ceased, but has constantly augmented.
>
> In my opinion, it will not cease, until a crisis shall have been reached, and passed. "A house divided against itself cannot stand." I believe this government cannot endure, permanently half slave and half free.
>
> I do not expect the Union to be dissolved – I do not expect the house to fall – but I do expect it will cease to be divided. It will become all one thing or all the other.
>
> Either the opponents of slavery, will arrest the further spread of it, and place it where the public mind shall rest in the belief that it is in the course of ultimate extinction; or its advocates will push it forward, till it shall become alike lawful in all the States, old as well as new – North as well as South.
>
> … The new year of 1854 found slavery excluded from more than half the States by State Constitutions, and from most of the national territory by congressional prohibition. Four days later, commenced the struggle, which ended in repealing that congressional prohibition (The Missouri Compromise). This opened all the national territory to slavery, and was the first point gained.
>
> Speaking of the 1856 election, Lincoln continued… Two years ago the Republicans of the nation mustered over thirteen hundred thousand strong… we gathered from the four winds, and formed and fought a battle though, under the constant hot fire of a disciplined, proud, and pampered enemy.
>
> Did we brave all then to falter now? – now – when that same enemy is wavering, dissevered and belligerent? The result is not doubtful. We shall not fail – if we stand firm, we shall not fail. Wise councils may accelerate or mistakes delay it, but sooner or later the victory is sure to come.[151]

Abraham Lincoln was not the first Republican candidate for president. That honor belonged to John C. Fremont who led the new party of former Whigs and anti-slavery Democrats. In opposition to the Kansas-Nebraska Act, the Republican Party was formed to defeat the party of slavery—the Democratic Party.[152] The 1856 Democratic National Platform threatened disunion if Congress tampered with "domestic slavery."[153] Fremont lost that 1856 election, but set the stage for Lincoln's victory in 1860.

To the right is a political map prepared in 1856 for John C. Fremont and William L. Dayton, the first candidates for president and vice president on the first Republican Party ticket. It was all about slavery.[154]

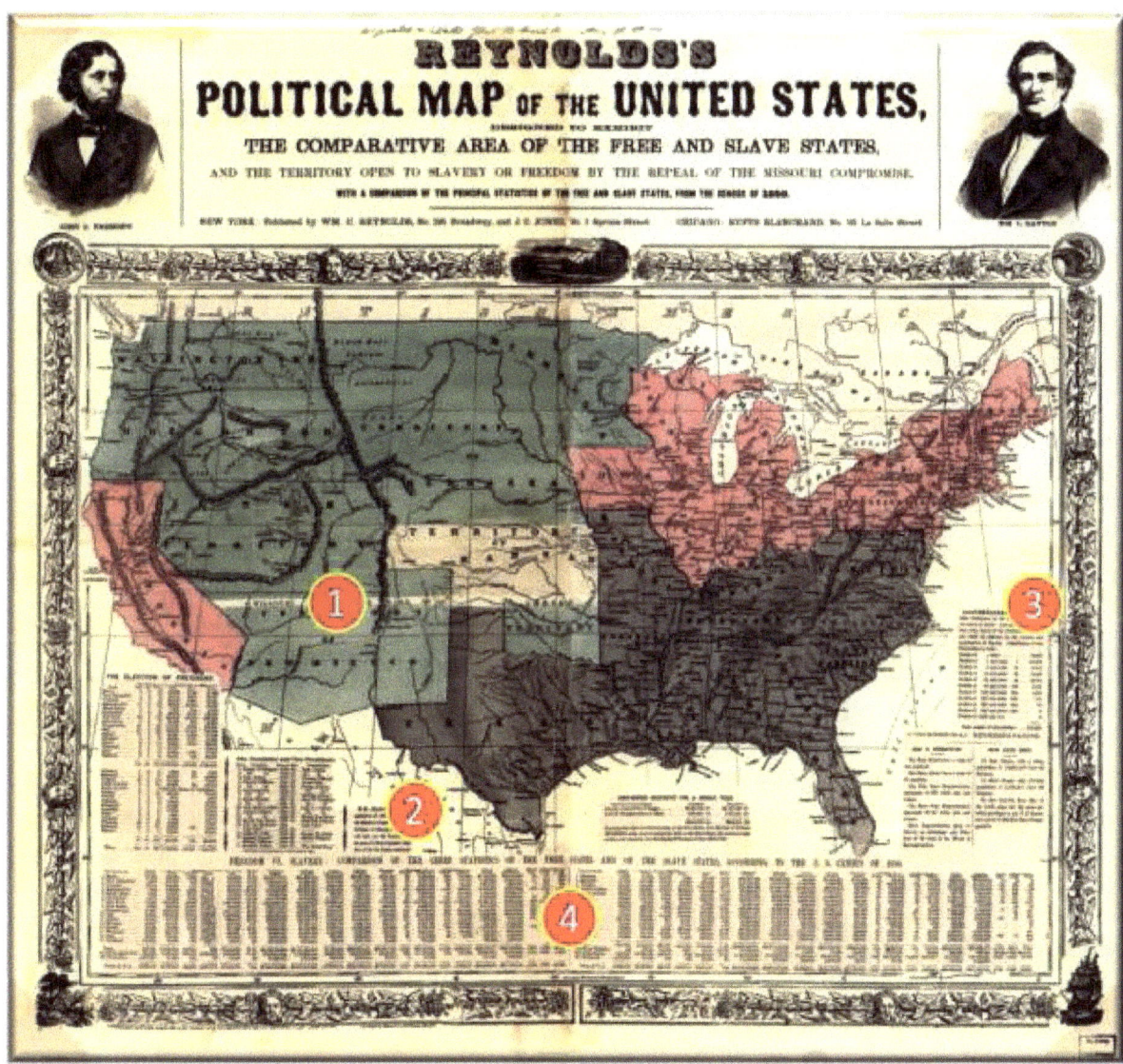

Key Points the Republican Party Stressed on Their 1856 Political Map

1. **36° 30' Slavery Line Erased:**
   The Missouri Compromise Slavery Demarcation Line was erased by the 1854 Democratic Party's Kansas/Nebraska Act. This allowed ALL Territories to vote whether to become Free States or Slave States.

2. **The Democratic legislation of 1854:**
   Repealed the Missouri Compromise, which banned slavery in new states above the southern boundary of Missouri. The institution of Slavery may be carried to all the Territories—the area of which is greater than that of all the States combined.

3. **Large Slaveholders Control Every Branch of the Federal Government:**
   Of the 6,222,418 white inhabitants of the South, only 347,525 are owners of slaves. And yet this faction controls every branch of the Federal Government, and wields its influence for the increase and perpetuation of Slavery.

Southern Slaveholders by the Numbers:

Own 1 slave	68,820	Own 50 – 99	6,196
2 - 4	105,683	100 – 199	1,479
5 – 9	80,765	200 – 299	187
10 – 19	54,595	300 – 499	56
20 – 49	29,744	500 – 999	9
		1,000 and over	2

During the Civil War, the Twenty-Slave Law was passed by the Confederate Congress October 11, 1862. It created an exemption from military conscription for the owners of 20 or more slaves. This law was controversial in that it enflamed social divisions and led to claims by drafted soldiers that they were fighting a "rich man's war."

4. **Industry, Agriculture, Transportation, Social Advancement:**
   The table at the bottom compares the overall prosperity and advancement between the North and South. The differences illustrate how slavery curses, rather than benefits the people—both slave and free.

Blood and Treasure: The Civil War

"**Once let the Black man get upon his person the brass letter, U.S.,** let him get an eagle on his button, and a musket on his shoulder and bullets in his pocket, **there is no power on earth that can deny that he has earned the right to citizenship.**"[155]

Frederick Douglas

Northern, Southern, and Union Black Casualties

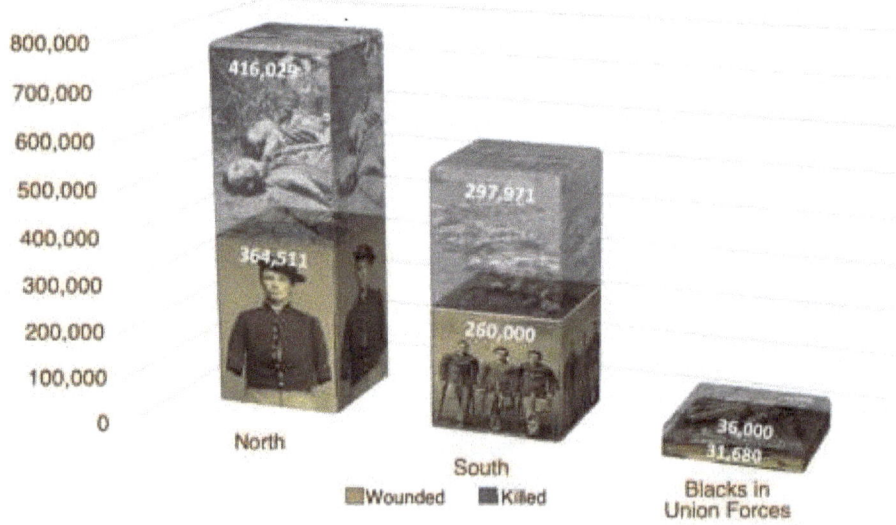

One-point-five million casualties represent the blood of soldiers to free four million slaves during the American Civil War…and they were not all White. 210,000 Black soldiers fought to free their brothers and sisters in chains. Altogether, **186,000 black soldiers served in the Union Army, while another 29,000 served in the Navy,**[156] accounting for nearly **10 percent of all Union forces and 68,178 of the Union dead or missing. Twenty-six African Americans received the Congressional Medal of Honor** for extraordinary bravery in battle.[157]

More Lives Were Lost in the Civil War than All Other Wars Combined

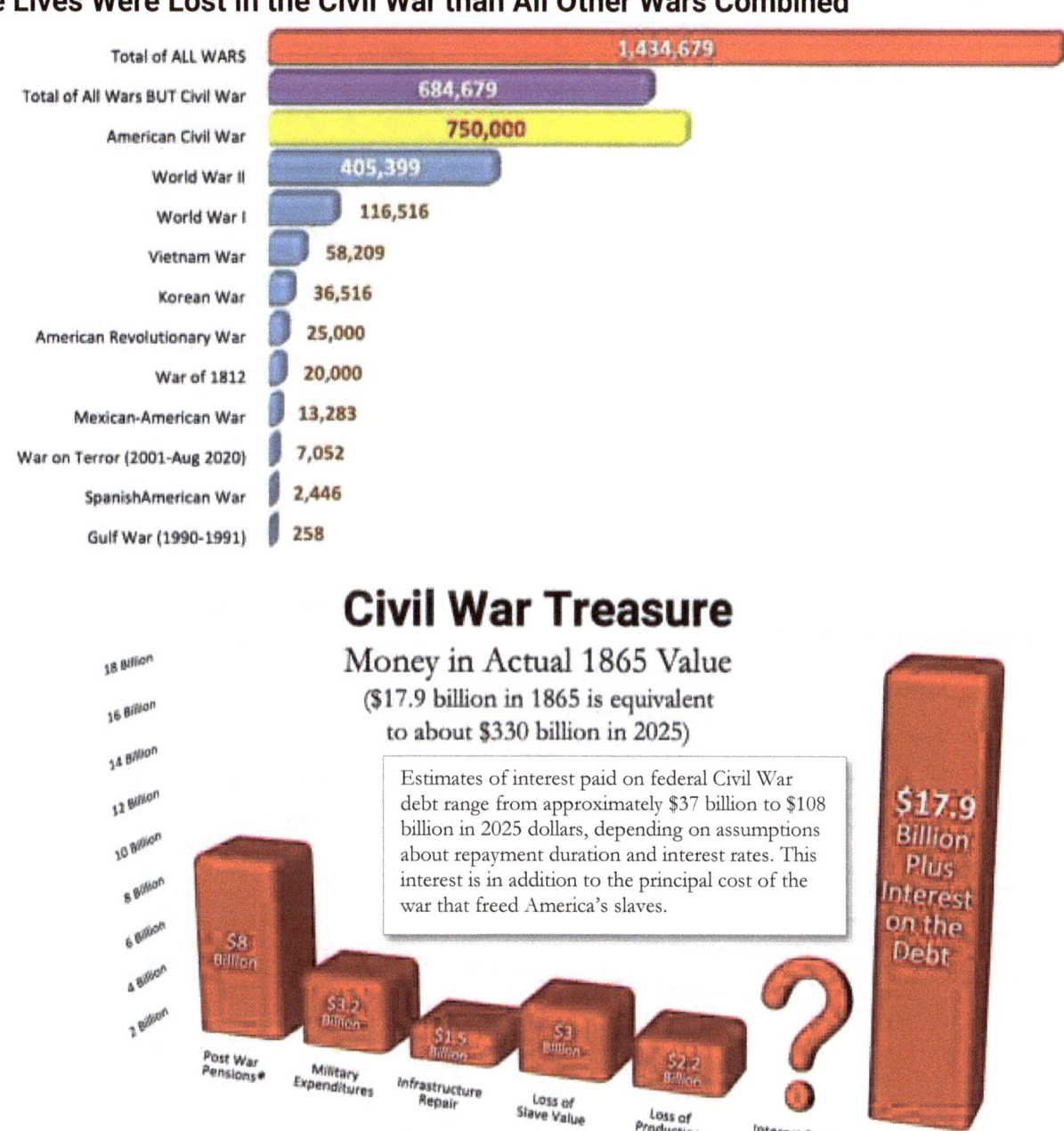

The blood and treasure spent on the Civil War was immense. More lives were lost in the Civil War than all other conflicts combined. New research estimates Civil War loss of life at 750,000[158] and casualties to have been 1.5 million. These sacrifices resulted in the freeing of over 4 million slaves at a cost of $330 billion in today's money.[159] The patriotism exhibited by Black soldiers who fought and died for the cause of freedom was inspiring.

Most Black soldiers enlisted after the **Emancipation Proclamation** of January 1863. The **Emancipation Proclamation freed few slaves**, but **held the promise of freedom for all slaves**. Slaves in states that did not secede (Missouri, Kentucky, West Virginia, Maryland, and Delaware) and areas in the South controlled by the Union were not affected. Nor did it free slaves controlled by states in rebellion. Fulfillment of **that promise was dependent upon winning the war and the Thirteenth Amendment, which passed in December 1865.**[160]

Forgotten Heroes
Black and Native Americans in Our Nation's Military

Throughout American history, Black and Native American soldiers have shown incredible courage, loyalty, and sacrifice—even when they were denied the very freedoms they fought to protect. Their contributions, though often overlooked, have been vital in shaping the history of our nation.

Fighting for a Nation That Didn't Always Fight for Them

During the Revolutionary War, about 5,000 Black men fought for independence, even though many of them were still enslaved. Some were promised freedom in exchange for their service, while others believed in the cause of liberty despite being denied its full benefits. Heroes like Crispus Attucks, Colonel George Middleton, and Salem Poor risked their lives in battles like Bunker Hill and Boston, proving that Black men were willing to fight for America's freedom—even when their own was not guaranteed.[161]

Native Americans also played a major role in the fight for independence, even though they were often caught between the British and the American colonists. Some tribes, like the Stockbridge-Mohican, fought alongside the Patriots, hoping it would protect their land and rights. Others sided with the British, believing they had a better chance of stopping American expansion into their territories. Regardless of their choice, Native warriors fought bravely, but their sacrifices were often met with broken promises after the war.

Unsung Heroes: The Buffalo Soldiers and Immune Troops

When people think of the Spanish-American War, they often picture Teddy Roosevelt and his Rough Riders charging up San Juan Hill. But the real heroes of the battle were the Buffalo Soldiers, the all-Black regiments of the U.S. Army, and the Immune Troops, Black soldiers believed to have resistance to tropical diseases.

At Las Guásimas and San Juan Hill, the Buffalo Soldiers saved Roosevelt and his men—twice. Fighting through intense enemy fire, they cleared paths, took key positions, and held the line against Spanish forces. Without them, the Rough Riders might have been wiped out. Yet their contributions are barely mentioned in many history books.

The bravery of Black soldiers had already been proven time and again. During the Civil War, at least 26 Black soldiers received the Medal of Honor, the nation's highest award for valor. From Fort Wagner to the Battle of Chaffin's Farm, they fought with unmatched courage, risking everything for a country that still denied them full citizenship.

World War I: The Harlem Hellfighters and Code Talkers

During World War I, more than 350,000 Black men served in the U.S. military. Many were assigned to labor and support roles rather than combat, but some fought on the front lines. The 369th Infantry Regiment, known as the Harlem Hellfighters, spent more time in battle than any other American unit and became legendary for their bravery. They fought under the French army, which treated them as equals, and many earned France's highest military honor, the Croix de Guerre.

Native Americans also served in high numbers, with over 12,000 enlisting despite not even being considered U.S. citizens at the time. While Choctaw Soldiers are the most documented group of World War I Code Talkers, the Army used nine tribal languages during the war. Cheyenne, Cherokee, Comanche, Ho-Chunk, Osage, and Yankton Sioux were used as "code talkers," using their Native languages to send secret military messages—an idea that would later become crucial in World War II.[162]

World War II: Breaking Barriers on the Battlefield

In World War II, Black and Native American soldiers once again answered the call to defend freedom. The Tuskegee Airmen, a group of elite Black fighter pilots, shattered stereotypes with their incredible skill and courage in the skies over Europe. Flying more than 15,000 missions, they proved that race had nothing to do with ability—and helped push for the eventual desegregation of the U.S. military.

Meanwhile, 44,000 Native Americans fought in World War II, including the famous Navajo Code Talkers. Their unbreakable code, based on the Navajo language, played a key role in the Pacific battles, including the victory at Iwo Jima. Messages that had taken more than 20 minutes to go through channels took less than 30 seconds for Code Talkers to send and receive. Their secret communication system saved thousands of lives, and decades later, they were finally honored as some of the war's greatest heroes.[163]

Korea, Vietnam, and Beyond: The Fight Continues

By the time of the Korean and Vietnam Wars, the U.S. military had officially ended segregation, allowing Black and Native American soldiers to serve alongside their White counterparts. However, challenges remained. Native Americans volunteered for service at five times the national average, showing their deep commitment to protecting their homeland—even as the U.S. government continued breaking treaties with their tribes.

Black soldiers also faced discrimination, despite making up nearly one-third of front-line troops in Vietnam. They fought bravely but often returned home to racial inequality and unrest. Still, their sacrifices helped push forward the Civil Rights Movement and led to greater opportunities in the military and beyond.[164]

Their Stories Still Matter

The bravery of these soldiers—many of whom never received the recognition they deserved—reminds us that the fight for freedom was never just for all groups of people. The same ideals that inspired *The Declaration of Independence* and the U.S. Constitution apply to everyone. From Crispus Attucks, the first man to die for American liberty, to the unsung heroes who broke barriers in every major war, their legacy is one of courage in the face of injustice. They fought, not just for themselves, but for the future of a country that did not always respect them. Their stories challenge us to ask: What does it really mean to be an American? It means standing up for what's right, even when it is difficult. It means recognizing the contributions of those who were overlooked. And it means continuing to build a country that truly honors the sacrifices made by all who serve.

Colonel George Middleton
Patriot, Protector, and Pioneer

George Middleton, born around 1735, was one of 5,000 African Americans who fought for American independence during the Revolutionary War. He wasn't just a soldier—he was a leader. Skilled in music and an expert horse trainer, Middleton was known and respected among Black and White communities in Boston. But we remember him today because he fought for liberty during the Revolution and long after it ended.[165]

The Bucks of America

During the Revolutionary War, Middleton helped form and lead a Black militia called the Bucks of America. At the time, the Continental Army did not allow all-Black units, so many Black soldiers fought in integrated regiments or worked as laborers. But Middleton's militia was different—it was one of the few all-Black units in the war.

While history hasn't recorded all their battles, the Bucks played a key role in defending Boston. They helped keep order, protect supply routes, and maintain security in the city as "The Protectors." They showed that Black Patriots had just as much at stake in America's future as anyone else. Their service was so valued that after the war, Governor John Hancock personally honored them with a special flag featuring a leaping buck and a pine tree, symbols of strength and freedom in New England. Today, that flag is carefully preserved by the Massachusetts Historical Society, one of the few surviving artifacts that prove the contributions of Black soldiers during the war.[166]

During the Battle of Bunker Hill, 103 Blacks and Native Americans fought with the colonial forces. Among these soldiers were George Middleton, Prince Hall, Salem Poor, Peter Salem, Caesar Brown, and Grant Cooper. Brown and Estabrook were killed in the battle. Peter Salem was credited with shooting British commander, Major Pitcairn, and forcing the British troops to regroup. This gave the smaller colonial force time to retreat rather than surrender. The efforts of these brave soldiers helped avoid a catastrophe.[167]

Fighting for Freedom—Even After the War

Middleton didn't stop fighting for his community once the war ended. He believed that freedom meant more than just independence from Britain—it also meant helping Black Americans build better lives. In 1796, he helped found the African Benevolent Society, one of the first Black-led organizations dedicated to helping those in need.

The society helped freed Black men and women find jobs, provided food and housing for those struggling, and supported widows and orphans. At the time, there weren't many safety nets for people of color, so Middleton and others stepped up to take care of their own. His work helped set an example for future Black mutual aid societies that would form across the country in the years to come.

Standing His Ground

Middleton was also known for his courage. One of the most famous stories about him happened later in his life, when a group of African Americans gathered in a Boston park to celebrate their freedom. Suddenly, a White mob showed up, trying to break up the gathering.

Though Middleton was older at this point, he refused to back down. He grabbed his musket, stood in front of the crowd, and warned the attackers that if they wanted a fight, he was ready. The mob, seeing Middleton's fearless stance, turned and ran. His bravery made him a legend among Boston's Black community.[168]

The Grand Master

Middleton wasn't just a military hero—he was also a leader in the world of Freemasonry, an important social and charitable organization. He worked closely with Prince Hall, one of the most famous Black leaders of the time, and helped run African Lodge No. 459, the first Black Masonic lodge in America.

By 1809, Middleton became the Grand Master of the lodge, helping it grow into a place where Black men could unite, educate themselves, and support one another. The lodge helped provide education, leadership, and community programs, proving that Middleton's dedication to service never ended.[169]

A Lasting Legacy

Middleton's home, located at 5 Pinckney Street in Boston, still stands today as part of the Boston Black Heritage Trail. His leadership—both on and off the battlefield—helped shape the future for Black Americans in Boston and beyond.

Middleton's efforts to defend freedom didn't end in 1783. He, and others like him, continued to push for equality, justice, and opportunity long after the war was won. His courage, leadership, and determination made him a true American hero—one whose name deserves to be honored.

John Howland
The Boy Who Fell Off the Mayflower

John Howland's story is one of survival, leadership, and legacy. At just 21 years of age, he nearly lost his life before the Pilgrims even reached land—falling overboard during a storm on the Mayflower and clinging to a trailing rope until he was rescued. Yet, this young, indentured servant would go on to sign the Mayflower Compact, help secure the colony's financial future, and become a patriarch whose descendants now number over two million people worldwide—including American presidents, world leaders, and cultural icons.

A Hand in Writing the Mayflower Compact
As the clerk and scribe for Governor John Carver, Howland was responsible for recording official documents. Some historians believe he may have actually penned the Mayflower Compact, and he signed it as an indentured servant, not yet a free man. This document laid the foundation for self-governance in America, ensuring that the new colony would be ruled by the consent of the people rather than by a single ruler.

Fur Trade, Diplomacy, and a Risky Encounter on the Kennebec River
After gaining his freedom, Howland became one of Plymouth's key leaders in trade and diplomacy with the Native nations. For 25 years, he traveled annually up the Kennebec River in present-day Maine, where he traded with the Abenaki and other tribes for valuable beaver pelts—essential to paying off the London merchants who financed the Pilgrims' journey.

One of his most harrowing moments came in 1634, when a rival English trader, John Hocking, defied an agreement and anchored his boat in Plymouth's trading territory. Howland sent men in a canoe to cut his boat loose, but Hocking drew his gun, threatening to shoot Howland's men. With tensions running high, Howland yelled at Hocking to aim the gun at him because the men were acting on his orders. Hocking shot a man in the canoe point blank, and his mates returned fire, killing Hocking.

Aiding a Native Leader and Navigating Political Upheaval

Howland is said to have played key roles in keeping peace with the Wampanoag and Abenaki tribes. When a powerful Native chief fell gravely ill, Edward Winslow, and possibly with Howland's assistance, helped him recover—solidifying goodwill between Plymouth and its Indigenous neighbors (*who actually lived forty miles away in what is not Rhode Island*). However, as the English Crown tightened its grip on colonial trade, events like the Hocking incident fueled growing resentment between the colonials. Some historians believe these early struggles over trade and self-rule foreshadowed the very conflicts that led to the American Revolution.

The Last Standing Mayflower Pilgrim Home

In his later years, Howland and his wife, Elizabeth, moved into their son's home, which still stands today as the only surviving home of a Mayflower Pilgrim. This historic site, part of the Plymouth Antiquarian Society, preserves Howland's story for future generations—giving visitors a direct connection to one of America's earliest settlers and leaders.

A Legacy That Shaped America…and the World

John Howland wasn't just a survivor—he was an early builder of the American Republic. He signed one of the first self-governing documents in the New World, helped finance the survival of Plymouth Colony, and played a role in the diplomatic struggles that shaped early American politics.

Howland lived into his eighty's, passing away in 1672 as one of Plymouth's most respected elders. His descendants include some of the most influential figures in history, among them:

- Franklin D. Roosevelt
- Winston Churchill
- Richard Nixon
- George H. W. Bush and George W. Bush
- Ralph Waldo Emerson
- Henry Wadsworth Longfellow
- Joseph Smith
- Laura Ingalls Wilder
- Astronaut John Glenn
- Humphrey Bogart
- Elvis Presley
- Jane Austin
- Dr. Benjamin Spock
- Henry Cabot Lodge, Jr

Howland's legacy isn't just about famous names—it's about the millions of people who carry his story forward today. His descendants now number over two million worldwide—proof that one person's resilience can echo through generations.

I know this well—John Howland is my 10th great-grandfather. His story isn't just history to me—it's family history. But what makes history so exciting is that it belongs to all of us. Whether or not you're one of Howland's descendants, his journey helped shape the nation we live in today. His story reminds us all that even those who fall overboard can rise to shape a nation. And maybe, just maybe, his adventurous spirit lives on in you.

Benjamin Lay
The "Quaker Comet"

Benjamin Lay was a dwarf—only 4½ feet tall—but his determination to end slavery made him a giant in the fight for justice. A Quaker with bold ideas and even bolder actions, Lay was never afraid to challenge people—even when it made him unpopular.

A Man Ahead of His Time

Born in 1682 in England, Lay grew up on a farm before becoming a glove maker, and then a sailor. His travels took him to Barbados, where he married and ran a store. He witnessed the horrifying brutality of slavery. The way enslaved people were treated shocked him to his core. He knew he could never be silent about it.

Lay and his wife, Sarah, moved to Philadelphia, expecting to find a more just society. But to their dismay, they discovered that Quakers—who preached peace and equality—were involved in slavery. More than half of Quakers in Pennsylvania owned enslaved people, including the colony's founder, William Penn.[170]

Lay, no hypocrite, refused to look the other way. He boycotted all goods produced by slave labor, including:

- Sugar
- Tobacco
- Coffee
- Cotton
- Rum
- Chocolate

He even made his own clothes out of flax so he wouldn't wear anything made from enslaved labor. Lay believed that if you truly opposed slavery, you had to live your values—not just talk about them.

Benjamin Lay's Big Protest

Lay wasn't just against slavery—he was willing to call people out for supporting it. And he didn't do it quietly.

One of his most famous protests happened in 1738 at a Quaker Yearly Meeting in New Jersey. Lay knew that many of the wealthy Quakers in the audience owned slaves. He stood before the assembly, holding a hollowed-out book filled with red pokeberry juice—a symbol of blood.

With fire in his eyes, Lay shouted, "God respects all people equally, be they rich or poor, man or woman, White or Black!" Then, he pulled out a dagger and stabbed the book—causing the "blood" to pour down his arm. He splattered the "blood" over the heads of slaveholders, warning that those who enslave others would face judgment—"of body and soul!" People gasped. Women fainted. But Lay didn't care. He had made his point.[171]

An Outcast, But a Legend

Lay's protests made him an outcast among the Quakers, but they also made people think. He lived in a cave outside Philadelphia, choosing a simple life over one that depended on enslaved labor. Even though he was disowned by the Quakers, he never stopped speaking out.

His 1738 book, All Slave-keepers that Keep the Innocent in Bondage, Apostates Pretending to Lay Claim to the Pure & Holy Christian Religion…, was published by Benjamin Franklin, who, at the time, was still involved in slavery himself and advertised for the capture of runaway slaves in his newspaper. But Lay's words were powerful, and Franklin eventually changed his views—becoming an abolitionist later in life.[172]

By the time Lay died in 1759, the Quakers had finally started turning against slavery. In 1776—the same year America declared independence—Quakers officially banned their members from owning slaves. It was a victory Lay didn't live to see, but one that happened because of his fearless fight for justice.

Benjamin Lay Anecdotes

The Snowy Protest – One winter morning, Benjamin Lay stood barefoot in the snow outside a Friends Meetinghouse, refusing to move. His pant-legs were pulled up and he looked like he was about to freeze to death. When concerned Quakers urged him to come inside, he rebuked them: "You pity me, but you do not pity the poor slaves who suffer far worse every day!" His dramatic protests left a lasting impression.

Calling Out Slaveholders – Lay had no patience for hypocrisy. If a Quaker slaveholder dared to speak in a meeting, he would leap to his feet and shout, "There's a man with the blood of slaves on his hands!" His fearless voice made slaveholders squirm—and made abolition impossible to ignore.

Why Benjamin Lay Still Matters

Lay wasn't just against slavery—he lived his beliefs every single day. Unlike Thomas Jefferson, who spoke against slavery but still owned enslaved people, Lay refused to compromise.

His story reminds us that one person can make a difference, even if they stand alone. Change doesn't happen overnight, and it is not always easy. But Lay's life proves that doing what's right is always worth it—even if it means shaking people up.

His nickname, **"The Quaker Comet,"** wasn't just because of his energy—it was because he lit up the sky and left a trail of change burning behind him. Today, he is remembered as one of the boldest voices against slavery in early America—**a man with the spirit of a giant** who refused to remain silent in the face of injustice.

Sarah Bradlee Fulton
"Mother of the Boston Tea Party" and Daughter of Liberty

Sarah Bradlee Fulton wasn't just a witness to history—she was a bold participant who helped shape the American Revolution. Known as the Mother of the Boston Tea Party, she played a critical role in one of the most famous acts of protest against British rule. But her courage didn't stop there. Fulton took action throughout the war, proving that women were just as vital to the Patriot cause as the men who took up arms.

A Patriot from the Beginning

Born in 1740 near Boston, Sarah Bradlee grew up surrounded by discussions of liberty and resistance to British rule. She married John Fulton in 1762, and together, they joined a growing movement of colonists determined to fight for their rights. Sarah became an active member of the **Daughters of Liberty**, a group of women who found creative ways to resist British oppression.

The Daughters of Liberty weren't soldiers, but they used their daily lives as acts of rebellion. They refused to buy British goods, organized spinning bees to make their own cloth, and encouraged colonial businesses to stop relying on imports from England. Their message was clear: America could stand on its own.

The Boston Tea Party: Her Defining Moment

By 1773, tensions between the colonies and Britain had reached a boiling point—especially over unfair taxes. When the British government imposed the Tea Act, colonists in Boston decided to send a clear message: **No taxation without representation!**

On the night of December 16, 1773, Sarah Bradlee Fulton played a key role in the event that would become known as the Boston Tea Party. She disguised the Sons of Liberty as Mohawk Indians, so they wouldn't be recognized when they boarded British ships and dumped 342 chests of tea into Boston Harbor. She also provided shelter for the men afterward, helping them remove their disguises and hide any evidence of their involvement.

Without her quick thinking, many of these Patriots might have been caught and punished by British authorities. Her bravery that night earned her the title **Mother of the Boston Tea Party**, a name that would follow her for the rest of her life.

Serving the Cause in Wartime

When war broke out in 1775, Sarah didn't hesitate to take action. After the Battle of Bunker Hill, she turned her home into a makeshift hospital for wounded soldiers, organizing local women to provide bandages and medical supplies.

She also took on one of the most dangerous missions of the war—delivering a secret message to General George Washington. The journey required her to travel through enemy-controlled territory, where she could have been captured at any moment. But Sarah succeeded, and when she handed the message to Washington, he personally thanked her for her bravery.

Another time, when British forces tried to steal firewood meant for the Continental Army, Sarah physically grabbed the oxen pulling the supply cart and turned them away from the Redcoats. Her defiant act left the British stunned, and she successfully delivered the much-needed firewood to the troops.

The Fight Didn't End in 1776

Sarah Bradlee Fulton's courage didn't just help win the Revolution—it also inspired future generations of women to take action for their country. The Daughters of Liberty set the stage for women's involvement in politics, protest, and community leadership. They proved that patriotism wasn't just about fighting on the battlefield—it was also about making sacrifices, organizing resistance, and standing up for what is right.

Even though she lived in a time when women had few legal rights, Sarah's bravery and leadership were undeniable. She didn't wait for permission to act—she saw what needed to be done and did it. Whether it was disguising the Sons of Liberty, nursing wounded soldiers, or standing up to the British, she proved that women were a force to be reckoned with in the fight for independence.

Her story reminds us that history isn't just made by famous generals or politicians. It's shaped by ordinary people who take extraordinary risks for freedom.

A Lasting Legacy

After the Revolution, Sarah Bradlee Fulton continued to support her country and community. She lived to be 95 years old, passing away in 1835. Sarah's story shows that not all Revolutionary War heroes carried muskets. There were many other patriots, men and women, who dared to take extraordinary risks for the promise of liberty.[173]

Mercy Otis Warren
The Revolutionary Woman Who Wielded a Mighty Pen

Most people involved in the American Revolution fought with muskets, but **Mercy Otis Warren fought with words**. At a time when women weren't supposed to be involved in politics, she used her writing to challenge British rule, inspire Patriots, and later, hold the new government accountable.

A Woman with a Powerful Voice

Born in Massachusetts in 1728, Mercy grew up in a family that believed in education—even for girls, which was unusual at the time. She loved to read and write, and when she married James Warren, a fellow Patriot, she became part of Boston's most important political circles. **The Sons of Liberty**, including leaders like Samuel Adams and John Hancock, **often met in her home to discuss how to resist British rule**.[174]

But Mercy didn't just listen—she took action. She wrote plays and poems that made fun of the Royal Governor and other leaders to expose unfair policies. Her first play, *The Adulator,* was published anonymously in 1772, mocking Massachusetts' governor, Thomas Hutchinson. Another play, *The Defeat,* was just as bold. These writings helped stir up support for the Patriot cause. People who read them began to see how British rule was limiting their freedoms.[175]

Mercy's influence extended beyond the political elite—her work reached ordinary men and women, encouraging them to question authority and fight for their rights. Unlike many political pamphlets of the time, her plays and satirical works were easy to understand, making them effective tools for rallying public opinion. Her ability to blend humor with sharp political critique made her a formidable force, proving that ridicule and wit could be just as powerful as muskets and cannons. At a time when women were expected to remain silent on public affairs, Mercy defied convention, showing that intellect and patriotism knew no gender.

Mercy's talent for writing earned her a place in Revolutionary circles. She exchanged letters with some of the most powerful men of her time, including George Washington, Thomas Jefferson, and John Adams. Many of them respected her sharp mind and political insights, even though it was rare for women to be part of these discussions.[176]

Writing Through the Revolution

During the war, Mercy continued to use her pen as a weapon. She and her husband worked closely with the **Committees of Correspondence**—groups of Patriots who spread news between the colonies. Mercy also helped manage important letters and messages while her husband served as paymaster in the Continental Army.

She was not afraid to speak her mind, even when it meant standing up to friends. After the war, when the U.S. Constitution was being debated, Mercy had serious concerns. She feared the new government might become too powerful—just like the British had been. **She argued that a Bill of Rights was needed** to protect individual freedoms. Her writings encouraged many people to push for these protections, which were finally added in 1791.

Historian of the Revolution

In 1805, **Mercy Otis Warren** published *History of the Rise, Progress, and Termination of the American Revolution*—a massive three-volume account of the war. It was one of the first books written about the Revolution from an American perspective, and the first by a woman.

Unlike other histories of the time, Mercy didn't just celebrate the victories. **She also pointed out mistakes and injustices, including the mistreatment of Native Americans**. She wrote about the Gnadenhutten Massacre of 1782, where nearly 100 peaceful Christian Native Americans were killed by American soldiers. She believed that history should tell the whole truth, even the uncomfortable parts.

Not everyone agreed with her views. John Adams, once one of her closest friends, dismissed her concerns about government power, saying history was "not the province of the ladies." But that didn't stop her. She kept writing, speaking, and fighting for the ideals of liberty, justice, and equality.

A Revolutionary Legacy

Mercy Otis Warren was more than a writer—**she was a voice for freedom when women's voices were often ignored**. She proved that words could change history, and her work continues to remind us that **freedom must be protected, not just won**.

Even today, her book remains an important record of the Revolutionary War, showing what life was like from a perspective that many history books leave out. Mercy's work also set an example for future generations of women who wanted to be involved in shaping their country's future.

More than just a chronicler of history, Mercy Otis Warren was a force in shaping it. As one of the most influential female voices of the Revolutionary era, **she defied expectations, wielding her pen as skillfully as any statesman wielded a sword**. Her sharp political satire exposed British tyranny, while her keen historical analysis ensured that the Revolution's ideals would not be forgotten. Warren understood that **liberty was not won on the battlefield alone—it had to be imprinted and defended in the hearts and minds of the people**. Through her writings, she preserved the Revolution's principles for future generations, proving that true patriotism is measured not just in action, but in **the courage to speak truth to power**.[177]

Benjamin Banneker
A Genius Who Read the Stars, and Saved Washington, D.C.

Benjamin Banneker was born in 1731 near Ellicott's Mills, Maryland. He grew up on a self-sufficient tobacco farm, where he developed a love for nature, science, and learning. Unlike most Black children of the time, Banneker had access to education—a rare privilege. A Quaker schoolteacher, Peter Heinrich, from Bucks County, Pennsylvania, briefly taught Benjamin and shared his books, igniting a passion for mathematics and astronomy. His incredible skill in math, paired with a photographic memory soon set Benjamin apart as a very special child.

Banneker's superior intellect was matched with an insatiable curiosity. He constantly experimented, questioned, and observed the world around him—qualities that would one day make him one of the most remarkable scientific minds in America.

The Boy Who Built a Clock

One of the most famous stories of Banneker's childhood involves a simple pocket watch. A neighbor lent it to him, and instead of just admiring the timepiece, Banneker carefully took it apart piece by piece, studying every tiny gear, wheel, and spring. Then, using only wood and his remarkable memory, he built a fully functional wooden clock—the first of its kind in America.

Even more astonishing? It kept perfect time until the day he died!

At a time when few people even owned watches, Banneker's handmade wooden clock amazed all who saw it. This was a clear sign that his mind was built for invention, precision, and discovery.

A Self-Taught Astronomer Who Corrected the Experts

Banneker wasn't just good with gears and wood—he was also fascinated by the stars. With no formal education in astronomy, he taught himself how to track celestial movements, predict eclipses, and calculate planetary orbits. Using homemade instruments and simple math tables, he charted the heavens with astonishing accuracy.

At a time when only the most elite scholars in Europe understood celestial mechanics, Banneker rivaled the greatest minds in the world. It has been said that his ancestors in Africa could read the stars and chart their courses. Some of this knowledge may have been passed to Benjamin by his father.

His skills were so advanced that he once discovered a major mathematical error in a highly respected British astronomy book. When Banneker corrected the mistake, scholars were stunned. His ability to predict eclipses and track the movements of planets years in advance proved that his brilliance was undeniable.

Saving Washington D.C.

In 1791, the newly formed United States needed a capital city, Banneker worked as an assistant to French engineer Pierre L'Enfant, who was hired to design Washington, D.C. But when L'Enfant had a falling-out with the government, he quit in frustration—taking all the city's plans with him!

It is said, that with the entire project at risk, Banneker was asked to help. Using his remarkable memory, he redrew the entire city layout from scratch, including the locations of its streets, squares, and major buildings. His incredible ability to recall every detail saved the capital's design.[178]

But that wasn't his only contribution. As an astronomer and surveyor, Banneker knew how to use the stars to set precise geographic locations. He is believed to have used the same star-based navigation techniques that Mason and Dixon used to lay out the Mason-Dixon Line a few years earlier. With only the night sky as his guide, Banneker set the cornerstone of Washington, D.C., marking the foundation of the nation's capital.

Challenging Jefferson

Banneker wasn't just a scientist—he was also a man of deep moral conviction. In 1791, he wrote a powerful letter to Thomas Jefferson, the author of *The Declaration of Independence*, challenging him on the hypocrisy of slavery. Jefferson had written that "all men are created equal," yet he enslaved people.

In his letter, Banneker reminded Jefferson that Black Americans were just as intelligent and capable as White Americans. He urged Jefferson to live up to the ideals of *The Declaration of Independence* and take action to end slavery.

> "Sir," he wrote, "how pitiable it is to reflect that although you were so fully convinced of the benevolence of the Father of mankind, you should at the same time counteract His mercies by detaining thousands of my brethren under groaning captivity and cruel oppression."

Surprisingly, Jefferson wrote back, expressing admiration for Banneker's talents and promising to forward a copy of Banneker's almanac to scientists in France. Though Jefferson did not take action by freeing his own slaves, Banneker's courage in speaking out set an example for generations to come.

The Man Who Measured the Stars
By the 1790s, almanacs were among the most widely read books in America. They contained vital information about:

- Solar and lunar eclipses
- Tide tables to help sailors navigate safely
- Weather forecasts for farmers to plant their crops
- Mathematical puzzles and proverbs for education and entertainment
- Anti-slavery essays, where Banneker boldly spoke out against injustice

The Struggle to Publish
Even though Banneker's almanacs were highly accurate and respected, he faced immense challenges in getting them published. Many White printers refused to work with a Black author. Some even doubted that Banneker could have written them himself.

Despite these obstacles, Banneker continued publishing almanacs from 1792 to 1797, distributing them in Pennsylvania, Maryland, Delaware, and Virginia. Thanks to Jefferson, copies even made it across the Atlantic to scientists in France, giving Banneker international recognition.

A Lasting Legacy—And a Tragic Fire
Benjamin Banneker never sought fame or fortune. He simply followed his curiosity, using his mind to better understand the world and help others.

- His wooden clock amazed all who saw it.
- His work in Washington, D.C. helped shape the capital of the United States.
- His letter to Jefferson challenged one of the most powerful men in America to reconsider his views on race and equality.
- His almanacs changed how people viewed African American intellect and ability.

But tragedy struck just hours after Banneker's death on October 19, 1806. His farmhouse, where he had spent years carefully studying the stars and recording his scientific discoveries, burned to the ground. The fire destroyed nearly all of his papers, books, and even the wooden clock he had built as a boy—the one that had kept perfect time for over 40 years.

Everything he had worked so hard to create—his lifetime of research, calculations, and observations—was lost forever. Some believe the fire was accidental, but others suspect it may have been set deliberately to erase his legacy. Despite this terrible loss, Banneker's story could not be erased. His ideas, his writings, and his influence had already spread far beyond his farm. He had changed minds, shattered barriers, and proven that intelligence, creativity, and brilliance know no race or background. Though we will never recover the pages that were lost in the flames, the impact of Benjamin Banneker's life still burns brightly in the history of America.

His almanacs, city maps, and fearless letters all remind us that true greatness comes not from where you are born—but from the fire inside you to learn, explore, and never give up. And so, every time you look up at the night sky, remember Benjamin Banneker—the boy who read the stars and helped shape a nation.

Big Ma-Ma and Prince Banneka

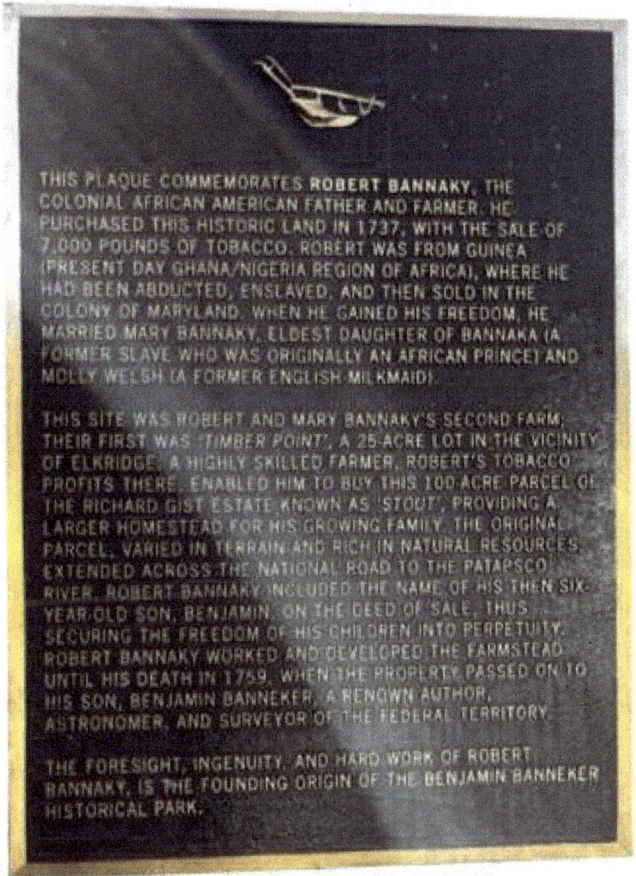

Photo taken by author Feb. 16, 2024
Benjamin Banneker Historical Park, Catonsville, MD

The story of Benjamin Banneker begins long before he was born, in an unlikely pairing that defied all odds—an African prince married an English convict.

His grandparents, Banneka, the son of a West African king, and Molly Welsh, a former indentured servant from England, built a life together in Maryland that would lay the foundation for their grandson's extraordinary mind.

Molly Welsh's journey to America began under cruel circumstances. As a young woman in England, she was falsely accused of theft after spilling a pail of milk and sentenced to seven years of indentured servitude in Maryland instead of execution (because she could read). Unlike many servants who never escaped their bonds, Molly not only survived but thrived, eventually securing land of her own. But she needed help to make it work.

That help came in an unusual form. At an auction of enslaved men, Molly purchased two African laborers fresh off the boat—one strong and muscular, the other lean and regal in demeanor. She soon discovered that the second man was Banneka, the son of an African king, captured in a raid and sold into slavery. Though many viewed him as ill-suited for labor, Molly recognized something different—a sharp mind and a quiet strength.

Over time, respect turned to love. Molly freed Banneka and married him, an astonishing act in colonial Maryland. Maryland law did not yet prohibit interracial marriage, but that would soon change. She called him "The Prince," and the family referred to her as "Big Ma-Ma"—a woman whose sheer willpower had built a life from nothing. Together, they raised four daughters, including Mary Banneky, Benjamin's mother.

The Prince, though weakened by the horrors of the Middle Passage, possessed remarkable skills that set him apart from other farmers. He was an expert hunter, ensuring the family always had food, but his most astonishing gift was his ability to predict the weather with uncanny accuracy. Long before scientific meteorology, he could sense shifts in the wind and patterns in the sky, allowing his crops to thrive while others struggled.

It's easy to see how young Benjamin inherited his grandfather's talents. Banneka's knowledge of the stars, seasons, and tides—passed down from the Dogon people of West Africa, acclaimed for their mastery of astronomy—seemed to take root in Benjamin's mind, preparing him for his own discoveries.

But it wasn't just nature that shaped Banneker—it was nurture, too. Big Ma-Ma saw something special in her grandson and poured every ounce of wisdom she had into him. She taught him to read using the same Bible that had saved her life in England and told him stories of survival, courage, and resilience.

This unusual heritage—a prince's knowledge, a convict's determination, and a family's belief in the power of education—shaped Benjamin Banneker into the genius he became—that and his photographic memory!

His destiny was written not just in the stars he studied, but in the courage of those who came before him.

Frances Ellen Watkins Harper
Activist, Poet, and Prophet of an American Dream

Plaque marking the Philadelphia home of Frances Ellen Watkins Harper, placed by the Pennsylvania Historical and Museum Commission, 1991. Used by permission. This home, where she lived here from 1870 until her death in 1911 was designated a National Historic Landmark in 1976. Her 1872 image is at the Library of Congress.

In the annals of American history, certain voices resonate across the centuries, echoing wisdom, resilience, and a profound call for justice. Among these voices, Frances Ellen Watkins Harper stands out as a poet, writer, educator, and activist whose life and work defined the struggle for equality in nineteenth-century America.

Known as the **"Dean of African American Writers"** of her time, Harper used her gifts with language to champion the causes of abolition, suffrage, temperance, and education, becoming a guiding light for her people in a deeply divided nation.

A Voice for Justice

Born free in Baltimore, Maryland, in 1825, Frances Ellen Watkins was raised by her uncle, a minister, after being orphaned at a young age. Her uncle operated a school for Black children, where Harper received an education that was rare for African Americans in the pre–Civil War era. From an early age, she displayed a keen intellect and a passion for learning, characteristics that would shape her life's work. By the age of twenty, she had published her first collection of poetry, *Forest Leaves*, which showcased her burgeoning literary talent and laid the foundation for a prolific career that spanned nearly seven decades.

Abolition and Women's Rights

Harper's path soon took her beyond the world of poetry and into the public sphere. In the 1850s, she became actively involved in abolitionist causes, writing and lecturing to for the end of slavery. She traveled extensively, speaking on behalf of the Pennsylvania Anti-Slavery Society and other organizations. These travels often placed her in hostile environments and physical hardships, yet she remained undeterred. One of her most compelling public addresses, *"We Are All Bound Up Together,"* delivered at the National Women's Rights Convention in 1866, captivated audiences with its moral force and impassioned plea for freedom and justice. She reflected on these experiences in writings that paint a vivid picture of the challenges faced in the fight against slavery.

Service and Sacrifice

The end of the Civil War marked a new chapter for Harper. With the abolition of slavery came the task of rebuilding the nation and ensuring the full participation of African Americans in society. Harper dedicated herself to this work, journeying into the heart of the post-war South to educate and support newly emancipated African Americans. Her accounts of these travels reveal the privations she endured: the long, uncomfortable journeys, the hostile environments, and the daily struggles of those she sought to help. Yet, her spirit remained unbroken. Harper viewed this work as both a duty and a calling, feeling a deep connection to the people she served.

Speaking Her Mind

Harper expressed deep disgust with President Lincoln's proposal to colonize the formerly enslaved outside of the United States. She saw the plan as both a betrayal of the very principles of freedom and a misguided notion that four million people could simply be removed from American society. Harper criticized this idea as an attempt to erase the contributions and future potential of freed Blacks, pointing out the absurdity of replacing such a vital part of the nation's workforce. The following selection, written in the midst of the Civil War in 1862, is from "Mrs. Frances E. Watkins Harper on the War and the President's Colonization Scheme:"

> Heavy is the guilt that hangs upon the neck of this nation, and where is the first sign of national repentance? The least signs of contrition for the wrongs of the Indian and the negro? As this nation has had glorious opportunities for standing as an example to the nations leading the van of the world's progress, and inviting the groaning millions to a higher destiny; but instead of that she has dwarfed herself to slavery's base and ignoble ends, and now, smitten of God and conquered by her crimes, she has become a mournful warning, a sad exemplification of the close connexion between national crimes and national judgments.

Harper's opinion was in response to a colonization movement which had never gained popularity among African Americans or abolitionists. Frederick Douglass condemned it in 1849, declaring, "We live here—have lived here—have a right to live here, and mean to live here." Yet, in 1862, President Lincoln met with Black leaders at the White House, advocating for their emigration as he argued, "It is better for us both…to be separated."[179]

In addition to her educational efforts, Harper's advocacy extended to the realms of women's suffrage and temperance. She recognized that the struggle for African American freedom was intrinsically linked to the rights of women, arguing eloquently for universal suffrage. Her speeches and writings on the topic showcased her ability to weave the threads of race, gender, and social justice into a coherent and compelling argument for equality. As she stated in her 1866 address: "We are all bound up together in one great bundle of humanity, and society cannot trample on the weakest and feeblest of its members without receiving the curse in its own soul." Her words exhibited prophetic clarity, insisting that the promise of the American republic could only be realized when all its citizens, regardless of race or gender, were granted their full rights.

The Dean of African American Writers

Her poetry often reflected a call for newly freed men to rise to the demands of newfound freedom and citizenship. In works *like "Aunt Chloe's Politics,"* Harper urged Black men not to squander their hard-won rights for fleeting pleasures, cautioning against selling their votes for a drink of liquor. Harper contrasted this with the steadfastness of women, whom she saw as more grounded and unwavering in their commitment to building a just society.

One of Harper's most poignant contributions was her novel, Iola Leroy, published in 1892. Through its narrative, Harper explored themes of race, identity, and the complexities of life for African Americans in the Reconstruction era. The novel not only offered readers a rare glimpse into the Black experience of the time but also served as a form of resistance, countering the prevailing stereotypes and assumptions about African Americans. *Iola Leroy* stands today as one of the earliest novels published by an African American woman and remains a testament to Harper's literary genius and her commitment to social justice.

Her poetry, often imbued with a prophetic tone, struck at the moral conscience of the nation. In works like *"Bury Me in a Free Land,"* she lamented the horrors of slavery and invoked a powerful vision of liberty and human dignity. Her words transcended the page, becoming a rallying cry for generations of activists who followed. Harper's pen was her sword, and she wielded it with unmatched skill, challenging her readers to confront the injustices of their time. **In** *"Bury Me in a Free Land,"* she wrote, **"I ask no monument, proud and high, to arrest the gaze of the passers-by; All that my yearning spirit craves, is bury me not in a land of slaves."**

A Life Among Legends

During her life, Harper enjoyed close associations with prominent figures of the abolitionist and suffrage movements, yet she carved out a unique space for herself as an independent thinker and leader. She corresponded with Frederick Douglass, admired Harriet Tubman for her courage and tenacity, and engaged with W. E. B. Du Bois, who at one time lived just down the street from her in Philadelphia. These connections placed her at the heart of the intellectual and social movements that shaped the course of African American history.

It was in Philadelphia that she spent the final years of her life, continuing her activism and writing until her death in 1911. Harper's presence in Philadelphia's vibrant community of African American leaders imbued her work with an unyielding sense of hope. Her house, now marked as a National Historic Site, was a gathering place for like-minded individuals who believed in the possibility of a better future. The city itself, home to so many luminaries like Tubman and Du Bois, became a symbol of the potential for progress and the perseverance of the African American spirit. Standing in front of Harper's former residence, one can almost hear the echoes of her words, urging us forward: *"We can do this."*

Note from the Author

In my journey through American history, I came across the works of Benson J. Lossing and felt compelled to order three volumes of his 1879 series, *Our Country*. When the books arrived, I noticed a beautifully inscribed signature on an otherwise blank page near the front of each volume. It was *"F. E. Watkins,"* the first owner of these three rare books. The significance of these signatures did not strike me until I compared them with an online sample. They were the same! **Imagine my astonishment when I realized these incredible books had once belonged to one of the most powerful voices for abolition and the dean of nineteenth-century African American literature!**

Polly Cooper, Oneida Angel of Valley Forge

Winter was bitter at Valley Forge. Rivers froze in silence beneath sheets of ice, trees stood skeletal and still, and snow fell heavy and unrelenting across the hills—as hungry soldiers froze.

"Allies in War, Partners in Peace," Smithsonian National Museum of the American Indian, Courtesy of Edward Hlavka, Rapid City, SD

But help was coming—from deep within the Northern forests, where tall pines whispered to the sky. General Lafayette had been sent from Valley Forge to Albany, New York, to lead an attack on Canada. The promised force did not materialize, and he learned the folly of the venture. Lafayette turned instead to the Oneida, heroes of the Battles of Oriskany and Saratoga, inviting 47 warriors to join him at Valley Forge.[180]

When old Chief Shenandoah heard of the suffering at Valley Forge, he was determined to help. Towering at six feet five and full of quiet strength, he was a man respected for both wisdom and courage. He had pledged his support to the rebels and was ready to help.

Shenandoah sent the warriors, including one of his two sons. Oneida legend says they brought with them six hundred baskets of dried white corn. This corn, used by the People of the Longhouse for generations, could nourish—but only if properly prepared. Its kernels were tough, its husks thick, and if eaten raw, would swell painfully in the stomach and sicken the starving men it was meant to save. And so, just as spring began to break winter's grip, the Oneida began their journey.

Walking beside the braves on the last part of the journey was Polly Cooper, a half-Oneida woman known for her strong heart and deep wisdom. She was neither warrior nor chief, but she carried something just as vital: the ancestral knowledge to turn that corn into life-saving food. When they arrived at Valley Forge, the weak and desperate soldiers began to reach for the corn, ready to eat it raw. But Polly stopped them. She told them plainly that doing so would make them sick.

Then she showed them the old ways—soaking and boiling the corn, stirring it into mush and soup, using the care her People had passed down through generations. She sometimes added dried berries, crushed nuts, or even husks, transforming simple food into something not just filling, but nourishing. She tended the pots, feeding the soldiers one bowl at a time. Slowly, strength returned to their bodies, and the light returned to their eyes.

For her kindness, the soldiers were deeply grateful. The wives of General Washington and his officers offered Polly money in thanks, but she gently refused. She had not come for pay. Instead, they gave her a gift: a finely woven black shawl and bonnet, offered with respect. Polly accepted the gifts. "I came because it was right," she told them. "Helping others is the way of the People."[181]

On May 20th, Lafayette led 2,200 soldiers who were about to be annihilated by a far superior British force at Barren Hill. Brave Oneida warriors protected the retreat, allowing the Continentals to escape across the river and return to Valley Forge. Six Oneida gave their lives that day, and may have saved not just an army, but a nation.

The Fight Goes On

Enslaved People Today:
- Nearly 25 million are in forced labor
- 15 million are in forced marriages
- Nearly three-quarters are female
- One in four is a child

Human trafficking generates an estimated $150 billion each year in illicit profits for traffickers and slave masters.

TOP 10 NATIONS WITH SLAVES TODAY
1. India — 8 million
2. China — 3.86 million
3. Pakistan — 3.19 million
4. North Korea — 2.64 million
5. Nigeria — 1.39 million
6. Iran — 1.29 million
7. Indonesia — 1.22 million
8. Dem. Republic of the Congo — 1 million
9. Russia — 794,000
10. Philippines — 784,000

HIGHEST RATES OF SLAVERY
- North Korea
- Eritrea
- Burundi

Today, over 150 products available to us are made with slave labor, generating $150 billion in profits annually for slave owners. The map above shows the top ten countries utilizing slave labor and the staggering numbers in each. Alongside, we see the nations with the highest rates of enslavement. In addition to the fifteen million forced into child marriages and sex slavery, twenty-five million are in forced labor today—many times the number enslaved during the Civil War. One-fourth of these enslaved individuals are children. Shockingly, we may be unwittingly supporting this modern slavery by purchasing goods tainted by forced labor.[182]

Products Made with Slave Labor

Alcoholic Beverages	Amber	Artificial Flowers	Baked Goods
Bamboo	Bananas	Beans	Beans (green beans)
Beans (green, soy, yellow)	Beef	Bidis (hand-rolled cigarettes)	Blueberries
Bovines	Brassware	Brazil Nuts/Chestnuts	Bricks
Broccoli	Cabbages	Carpets	Carrots
Cashews	Cattle	Cement	Ceramics
Cereal Grains	Charcoal	Chile Peppers	Christmas Decorations
Citrus Fruits	Cloves	Coal	Cobalt ore
Coca (stimulant plant)	Cocoa	Coconuts	Coffee
Copper	Corn	Cotton	Cottonseed (hybrid)
Cucumbers	Cumin	Diamonds	Dried Fish
Eggplants	Electronics	Embellished Textiles	Emeralds
Fashion Accessories	Fireworks	Fish	Flowers
Fluorspar (mineral)	Footwear	Footwear (sandals)	Fruits (Pome and Stone)
Furniture	Furniture (steel)	Garlic	Garments
Gems	Glass	Glass Bangles	Gloves
Goats	Granite	Granite (crushed)	Grapes
Gravel (crushed stones)	Gypsum (mineral)	Hair Products	Hazelnuts
Hogs	Incense (agarbatti)	Iron	Jade

Khat	Khat/Miraa (stimulant plant)	Leather	Leather Goods
Lettuce	Lobsters	Locks	Manioc/Cassava
Matches	Meat	Melons	Mica
Nails	Nile Perch (fish)	Oil (palm)	Olives
Onions	Palm Thatch	Peanuts	Pepper
Peppers	Pineapples	Poppies	Pornography
Potatoes	Poultry	Pulses (legumes)	Pyrotechnics
Rice	Rubber	Rubber Gloves	Rubies
Salt	Sand	Sandstone	Sapphires
Sesame	Sheep	Shellfish	Shrimp
Silk Cocoons	Silk Fabric	Silk Thread	Silver
Sisal	Soap	Soccer Balls	Stones (limestone)
Stones (pumice)	Strawberries	Sugar Beets	Sugarcane
Sunflowers	Surgical Instruments	Sweet Potatoes	Tantalum ore (coltan)
Tanzanite (gems)	Tea	Textiles	Textiles (hand-woven)
Textiles (jute)	Thread/Yarn	Tilapia (fish)	Timber
Tin	Tin ore (cassiterite)	Tobacco	Tomato Products
Tomatoes	Toys	Trona (mineral)	Tungsten ore (wolframite)
Vanilla	Wheat	Yerba Mate (stimulant plant)	Zinc[183]

A Call to Action

It is not easy to discern which products are made with slave labor. It will require a concerted effort from governments, industries, and consumers to eliminate these products from global supply chains. Sadly, some would rather focus solely on our nation's past sins while ignoring these current injustices that continue to plague society. Real change demands a unified and determined effort.

When I brought this issue to one of my congressional representatives, he responded that federal laws implemented in the 1930s are sufficient to regulate the production, import, and sale of items made by slave labor. But these laws, quite simply, are not adequate.

What Can WE Do?

By purchasing products made with slave labor, we become complicit in the cycle of exploitation. We can look to Benjamin Lay as an example, but in today's interconnected world, it is nearly impossible to produce everything ourselves as he once did. Nevertheless, we can demand transparency and ethical practices from government, industry, and merchants. Are we buying products made with slave labor? How can we encourage businesses to ensure no slave labor is involved in their supply chains?

PITY FOR POOR AFRICANS

I OWN I am shock'd at the purchase of slaves,
And fear those who buy them and sell them are knaves;
What I hear of their hardships, their tortures, and groans,
Is almost enough to draw pity from stones.
I pity them greatly, but I must be mum,
For how could we do without sugar and rum?

(William Cowper, Pity for Poor Africans, 1788)

A Final Reflection

America did not win the right to govern itself as a free nation just by declaring its independence. It took winning a war for self-determination and enshrining their new-found liberty in law, in the form of the Constitution of the United States and the Bill of Rights.

About three generations later, the pattern repeated itself. Abraham Lincoln, who abhorred slavery, issued the Emancipation Proclamation on January 1, 1863. Yet, this proclamation did not immediately free any enslaved people—it was only a promise of freedom, dependent on the Union's victory in the Civil War. It applied only to states still in rebellion, leaving slavery untouched in border states that had not seceded and in southern counties already under Union control. Even so, the proclamation inspired 210,000 African American men to don the Union blue and fight for the cause of liberty. Their sacrifices were immense—approximately 67,680 became casualties of battle or disease, with 36,000 making the ultimate sacrifice to help free four million of their brothers and sisters. For extraordinary bravery in combat, **twenty-six African Americans were awarded the Congressional Medal of Honor. They were heroes!**

The proclamation freed no slaves in the border states that had not seceded. Neither had it freed the slaves in many counties in the South that were firmly under the control of the Union. Enslaved persons in these areas were spelled out in the proclamation as if no proclamation had been issued. It only "freed" slaves in states still in rebellion as of January 1, 1863, but that was freedom in name only. They were still under the control of Confederate forces and needed to escape to become free. Even so, many were kept in Union encampments and were classified as "contraband," a derogatory term for "illicit goods," or property relieved from their masters.

It took winning the war and the rebellious states returning to the Union with the promise that their citizens would support the Emancipation Proclamation. Our founding documents worked just as before, following that inspired pattern of Liberty Enshrined in Law, culminating in the Thirteenth Amendment. The fight for freedom did not end there, however, as Jim Crow, the Klan, and lynchings left ugly stains upon our nation.

As we reflect on the legacies of Jefferson and Lincoln's, we are reminded of the enduring struggle for freedom and equality that defines the American experience. This journey is marked by progress and setbacks, triumphs and tragedies, yet the timeless principles of liberty, justice, and equality also fuel this journey.

Learning how each Grievance lent teeth to the arguments surrounding the king's *"long train of abuses"* helps us realize that these *Charters of Freedom* were not merely flowery prose and lofty ideals but each had history behind it. Those men of a bygone era looked forward to our time with dreams and hope that we would understand their difficulties, appreciate the enormity of their tasks, and improve upon their efforts.

In navigating the complexities of our present moment, let us draw inspiration from the courage and conviction of those who came before. Let us reaffirm our commitment to the principles that have guided our nation through its darkest hours. We can build a future worthy of the sacrifices made by those who dared to dream of a *More Perfect Union*. This was said quite well in a poem by Francis Daniel Pastorius, leader of the 1688 Germantown Protest Against Slavery. During that very year, Pastorius wrote a poem entitled ***"Greeting to Posterity"*** in the first official document of Germantown. Translated from Latin by John Greenleaf Whittier, it reads in part:

HAIL to posterity! …

Remember, and wherein we have done well

Follow our footsteps, men of coming years!

Where we have failed to do aright, or wisely live,

Be warned by us, the better way pursue,

And, knowing we were human, even as you,

Pity us and forgive!

Farewell, Posterity! …

…Forevermore farewell.

Francis Daniel Pastorius
German-born educator, lawyer, poet, and public official
Founder of Germantown, Pennsylvania
September 26, 1651—c. 1720

Pastorius' poem serves as a timeless challenge to future generations, urging us to learn from the past, build upon its successes, and correct the failures. His words remind us that history is not just a record of what was, but a guide for what may be. We are the posterity Pastorius was speaking to, entrusted with the responsibility to advance the cause of liberty, justice, and human dignity. If we truly honor those who laid the foundation of liberty, we must ensure their sacrifices were not in vain by standing against injustice in our own time.

The Choice is Ours

It is easy to view the distant past and harshly judge former generations and men like Thomas Jefferson for their failures in ending slavery. We blame them for tolerating and supporting slave labor. Their legacies are dimmed by the evils and darkness of slavery. Yet, we ignorantly support slavery today with our purchases and allow it to continue through our complacency.

The reality of slavery today, including the sex slave trade, should shake our souls and stir our hearts. It presents an urgent call to rally together and extend the inalienable rights of life and liberty to every individual. This is not just a problem of the past—it is our problem.

Will we rise to the challenge and take a stand for liberty, as many of our ancestors fearlessly did? The choice is ours. OUR legacy rests upon it.

This is OUR Jefferson moment.

Bibliography

Books

Barton, David. *American History in Black & White*. Aledo, TX: WallBuilder Press, 2004. ISBN: 978-1-932225-27-3.

Banneker, Benjamin. Banneker's Almanack, 1795. Facsimile reprint. Delhi, India: Facsimile Publisher, 2018.

Beck, Derek W. *Igniting the American Revolution 1773-1775*. ISBN: 978-1-4926-3132-3.

Bedini, Silvio A. The Life of Benjamin Banneker: The First African-American Man of Science. New York: Scribner, 1972.

Boyd, Julian P., ed. *The Papers of Thomas Jefferson, Volume 1: 1760-1776*. Princeton, NJ: Princeton University Press, 1950.

Braght, Thieleman J. van. *Martyrs Mirror: The Story of Seventeen Centuries of Christian Martyrdom from the Time of Christ to A.D. 1660*. Scottdale, PA: Herald Press, 1950. ISBN: 978-0-8361-1390-7.

Cappon, Lester J., ed. *The Adams-Jefferson Letters: The Complete Correspondence Between Thomas Jefferson and Abigail and John Adams*. Chapel Hill, NC: University of North Carolina Press, 1988. ISBN: 978-0-8078-4230-0.

Captivating History. *History of Colonial America*. ISBN: 9781637165546.

Channing, Edward. *A History of the United States*. Vol. 3. New York: Macmillan, 1907–1929.

Chernow, Ron. *Alexander Hamilton*. New York: Penguin Press, 2004. ISBN: 978-1-59420-009-0.

Cook, Jane Hampton. *Stories of Faith and Courage from the Revolutionary War*. ISBN: 9780899570426.

Davis, Burke. *Black Heroes of the American Revolution*. New York: Harcourt, Inc., 1976. ISBN: 0-15-238739-8.

Ellis, Joseph J. *Friends Divided: John Adams and Thomas Jefferson*. New York: Penguin Press, 2017. ISBN: 978-0-7352-2471-1.

Fried, Stephen. *Rush: Revolution, Madness, and the Visionary Doctor Who Became a Founding Father*. New York: Crown, 2018. ISBN: 978-0-8041-4006-5.

Glubok, Shirley. *Home and Child Life in Colonial Days*. New York: Macmillan, 1969.

Goodrich, Charles Augustus, and Thomas W. Lewis. *Lives of the Signers to the Declaration of Independence*. WallBuilders Press, 1995. ISBN: 978-1-946100-10-8.

Herrick, Cheesman A. *White Servitude in Pennsylvania: Indentured and Redemption Labor in Colony and Commonwealth*. Philadelphia: John Joseph McVey, 1926.

Hull, William I. *William Penn and the Dutch Quaker Migration to Pennsylvania*. ISBN: 9781163453209.

Jennings, Francis. *Benjamin Franklin, Politician: The Mask and the Man*. ISBN: 0-393-03983-8.

Jordan, Don, and Michael Walsh. *White Cargo: The Forgotten History of Britain's White Slaves in America*. New York: New York University Press, 2008. ISBN: 978-0-8147-4296-9.

Lay, Benjamin. *All Slave-Keepers That Keep the Innocent in Bondage, Apostates Pretending to Lay Claim to the Pure & Holy Christian Religion; Of What Congregation So Ever; But Especially in Their Ministers*. Philadelphia: Printed by Benjamin Franklin, 1737.

Lewis, Claude. *Benjamin Banneker: The Man Who Saved Washington*. New York: McGraw-Hill, 1970.

Lynch, John Roy. *Reminiscences of an Active Life: The Autobiography of John Roy Lynch*. Edited by John Hope Franklin. Chicago: University of Chicago Press, 1970. ISBN: 0-226-49818-2.

Lynch, P.J. The Boy Who Fell Off the Mayflower, or John Howland's Good Fortune. Candlewick Press, 2015.

Maier, Pauline. *American Scripture: Making the Declaration of Independence*. ISBN: 0-679-45492-6.

McCullough, David. *1776*. New York: Simon & Schuster, 2005. ISBN: 978-0-7432-2672-1.

Memoirs of the Private and Public Life of William Penn. ISBN: 9781162949710.

Miller, John Chester. *The Wolf by the Ears: Thomas Jefferson and Slavery*. The Free Press, a Division of Macmillan Publishing Co., Inc., New York, 1977. ISBN: 0-02-921500-5.

Nell, William Cooper. *The Colored Patriots of the American Revolution*. Boston: Robert F. Wallcut, 1855. ISBN: 978-1-9733-7947-8.

Oakley, Violet. *The Holy Experiment: Our Heritage from William Penn 1644-1944*. Philadelphia: Cogslea Studio Publications, 1950.

Pennypacker, Samuel W. *The Autobiography of a Pennsylvanian*. ISBN: 9781345867589.

Petersen, Eric S., ed. *Light and Liberty: Reflections on the Pursuit of Happiness*. New York: Modern Library, 2004. ISBN: 978-0-8129-7432-4.

Ragosta, John A. *For the People, for the Country: Patrick Henry's Final Political Battle*. ISBN: 978-0-8139-5022-8.

Raphael, Ray. *Founding Myths: Stories That Hide Our Patriotic Past*. New York: The New Press, 2004. ISBN: 978-1-56584-921-1.

Rankin, Hugh F. *Francis Marion: The Swamp Fox*. New York: Thomas Y. Crowell Company, 1973. ISBN: 0-690-00097-9.

Schiapp, Stacy. *The Revolutionary: Samuel Adams*. New York: Little, Brown and Company, 2020. ISBN: 978-0-316-44111-7.

Souter, Gerry, and Janet Souter. *The Constitution: The Story of the Creation and Adaptation of the Most Important Document in the History of the United States of America*. London: Arcturus Publishing, 2019. ISBN: 978-1-83861-007-4.

The Complete Frances Harper. ISBN: 978-1-5131-3348-5.

Warren, Mercy Otis. *History of the Rise, Progress and Termination of the American Revolution*. ISBN: 9781015707108.

Webb, Simon. *Jeremiah Dixon: Surveyor of the Mason-Dixon Line*. CreateSpace Independent Publishing Platform, 2015. ISBN: 978-1-5229-4825-4.

Wood, Gordon S. *Revolutionary Characters: What Made the Founders Different*. New York: Penguin Press, 2006. ISBN: 1-59420-093-9.

Anthologies and Compilations

The Constitution of the United States of America and Selected Writings of the Founding Fathers. New York: Barnes & Noble, 2012. ISBN: 978-1-4351-3930-5.

The Essential Debate on the Constitution: Federalist and Anti-Federalist Speeches, Articles, and Letters During the Struggle Over Ratification. Edited by Bernard Bailyn. New York: Library of America, 2018. ISBN: 978-1-59853-583-9.

Lives of the Signers to the Declaration of Independence. Edited by B. J. Lossing. WallBuilders Press, 1995. ISBN: 978-1-932225-10-5.

The Founding Fathers: The Essential Guide to the Men Who Made America. Hoboken, NJ: Wiley, 2007. ISBN: 978-0-470-11792-7.

The Signers: The 56 Stories Behind the Declaration of Independence. Edited by Dennis Brindell Fradin. New York: Scholastic, 2002. ISBN: 0-439-49560-1.

End Notes

1. St. James Episcopal Church, "Our History," last accessed January 16, 2025, https://stjames-episcopal.org/our-history/.
2. "May 27, 1776: Six Nations Meet with Continental Congress," *Nations & Cannons*, accessed February 20, 2025, https://www.nationsandcannons.com/blog/may-27-1776-six-nations-meet-with-continental.
3. "Fast Facts: Democracy and the Haudenosaunee," Oneida Indian Nation, accessed February 20, 2025, https://www.oneidaindiannation.com/fast-facts-democracy-and-the-haudenosaunee/.
4. Oneida Indian Nation, "There Is Strength in Unity," last accessed January 16, 2025, https://www.oneidaindiannation.com/there-is-strength-in-unity/.
5. Oneida Indian Nation, "There Is Strength in Unity," last accessed January 16, 2025, https://www.oneidaindiannation.com/there-is-strength-in-unity/.
6. Great Law of Peace, *Haudenosaunee (Iroquois) Confederacy*, Portland State University, accessed February 24, 2025, https://web.pdx.edu/~caskeym/iroquois_web/html/greatlaw.html.
7. "The Great Tree of Peace (Skaehetsi'kona)," Indigenous Values Initiative, accessed February 20, 2025, https://indigenousvalues.org/haudenosaunee-values/great-tree-peace-skaehetsi%CB%80kona/.
8. Library of Congress, "Broadside Collection: Rare Book and Special Collections Division," last accessed January 16, 2025, https://www.loc.gov/resource/rbpe.1900040a/?sp=1&st=text.
9. Akhil Reed Amar, *America's Constitution: A Biography* (New York: Random House, 2005), 15–20.
10. Akhil Reed Amar, *The Bill of Rights: Creation and Reconstruction* (New Haven: Yale University Press, 1998), 245–252.
11. "Abraham Lincoln, Collected Works of Abraham Lincoln: Volume 4, Mar. 5, 1860–Oct. 24, 1861," last accessed January 16, 2025, https://constitutingamerica.org/90day-dcin-apple-gold-picture-silver-declaration-of-independence-influence-on-united-states-constitution-guest-essayist-tony-williams/#:~:text=the%20American%20Founding.-,Using%20a%20biblical%20metaphor%2C%20he%20thought%20.
12. Abraham Lincoln, *Fragment on the Constitution and the Union*, ca. January 1861, in Roy P. Basler, ed., *The Collected Works of Abraham Lincoln, Vol. 4* (New Brunswick: Rutgers University Press, 1953), 168.
13. Pauline Maier, *Ratification: The People Debate the Constitution, 1787–1788* (New York: Simon & Schuster, 2010), 50–57.
14. James Madison, *The Federalist No. 45*, in *The Federalist Papers*, ed. Clinton Rossiter (New York: Signet Classic, 2003), 292. Madison reassured skeptics that the federal government's powers would be "few and defined," primarily concerning national defense, foreign affairs, and interstate matters, while the states would retain "numerous and indefinite" powers affecting daily life.
15. *History Today*, "Waves of Revolution," last accessed January 16, 2025, https://www.historytoday.com/archive/waves-revolution#:~:text=They%20sparked%20the%20Haitian%20Revolution,the%20barricades%20to%20confront%20absolutism.
16. National Archives, "The Virginia Declaration of Rights," last accessed January 16, 2025, https://www.archives.gov/founding-docs/virginia-declaration-of-rights.
17. George Mason, The Virginia Declaration of Rights, June 12, 1776, National Constitution Center, accessed February 18, 2025, https://constitutioncenter.org/the-constitution/historic-document-library/detail/the-virginia-declaration-of-rights.
18. Project Gutenberg, "The Project Gutenberg eBook of Second Treatise of Government," by John Locke, last accessed January 16, 2025, https://www.gutenberg.org/files/7370/7370-h/7370-h.htm?ref=americanpurpose.com.
19. Lawrence A. Harper, *The English Navigation Laws: A Seventeenth-Century Experiment in Social Engineering* (New York: Columbia University Press, 1939), 112–118.
20. Thomas C. Barrow, *Trade and Empire: The British Customs Service in Colonial America, 1660–1775* (Cambridge, MA: Harvard University Press, 1967), 145–150.
21. Joseph Albert Ernst, *Money and Politics in America, 1755–1775: A Study in the Currency Act of 1764 and the Political Economy of Revolution* (Chapel Hill: University of North Carolina Press, 1973), 45–50.
22. Peter J. Kastor, *The Nation's Crucible: The Louisiana Purchase and the Creation of America* (New Haven: Yale University Press, 2004), 28–33.
23. Colin G. Calloway, *The Scratch of a Pen: 1763 and the Transformation of North America* (Oxford: Oxford University Press, 2006), 78–84.
24. Edmund S. Morgan and Helen M. Morgan, *The Stamp Act Crisis: Prologue to Revolution* (Chapel Hill: University of North Carolina Press, 1953), 48–53.

[25] Joseph Albert Ernst, *Money and Politics in America, 1755–1775: A Study in the Currency Act of 1764 and the Political Economy of Revolution* (Chapel Hill: University of North Carolina Press, 1973), 85–90.

[26] Edmund S. Morgan and Helen M. Morgan, *The Stamp Act Crisis: Prologue to Revolution* (Chapel Hill: University of North Carolina Press, 1953), 85–92.

[27] David Ammerman, *In the Common Cause: American Response to the Coercive Acts of 1774* (Charlottesville: University Press of Virginia, 1974), 75–79.

[28] Jack P. Greene, *The Constitutional Origins of the American Revolution* (Cambridge: Cambridge University Press, 2011), 155–160.

[29] Benjamin L. Carp, *Defiance of the Patriots: The Boston Tea Party and the Making of America* (New Haven: Yale University Press, 2010), 45–50.

[30] Hiller B. Zobel, *The Boston Massacre* (New York: W.W. Norton, 1970), 145–150.

[31] Benjamin L. Carp, *Defiance of the Patriots: The Boston Tea Party and the Making of America* (New Haven: Yale University Press, 2010), 60–65.

[32] Benjamin L. Carp, *Defiance of the Patriots: The Boston Tea Party and the Making of America* (New Haven: Yale University Press, 2010), 75–82.

[33] David Ammerman, *In the Common Cause: American Response to the Coercive Acts of 1774* (Charlottesville: University Press of Virginia, 1974), 80–85.

[34] David Ammerman, *In the Common Cause: American Response to the Coercive Acts of 1774* (Charlottesville: University Press of Virginia, 1974), 85–90.

[35] David Ammerman, *In the Common Cause: American Response to the Coercive Acts of 1774* (Charlottesville: University Press of Virginia, 1974), 90–95.

[36] John Phillip Reid, *Constitutional History of the American Revolution: The Authority of Law* (Madison: University of Wisconsin Press, 1993), 175–180.

[37] David Ammerman, *In the Common Cause: American Response to the Coercive Acts of 1774* (Charlottesville: University Press of Virginia, 1974), 95–100.

[38] Pauline Maier, *American Scripture: Making the Declaration of Independence* (New York: Knopf, 1997), 120–126.

[39] Thomas Jefferson, *A Summary View of the Rights of British America* (Williamsburg, VA: Clementina Rind, 1774), in *The Papers of Thomas Jefferson*, vol. 1, ed. Julian P. Boyd (Princeton: Princeton University Press, 1950), 121–126; Jack N. Rakove, *Original Meanings: Politics and Ideas in the Making of the Constitution* (New York: Alfred A. Knopf, 1996), 183–189; Gordon S. Wood, *The Creation of the American Republic, 1776–1787* (Chapel Hill: University of North Carolina Press, 1969), 143–148.

[40] Thomas Jefferson, *A Summary View of the Rights of British America* (Williamsburg, VA: Clementina Rind, 1774), in *The Papers of Thomas Jefferson*, vol. 1, ed. Julian P. Boyd (Princeton: Princeton University Press, 1950), 121–126; Bernard Bailyn, *The Ideological Origins of the American Revolution* (Cambridge, MA: Harvard University Press, 1992), 198–203; Gordon S. Wood, *The American Revolution: A History* (New York: Modern Library, 2002), 64–67.

[41] Thomas Jefferson, *A Summary View of the Rights of British America* (Williamsburg, VA: Clementina Rind, 1774), in *The Papers of Thomas Jefferson*, vol. 1, ed. Julian P. Boyd (Princeton: Princeton University Press, 1950), 121–126; Gordon S. Wood, *The Radicalism of the American Revolution* (New York: Alfred A. Knopf, 1992), 174–178; Jack P. Greene, *The Constitutional Origins of the American Revolution* (Cambridge: Cambridge University Press, 2011), 92–97.

[42] *Journals of the House of Burgesses of Virginia, 1773–1776*, ed. H. R. McIlwaine (Richmond: The Colonial Press, 1905), 154–155.

See also: Paul Leicester Ford, The Writings of Thomas Jefferson, vol. 1 (New York: G. P. Putnam's Sons, 1892), 426–427.

[43] David Ammerman, *In the Common Cause: American Response to the Coercive Acts of 1774* (Charlottesville: University Press of Virginia, 1974), 45–49; Jack P. Greene, *The Constitutional Origins of the American Revolution* (Cambridge: Cambridge University Press, 2011), 102–107; Bernard Bailyn, *The Ideological Origins of the American Revolution* (Cambridge, MA: Harvard University Press, 1992), 210–214.

[44] Jack P. Greene, *The Constitutional Origins of the American Revolution* (Cambridge: Cambridge University Press, 2010), 146–149

[45] J.R. Jones, *The Revolution of 1688 in England* (New York: W.W. Norton, 1972), 189–192; Mark Kishlansky, *A Monarchy Transformed: Britain 1603–1714* (London: Penguin Books, 1997), 311–315; David L. Smith, *A History of the British Bill of Rights* (Cambridge: Cambridge University Press, 2019), 78–81.

[46] J.R. Jones, *The Revolution of 1688 in England* (New York: W.W. Norton, 1972), 189–192; Mark Kishlansky, *A Monarchy Transformed: Britain 1603–1714* (London: Penguin Books, 1997), 311–315; Jack P. Greene, *The Constitutional Origins of the American Revolution* (Cambridge: Cambridge University Press, 2011), 92–97; Pauline Maier, *From Resistance to Revolution: Colonial Radicals and the Development of American Opposition to Britain, 1765-1776* (New York: W.W. Norton, 1991), 154–159.

[47] Thomas Jefferson, *A Summary View of the Rights of British America* (Williamsburg, VA: Clementina Rind, 1774), in *The Papers of Thomas Jefferson*, vol. 1, ed. Julian P. Boyd (Princeton: Princeton University Press, 1950), 121–126; Jack P. Greene, *The Constitutional Origins of*

the American Revolution (Cambridge: Cambridge University Press, 2011), 97–102; David Ammerman, *In the Common Cause: American Response to the Coercive Acts of 1774* (Charlottesville: University Press of Virginia, 1974), 53–57; Pauline Maier, *From Resistance to Revolution: Colonial Radicals and the Development of American Opposition to Britain, 1765-1776* (New York: W.W. Norton, 1991), 162–167.

48 Jack P. Greene, *The Constitutional Origins of the American Revolution* (Cambridge: Cambridge University Press, 2010), 93–98.

49 The Second Charter of Virginia (1609), in The Avalon Project: Documents in Law, History and Diplomacy (Yale Law School), accessed October 2025, https://avalon.law.yale.edu/17th_century/va02.asp

50 *Charter of Maryland (1632)*, in *Archives of Maryland Online*, vol. 3, ed. William Hand Browne (Baltimore: Maryland Historical Society, 1885), 7–17.

51 Francis Parkman, *La Salle and the Discovery of the Great West* (Boston: Little, Brown, 1869), 225–232.

52 Royal Proclamation of 1763, in The Avalon Project: Documents in Law, History and Diplomacy (Yale Law School), accessed October 2025, https://avalon.law.yale.edu/18th_century/proc1763.asp

53 Thomas Jefferson, Albemarle County Resolves (July 26, 1774), in The Papers of Thomas Jefferson, vol. 1, 1760–1776, ed. Julian P. Boyd (Princeton, NJ: Princeton University Press, 1950), 127–128.

54 Robert M. Calhoon, Timothy M. Barnes, and Robert S. Davis, eds., *The Loyalist Perception and Other Essays* (Columbia: University of South Carolina Press, 1989), 45–47; John Phillip Reid, *Constitutional History of the American Revolution: The Authority of Law* (Madison: University of Wisconsin Press, 1993), 106–109; James M. Volo and Dorothy Denneen Volo, *Daily Life During the American Revolution* (Westport, CT: Greenwood Press, 2003), 224–226.

55 David Ammerman, In the Common Cause: American Response to the Coercive Acts of 1774 (Charlottesville: University Press of Virginia, 1974), 45–49; Jack P. Greene, The Constitutional Origins of the American Revolution (Cambridge: Cambridge University Press, 2011), 102–107; John Phillip Reid, Constitutional History of the American Revolution: The Authority of Law (Madison: University of Wisconsin Press, 1993), 106–109; Pauline Maier, From Resistance to Revolution: Colonial Radicals and the Development of American Opposition to Britain, 1765–1776 (New York: W.W. Norton, 1991), 154–159.

56 *An Act for Establishing a General Post-Office for all Her Majesty's Dominions, 1710*, Great Britain Philatelic Society, accessed February 15, 2025, https://www.gbps.org.uk/information/sources/acts/1710-11-25_Act-9-Anne-cap-10.php.

57 Smithsonian National Postal Museum, "Queen Anne 10th Act in 9th Year of Her Reign," *Smithsonian National Postal Museum*, accessed February 15, 2025, https://postalmuseum.si.edu/object/npm_1984.1127.1.

58 Jack P. Greene, *The Constitutional Origins of the American Revolution* (Cambridge: Cambridge University Press, 2011), 109–113; John Phillip Reid, *Constitutional History of the American Revolution: The Authority of Law* (Madison: University of Wisconsin Press, 1993), 119–123; Mary Sarah Bilder, *The Transatlantic Constitution: Colonial Legal Culture and the Empire* (Cambridge, MA: Harvard University Press, 2004), 152–157; Gordon S. Wood, *The Creation of the American Republic, 1776–1787* (Chapel Hill: University of North Carolina Press, 1969), 296–301.

59 Thomas Jefferson, *The Declaration of Independence: The Fair Copy*, July 1776, in The Papers of Thomas Jefferson, vol. 1, 1760–1776, ed. Julian P. Boyd (Princeton, NJ: Princeton University Press, 1950), 423–429.

60 The Townshend Acts (1767), in The Avalon Project: Documents in Law, History and Diplomacy (Yale Law School), accessed October 2025, https://avalon.law.yale.edu/18th_century/townshend.asp

61 John Phillip Reid, *Constitutional History of the American Revolution: The Authority of Law* (Madison: University of Wisconsin Press, 1993), 132–136; Jack P. Greene, *The Constitutional Origins of the American Revolution* (Cambridge: Cambridge University Press, 2011), 118–122; William R. Leslie, *The Enforcement of the American Revolution: A Study of the British Customs Service in Colonial America* (New York: Octagon Books, 1980), 64–69; Pauline Maier, *From Resistance to Revolution: Colonial Radicals and the Development of American Opposition to Britain, 1765–1776* (New York: W.W. Norton, 1991), 171–175.

62 John Shy, *A People Numerous and Armed: Reflections on the Military Struggle for American Independence* (Ann Arbor: University of Michigan Press, 1990), 83–88; David Ammerman, *In the Common Cause: American Response to the Coercive Acts of 1774* (Charlottesville: University Press of Virginia, 1974), 58–62; Fred Anderson, *Crucible of War: The Seven Years' War and the Fate of Empire in British North America, 1754–1766* (New York: Vintage, 2000), 634–639; Pauline Maier, *From Resistance to Revolution: Colonial Radicals and the Development of American Opposition to Britain, 1765–1776* (New York: W.W. Norton, 1991), 183–187.

63 David Hackett Fischer, *Paul Revere's Ride* (New York: Oxford University Press, 1994), 195–201; David Ammerman, *In the Common Cause: American Response to the Coercive Acts of 1774* (Charlottesville: University Press of Virginia, 1974), 64–68; John Phillip Reid, *Constitutional History of the American Revolution: The Authority of Law* (Madison: University of Wisconsin Press, 1993), 140–145; Jack P. Greene, *The Constitutional Origins of the American Revolution* (Cambridge: Cambridge University Press, 2011), 125–130.

64 Brennan Center, "The Posse Comitatus Act Explained," last accessed January 16, 2025, https://www.brennancenter.org/our-work/research-reports/posse-comitatus-act-explained.

65 John Phillip Reid, *Constitutional History of the American Revolution: The Authority of Law* (Madison: University of Wisconsin Press, 1993), 148–152; *Jack P. Greene, The Constitutional Origins of the American Revolution* (Cambridge: Cambridge University Press, 2011), 135–140; Mary Sarah Bilder, *The Transatlantic Constitution: Colonial Legal Culture and the Empire* (Cambridge, MA: Harvard University Press, 2004), 162–167; David Ammerman, *In the Common Cause: American Response to the Coercive Acts of 1774* (Charlottesville: University Press of Virginia, 1974), 70–74.

66 John Phillip Reid, Constitutional History of the American Revolution: The Authority of Law (Madison: University of Wisconsin Press, 1993), 148–152; Jack P. Greene, The Constitutional Origins of the American Revolution (Cambridge: Cambridge University Press, 2011), 135–140; Mary Sarah Bilder, The Transatlantic Constitution: Colonial Legal Culture and the Empire (Cambridge, MA: Harvard University Press, 2004), 162–167; William R. Leslie, The Enforcement of the American Revolution: A Study of the British Customs Service in Colonial America (New York: Octagon Books, 1980), 74–79.

67 Stephen Conway, *Britain's War of American Independence: A New History* (New York: Cambridge University Press, 2000), 54–58; Benjamin L. Carp, *Rebels Rising: Cities and the American Revolution* (Oxford: Oxford University Press, 2007), 133–137; H.T. Dickinson, *A Companion to Eighteenth-Century Britain* (Malden, MA: Blackwell, 2002), 426–429; Peter D. G. Thomas, *Tea Party to Independence: The Third Phase of the American Revolution, 1773–1776* (Oxford: Clarendon Press, 1991), 94–99.

68 Hiller B. Zobel, The Boston Massacre (New York: W.W. Norton, 1970), 245–250; John Phillip Reid, Constitutional History of the American Revolution: The Authority of Law (Madison: University of Wisconsin Press, 1993), 160–164; David Ammerman, In the Common Cause: American Response to the Coercive Acts of 1774 (Charlottesville: University Press of Virginia, 1974), 80–84; Pauline Maier, From Resistance to Revolution: Colonial Radicals and the Development of American Opposition to Britain, 1765–1776 (New York: W.W. Norton, 1991), 190–195.

69 Bernard Bailyn, *The Ideological Origins of the American Revolution* (Cambridge, MA: Harvard University Press, 1992), 229–235; Jack P. Greene, *The Constitutional Origins of the American Revolution* (Cambridge: Cambridge University Press, 2011), 145–150; David Ammerman, *In the Common Cause: American Response to the Coercive Acts of 1774* (Charlottesville: University Press of Virginia, 1974), 85–89; Thomas Jefferson, *A Summary View of the Rights of British America* (Williamsburg, VA: Clementina Rind, 1774), in *The Papers of Thomas Jefferson*, vol. 1, ed. Julian P. Boyd (Princeton: Princeton University Press, 1950), 121–126.

70 John Phillip Reid, *Constitutional History of the American Revolution: The Authority of Law* (Madison: University of Wisconsin Press, 1993), 165–170; *Jack P. Greene, The Constitutional Origins of the American Revolution* (Cambridge: Cambridge University Press, 2011), 150–155; David Ammerman, *In the Common Cause: American Response to the Coercive Acts of 1774* (Charlottesville: University Press of Virginia, 1974), 90–94; William E. Nelson, The Common Law in Colonial America, Vol. 2: The Middle Colonies and the Carolinas, 1660–1730 (Oxford: Oxford University Press, 2013), 201–206.

71 John Phillip Reid, *Constitutional History of the American Revolution: The Authority of Law* (Madison: University of Wisconsin Press, 1993), 172–176; Jack P. Greene, *The Constitutional Origins of the American Revolution* (Cambridge: Cambridge University Press, 2011), 157–162; David Ammerman, *In the Common Cause: American Response to the Coercive Acts of 1774* (Charlottesville: University Press of Virginia, 1974), 95–99; Thomas Jefferson, *A Summary View of the Rights of British America* (Williamsburg, VA: Clementina Rind, 1774), in *The Papers of Thomas Jefferson*, vol. 1, ed. Julian P. Boyd (Princeton: Princeton University Press, 1950), 121–126.

72 The Papers of Thomas Jefferson, vol. 1, 1760–1776, ed. Julian P. Boyd [Princeton: Princeton University Press, 1950], 187–192.

73 Jack P. Greene, The Constitutional Origins of the American Revolution (Cambridge: Cambridge University Press, 2010), 98–102.

74 The Canadian Encyclopedia, s.v. "Quebec Act, 1774," last accessed January 16, 2025, https://www.thecanadianencyclopedia.ca/en/article/quebec-act.

75 Fred Anderson, *Crucible of War: The Seven Years' War and the Fate of Empire in British North America, 1754–1766* (New York: Vintage, 2000), 562–568; Colin G. Calloway, *The Scratch of a Pen: 1763 and the Transformation of North America* (Oxford: Oxford University Press, 2006), 94–101; Jack P. Greene, *The Constitutional Origins of the American Revolution* (Cambridge: Cambridge University Press, 2011), 165–170; H.T. Dickinson, *The British Empire and the American Revolution* (London: Pickering & Chatto, 2014), 210–215.

76 Samuel Flagg Bemis, *Diplomacy of the American Revolution* (Bloomington: Indiana University Press, 1957), 225–230; Richard B. Morris, *The Peacemakers: The Great Powers and American Independence* (New York: Harper & Row, 1965), 318–324; Jonathan R. Dull, *A Diplomatic History of the American Revolution* (New Haven: Yale University Press, 1985), 152–157; George C. Herring, *From Colony to Superpower: U.S. Foreign Relations Since 1776* (New York: Oxford University Press, 2008), 24–29.

77 Massachusetts Historical Society, "Signed, Sealed, and Delivered: The Treaty that Ended the Revolutionary War," last accessed January 16, 2025, https://www.masshist.org/beehiveblog/2014/09/signed-sealed-and-delivered-the-treaty-that-ended-the-revolutionary-war/.

78 Fred Anderson, *Crucible of War: The Seven Years' War and the Fate of Empire in British North America, 1754–1766* (New York: Vintage, 2000), 562–568; Colin G. Calloway, *The Scratch of a Pen: 1763 and the Transformation of North America* (Oxford: Oxford University Press, 2006), 94–101; Jack P. Greene, *The Constitutional Origins of the American Revolution* (Cambridge: Cambridge University Press,

2011), 165–170; H.T. Dickinson, *The British Empire and the American Revolution* (London: Pickering & Chatto, 2014), 210–215; Francis D. Cogliano, *Revolutionary America, 1763–1815: A Political History* (New York: Routledge, 2000), 38–42.

[79] Jack P. Greene, *The Constitutional Origins of the American Revolution* (Cambridge: Cambridge University Press, 2011), 85–89; Bernard Bailyn, *The Ideological Origins of the American Revolution* (Cambridge, MA: Harvard University Press, 1992), 203–207; Mary Sarah Bilder, *The Transatlantic Constitution: Colonial Legal Culture and the Empire* (Cambridge, MA: Harvard University Press, 2004), 145–149.

[80] David Ammerman, *In the Common Cause: American Response to the Coercive Acts of 1774* (Charlottesville: University Press of Virginia, 1974), 67–72; John Phillip Reid, *Constitutional History of the American Revolution: The Authority of Law* (Madison: University of Wisconsin Press, 1993), 142–147; Jack P. Greene, *The Constitutional Origins of the American Revolution* (Cambridge: Cambridge University Press, 2011), 128–133; H.T. Dickinson, *The British Empire and the American Revolution* (London: Pickering & Chatto, 2014), 218–223.

[81] Battlefields.org, "Massachusetts Government Act, May 20, 1774," last accessed January 16, 2025, https://www.battlefields.org/learn/primary-sources/massachusetts-government-act-may-20-1774.

[82] See *Journals of the Continental Congress*, Vol. 1 (Washington: Government Printing Office, 1904), pp. 67–69; "Declaration and Resolves of the First Continental Congress" (October 14, 1774), which condemned Parliamentary acts that "abolish the free system of English laws in a neighboring province, establishing therein an arbitrary government." Also see Bernard Bailyn, *The Ideological Origins of the American Revolution* (Cambridge: Harvard University Press, 1967), 107–112; Jack P. Greene, *The Constitutional Origins of the American Revolution* (Cambridge: Cambridge University Press, 2011), 87–94; and Merrill Jensen, *The Founding of a Nation: A History of the American Revolution, 1763–1776* (New York: Oxford University Press, 1968), 406–410.

[83] David Ammerman, *In the Common Cause: American Response to the Coercive Acts of 1774* (Charlottesville: University Press of Virginia, 1974), 72–77; John Phillip Reid, *Constitutional History of the American Revolution: The Authority of Law* (Madison: University of Wisconsin Press, 1993), 150–155; Jack P. Greene, *The Constitutional Origins of the American Revolution* (Cambridge: Cambridge University Press, 2011), 135–140; H.T. Dickinson, *The British Empire and the American Revolution* (London: Pickering & Chatto, 2014), 225–230.

[84] David Ammerman, *In the Common Cause: American Response to the Coercive Acts of 1774* (Charlottesville: University Press of Virginia, 1974), 80–85; John Phillip Reid, *Constitutional History of the American Revolution: The Authority of Law* (Madison: University of Wisconsin Press, 1993), 175–180; Jack P. Greene, *The Constitutional Origins of the American Revolution* (Cambridge: Cambridge University Press, 2011), 145–150; H.T. Dickinson, *The British Empire and the American Revolution* (London: Pickering & Chatto, 2014), 235–240; James H. Merrell, *Into the American Woods: Negotiators on the Pennsylvania Frontier* (New York: W.W. Norton, 1999), 312–318.

[85] David Hackett Fischer, *Paul Revere's Ride* (New York: Oxford University Press, 1994), 256–261; John Ferling, *A Leap in the Dark: The Struggle to Create the American Republic* (New York: Oxford University Press, 2003), 211–215; Mary Beth Norton, *1774: The Long Year of Revolution* (New York: Alfred A. Knopf, 2020), 305–311.

[86] Rodney Atwood, *The Hessians: Mercenaries from Hessen-Kassel in the American Revolution* (Cambridge: Cambridge University Press, 1980), 95–102; Stephen Conway, *Britain's War of American Independence: A New History* (New York: Cambridge University Press, 2000), 215–221; David Hackett Fischer, *Washington's Crossing* (New York: Oxford University Press, 2004), 150–155; Richard M. Ketchum, *Saratoga: Turning Point of America's Revolutionary War* (New York: Henry Holt, 1997), 276–282.

[87] Isaac Land, "Anti-Impressment Riots and the Origins of the Age of Revolution," International Review of Social History 58, no. 2 (August 2013): 177–202

[88] David Brion Davis, *The Problem of Slavery in the Age of Revolution, 1770–1823* (Ithaca, NY: Cornell University Press, 1975), 124–130;

[89] Thomas Jefferson, *Draft Constitution for Virginia*, 1760-1776, in *The Papers of Thomas Jefferson*, vol. 1, ed. Julian P. Boyd (Princeton: Princeton University Press, 1950). 337-365.

[90] George Washington, "Fairfax County Resolves, 18 July 1774," *Founders Online*, National Archives, last accessed January 16, 2025, https://founders.archives.gov/documents/Washington/02-10-02-0080.

[91] Monticello, "George Wythe," last accessed January 16, 2025, https://www.monticello.org/research-education/thomas-jefferson-encyclopedia/george-wythe/.

[92] Benjamin Franklin, "A Conversation between an Englishman, a Scotchman, and an American, on the Subject of Slavery," The Papers of Benjamin Franklin, vol. 17, January 1 through December 31, 1770, last accessed January 20, 2025, https://founders.archives.gov/documents/Franklin/01-17-02-0019.

[93] Lossing, Benson J. *Our Country: A Household History for All Readers*. Vol. 1. New York: Johnson & Miles, 1878, 409–410.

[94] Pauline Maier, *American Scripture: Making the Declaration of Independence* (New York: Knopf, 1997), 143–148.

[95] Connecticut Society of the Sons of the American Revolution, *The Price They Paid*, last accessed February 15, 2025, https://www.sarconnecticut.org/the-price-they-paid/.

96 Walter Isaacson, "Benjamin Franklin Joins the Revolution," Smithsonian Magazine, July 31, 2003, https://www.smithsonianmag.com/history/benjamin-franklin-joins-the-revolution-87199988/.

97 Daniel Webster, Adams and Jefferson, American Literature, last accessed February 15, 2025, https://americanliterature.com/history/daniel-webster/speech/adams-and-jefferson.

98 National Archives, Founding Fathers: *Signers of the Declaration of Independence* Fact Sheet, last accessed February 15, 2025, https://www.archives.gov/founding-docs/signers-factsheet.

99 Paul H. Smith, *Letters of Delegates to Congress*, 1774-1789, Vol. 4: July 17, 1776 - October 15, 1776 (Washington, D.C.: Library of Congress, 1979), 265–270.

100 Benson Bobrick, *Angel in the Whirlwind: The Triumph of the American Revolution* (New York: Simon & Schuster, 1997), 298–305.

101 Jefferson, Thomas. *The Writings of Thomas Jefferson*, edited by Paul Leicester Ford, vol. 4. New York: G.P. Putnam's Sons, 1893, 66.

102 Thomas Jefferson, *Extract from Thomas Jefferson's Notes of Proceedings in the Continental Congress*, July 2, 1776, in *Jefferson Quotes & Family Letters*, Monticello, accessed May 9, 2025, https://tjrs.monticello.org/letter/54.

103 Thomas Jefferson, *Draft Constitution for Virginia*, 1760-1776, in *The Papers of Thomas Jefferson*, vol. 1, ed. Julian P. Boyd (Princeton: Princeton University Press, 1950). 340.

104 Thomas Jefferson, *Draft Constitution for Virginia*, 1760-1776, in *The Papers of Thomas Jefferson*, vol. 1, ed. Julian P. Boyd (Princeton: Princeton University Press, 1950). 337.

105 Gregg, Edward. *Queen Anne*. New Haven: Yale University Press, 2001.

106 Library of Congress Magazine, "An Important Revision," last accessed January 16, 2025, https://loc.gov/lcm/pdf/LCM_2015_0102.pdf.

107 Patrick Henry, speech to the Second Virginia Convention, March 23, 1775, St. John's Church, Richmond, Virginia, in William Wirt, *Sketches of the Life and Character of Patrick Henry* (Philadelphia: James Webster, 1817), 120–121.

108 John Adams, Thoughts on Government: Applicable to the Present State of the American Colonies (Philadelphia: John Dunlap, 1776).

109 Source: Jefferson, *Itinerary and Chronology, May 7–14, 1776*, The Works of Thomas Jefferson, vol. 2 (1904–1905), pp. xxv–xxvi (Liberty Fund Online Edition).

110 Thomas Jefferson, Autobiography (1821), in The Papers of Thomas Jefferson: Retirement Series, vol. 1 (Princeton University Press).

111 *"Resolutions of the Freeholders of Albemarle County, Virginia, July 26, 1774,"* Founders Online, National Archives.

112 Hastings, Patrick. "Jefferson's Revisions to *Summary View*." *Bibliomania: The Library of Congress Blog*, February 11, 2026. https://blogs.loc.gov/bibliomania/2026/02/11/jeffersons-revisions-to-summary-view/

113 *"A declaration by the representatives of the united colonies of North America, now met in Congress at Philadelphia, setting forth the causes and necessity of their taking up arms."*—Journals of the Continental Congress, 1774–1789, Vol. 2 (Washington: Library of Congress, 1905), pp. 140–147.

114 Jefferson, Thomas. *Draft Constitution for Virginia (Proposed Constitution for Virginia)*, June 1776. Manuscript Division, The New York Public Library, New York. [Also printed in Paul L. Ford (ed.), *The Writings of Thomas Jefferson*, Federal Edition, Vol. 2 (New York & London: G.P. Putnam's Sons, 1904–05), p. 7.]

115 Adams, John. *The Works of John Adams, Second President of the United States*, edited by Charles Francis Adams, vol. 2. Boston: Little, Brown and Company, 1850, p. 514.

116 John Adams, Autobiography of John Adams, in *The Works of John Adams*, ed. Charles Francis Adams, vol. 3 (Boston: Little, Brown and Company, 1851), 293.

117 New York Public Library. "The Declaration of Independence, Handwritten." Exhibition page. https://www.nypl.org/events/exhibitions/declaration-independence-handwritten

118 John F. Kennedy, remarks at a White House dinner honoring Nobel Prize winners, April 29, 1962, Public Papers of the Presidents of the United States: John F. Kennedy, 1962 (Washington, D.C.: U.S. Government Printing Office, 1963), 347.

119 Thomas Jefferson, *Notes on the State of Virginia* (Paris, 1785), Avalon Project, Yale Law School, https://avalon.law.yale.edu/18th_century/jeffvir.asp

120 Thomas Jefferson to John Holmes, April 22, 1820, in *The Papers of Thomas Jefferson: Retirement Series*, vol. 15 (Princeton University Press).

[121] Lucas Vázquez de Ayllón expedition, 1526, San Miguel de Gualdape; see Paul E. Hoffman, *A New Andalusia and a Way to the Orient: The American Southeast during the Sixteenth Century* (Baton Rouge: LSU Press, 1990).

[122] Reuters, *"Chronology – Who Banned Slavery When?"* last accessed February 16, 2025, https://www.reuters.com/article/economy/chronology-who-banned-slavery-when-idUSL15614649/.

[123] Seymour Drescher, *Abolition: A History of Slavery and Antislavery* (Cambridge: Cambridge University Press, 2009), 223-225; David Eltis, *Economic Growth and the Ending of the Transatlantic Slave Trade* (New York: Oxford University Press, 1987), 100-102; and Michael Craton, *Testing the Chains: Resistance to Slavery in the British West Indies* (Ithaca, NY: Cornell University Press, 1982), 276-280.

[124] Wikipedia, s.v. "Indentured Servitude," last accessed January 16, 2025, https://en.wikipedia.org/wiki/Indentured_servitude#:~:text=Colonial%20Indian%20indenture%20system,-Main%20article%3A%20Indian&text=It%20started%20from%20the%20end,1833%20and%20continued%20until%201920.

[125] David W. Galenson, *White Servitude in Colonial America: An Economic Analysis* (Cambridge: Cambridge University Press, 1981), 14-18; Richard S. Dunn, *Sugar and Slaves: The Rise of the Planter Class in the English West Indies, 1624-1713* (Chapel Hill: University of North Carolina Press, 1972), 243-247; and Don Jordan and Michael Walsh, *White Cargo: The Forgotten History of Britain's White Slaves in America* (New York: NYU Press, 2008), 65-70.

[126] Don Jordan and Michael Walsh, White Cargo: The Forgotten History of Britain's White Slaves in America (New York: New York University Press, 2008), 76–86.

[127] Learning for Justice, Indentured Servitude (PDF file), accessed February 15, 2025, https://www.learningforjustice.org/sites/default/files/general/tt_indentured_servitude_09_h2.pdf.

[128] Stephen Winick, "Beyond 1619: Slavery and the American Folklife Center," Folklife Today (blog), Library of Congress, August 27, 2019, https://blogs.loc.gov/folklife/2019/08/beyond-1619/.

[129] "European Migrations Before the American Revolution," U.S. Immigration History (Pressbooks, City University of New York), accessed February 16, 2025, https://pressbooks.cuny.edu/immigrationhistory/chapter/chapter-1-european-migrations-before-the-american-revolution/.

[130] Encyclopedia Virginia, s.v. "Convict Labor during the Colonial Period," accessed February 16, 2025, https://encyclopediavirginia.org/entries/convict-labor-during-the-colonial-period/.

[131] South Carolina Encyclopedia, s.v. "Lucas Vasquez de Ayllón," last accessed January 16, 2025, https://www.scencyclopedia.org/sce/entries/ayllon-lucas-vasquez-de/.

[132] "Negro Women's Children to Serve According to the Condition of the Mother, 1662," Encyclopedia Virginia, accessed February 16, 2025, https://encyclopediavirginia.org/primary-documents/negro-womens-children-to-serve-according-to-the-condition-of-the-mother-1662/.

[133] *The Brookes Slave Ship, 1807 Commemorated, Institute of Historical Research*, accessed February 15, 2025, https://archives.history.ac.uk/1807commemorated/exhibitions/museums/brookes.html.

[134] *Model of the Brookes Slave Ship, Understanding Slavery Initiative*, accessed February 15, 2025, https://understandingslavery.com/artefact/model-of-the-brookes-slave-ship/.

[135] Slave Voyages: The Trans-Atlantic Slave Trade Database, last accessed February 11, 2025, https://www.slavevoyages.org/voyage/database.

[136] "H.M. King Leopold II of the Belgians," Henry Poole & Co., accessed February 15, 2025, https://henrypoole.com/individual/hm-king-leopold-ii-belgians/.

[137] Mac Mckinney, "Congo: The Horror Crescendos," LA Progressive, March 1, 2012, accessed February 15, 2025, https://www.laprogressive.com/foreign-policy/congo-horror-crescendos.

[138] "King Leopold's Ghost: A Story of Greed, Terror, and Heroism in Colonial Africa," Harvard Kennedy School Library & Research Services, accessed February 15, 2025, https://www.hks.harvard.edu/faculty-research/library-research-services/collections/diversity-inclusion-belonging/king-leopolds.

[139] "H.M. King Leopold II of the Belgians," Henry Poole & Co., accessed February 15, 2025, https://henrypoole.com/individual/hm-king-leopold-ii-belgians/.

[140] Marcus Rediker, *The Slave Ship: A Human History* (New York: Viking, 2007), 98–105.

[141] SlaveVoyages, *Trans-Atlantic Slave Trade Database*, accessed February 19, 2025, https://www.slavevoyages.org.

[142] Paul Finkelman, *Slavery and the Founders: Race and Liberty in the Age of Jefferson* (Armonk, NY: M.E. Sharpe, 1996), 45–50.

143. Christopher Klein, "Alexander Hamilton's Complicated Relationship to Slavery," HISTORY, last modified October 16, 2020, https://www.history.com/news/alexander-hamilton-slavery-facts.
144. Paul Finkelman, *Slavery and the Founders: Race and Liberty in the Age of Jefferson* (Armonk, NY: M.E. Sharpe, 1996), 60–65; David Brion Davis, *Inhuman Bondage: The Rise and Fall of Slavery in the New World* (New York: Oxford University Press, 2006), 189–194.
145. Politico, "Congress Votes to Ban Slave Importation, March 2, 1807," Politico, March 2, 2018, accessed February 12, 2025, https://www.politico.com/story/2018/03/02/congress-votes-to-ban-slave-importation-march-2-1807-430820.
146. Sheila Scarborough Fitzgerald, "Newport Rum and Slavery History," Perceptive Travel Blog, July 5, 2011, accessed February 12, 2025, https://perceptivetravel.com/blog/2011/07/05/newport-rum-slavery-history/.
147. *Thomas Cresap and the Border War*, The Historical Marker Database, last modified [date if available], https://www.hmdb.org/m.asp?m=242835.https://www.hmdb.org/m.asp?m=242835.
148. Francis Daniel Pastorius et al., *1688 Germantown Petition Against Slavery*, Haverford College Quaker & Special Collections, Haverford, PA.
149. National Park Service, "1688 Germantown Quaker Petition Against Slavery," U.S. National Park Service, accessed February 12, 2025, https://www.nps.gov/articles/quakerpetition.htm.
150. Library of Congress, "Memorial Against Slavery, Germantown, Pennsylvania, 1688," Library of Congress, accessed February 12, 2025, https://www.loc.gov/resource/rbpe.14000200/?st=text.
151. National Park Service, "A House Divided," Lincoln Home National Historic Site, U.S. Department of the Interior, accessed February 12, 2025, https://www.nps.gov/liho/learn/historyculture/housedivided.htm.
152. Institute, "The Free Soil Party," Bill of Rights Institute, accessed February 12, 2025, https://billofrightsinstitute.org/essays/the-free-soil-party.
153. Democratic Party, "1856 Democratic Party Platform," The American Presidency Project, University of California, Santa Barbara, accessed February 12, 2025, https://www.presidency.ucsb.edu/documents/1856-democratic-party-platform.
154. Harvard University, "1852 Bill of Sale for an Enslaved Woman and Child," HIST 1952: Harvard & Slavery, accessed February 12, 2025, https://hist1952.omeka.fas.harvard.edu/items/show/104.
155. National Archives, "Black Soldiers in the U.S. Military During the Civil War," last reviewed August 23, 2021, https://www.archives.gov/education/lessons/blacks-civil-war.
156. Gilder Lehrman Institute of American History, "Historical Context: Black Soldiers in the Civil War," Gilder Lehrman Institute of American History, accessed February 12, 2025, https://www.gilderlehrman.org/history-resources/teacher-resources/historical-context-black-soldiers-civil-war.
157. U.S. Army, "Meet Sgt. William Carney: The First African American Medal of Honor Recipient," Army.mil, accessed February 12, 2025, https://www.army.mil/article/181896/meet_sgt_william_carney_the_first_african_american_medal_of_honor_recipient.
158. J. David Hacker, "New Estimate Raises Civil War Death Toll," The New York Times, April 2, 2012, accessed February 12, 2025, https://www.nytimes.com/2012/04/03/science/civil-war-toll-up-by-20-percent-in-new-estimate.html.
159. Roger L. Ransom, "The Economics of the Civil War," EH.net, Economic History Association, accessed February 12, 2025, https://eh.net/encyclopedia/the-economics-of-the-civil-war/.
160. National Archives, "Emancipation Proclamation," Milestone Documents, accessed February 12, 2025, https://www.archives.gov/milestone-documents/emancipation-proclamation.
161. Museum of the American Revolution, "Black Founders Big Idea 2: Black Soldiers and Sailors in the Revolutionary War," last accessed January 20, 2025,
162. National Park Service, "The Iconic 369th Infantry Regiment," last accessed January 20, 2025, https://www.nps.gov/articles/000/iconic369thphoto.htm#:~:text=The%20369th%20Infantry%2C%20whose%20members,Guerre%20medals%20for%20their%20valor.
163. Partnership With Native Americans, "Code Talkers," last accessed January 20, 2025.
164. National Indian Council on Aging (NICOA), "American Indian Veterans Have Highest Record of Military Service," last accessed January 20, 2025, https://www.nicoa.org/american-indian-veterans-have-highest-record-of-military-service/.
165. Wikipedia, s.v. "George Middleton (Activist)," last accessed January 16, 2025, https://en.wikipedia.org/wiki/George_Middleton_(activist).

[166] Wikipedia, s.v. "Bucks of America," last accessed January 16, 2025, https://en.wikipedia.org/wiki/Bucks_of_America#:~:text=Governor%20John%20Hancock%20and%20his,benefactor%2C%20John%20George%20Washington%20Hancock.

[167] https://thewestendmuseum.org/history/era/west-boston/colonel-george-middleton/

[168] Burke Davis, *Black Heroes of the American Revolution* (New York: Harcourt, Inc., 1976), 64–66.

[169] African American Registry, "George Middleton, Patriot Born," last accessed January 16, 2025, https://aaregistry.org/story/george-middleton-patriot-born/.

[170] Friends Journal, "Rethinking William Penn," last accessed January 16, 2025, https://www.friendsjournal.org/rethinking-william-penn/.

[171] BBC, "Benjamin Lay: The Quaker Dwarf Who Fought Slavery," last accessed January 16, 2025, https://www.bbc.com/news/uk-england-essex-42640782.

[172] Smithsonian Institution, "Benjamin Lay," last accessed January 16, 2025, https://www.si.edu/object/benjamin-lay%3Anpg_NPG.79.171.

[173] Battlefields.org, "Sarah Bradlee Fulton, Mother of the Boston Tea Party," last accessed January 16, 2025, https://www.battlefields.org/learn/biographies/sarah-bradlee-fulton.

[174] Mount Vernon, "Mercy Otis Warren," last accessed January 16, 2025, https://www.mountvernon.org/library/digitalhistory/digital-encyclopedia/article/mercy-otis-warren-1728-1814.

[175] National Women's History Museum, "Mercy Otis Warren," last accessed January 20, 2025, https://www.womenshistory.org/education-resources/biographies/mercy-otis-warren.

[176] "Mercy Otis Warren's Revolutionary Impact," last accessed January 20, 2025, https://www.usconstitution.net/mercy-otis-warrens-revolutionary-impact/.

[177] Mercy Otis Warren, *History of the Rise, Progress and Termination of the American Revolution* (ISBN: 9781015707108).

[178] Library of Congress, "Benjamin Banneker: Surveyor, City Planner, Astronomer?" *In Custodia Legis: Law Librarians of Congress* (blog), February 2, 2024, https://blogs.loc.gov/law/2024/02/benjamin-banneker-surveyor-city-planner-astronomer.

[179] History.com, "Abraham Lincoln and Black Resettlement in Haiti," last accessed January 16, 2025, https://www.history.com/news/abraham-lincoln-black-resettlement-haiti.

[180] William L. Stone, *Life of Joseph Brant—Thayendanegea*, Vol. 1 (New York: George Dearborn & Co., 1838), 281–283; see also Charles S. Hall, *The Oneida Indians and the Coming of the Revolution* (Boston: Grafton Press, 1905), 198–201.

[181] "Report on Lafayette's Reconnaissance Expedition," *Papers of George Washington: Revolutionary War Series*, ed. Philander D. Chase, Vol. 14 (Charlottesville: University of Virginia Press, 2004), 120–123; Robert S. Allen, *His Majesty's Indian Allies: British Indian Policy in the Defence of Canada, 1774–1815* (Toronto: Dundurn Press, 1992), 46.

[182] Relief Web, "Modern Slavery by Country," last accessed January 16, 2025,

[183] U.S. Department of Labor, "Child Labor Report," last accessed January 16, 2025, https://www.dol.gov/agencies/ilab/reports/child-labor/list-of-goods-print.

www.ingramcontent.com/pod-product-compliance
Lightning Source LLC
Chambersburg PA
CBHW061354010526
44107CB00011B/930